WALKING
on WATER

WALKING
on WATER

AND OTHER CLASSIC MESSAGES

S. MICHAEL WILCOX

DESERET
BOOK

SALT LAKE CITY, UTAH

Library of Congress Cataloging-in-Publication Data

Wilcox, S. Michael, author.
  Walking on water and other classic messages / S. Michael Wilcox.
     p. cm.
  Includes bibliographical references and index.
  Summary: Compilation of nine messages by S. Michael Wilcox from previously published audio talks.
  ISBN 978-1-60908-362-5 (hardbound : alk. paper)
  1. Mormons—Conduct of life. 2. Jesus Christ. 3. The Church of Jesus Christ of Latter-day Saints—Doctrines. 4. Mormon Church—Doctrines. I. Title.
  BX8639.W49W35 2011
  252'.093—dc22   2011001528

Printed in the United States of America
Publishers Printing, Salt Lake City, UT

10   9   8   7   6   5   4   3   2   1

CONTENTS

CHAPTER ONE

WALKING ON WATER

When the Lord Asks the Impossible

HAYSTACKS AND DRIVING LESSONS

When I was young, I spent many of my summers on a cattle ranch in Northern Nevada. I had a wonderful uncle, Uncle Verland, who taught me a great many things. He raised cattle and he raised horses, but he was also deeply engaged in raising boys. He had a certain technique in raising boys that has helped me a great deal in life.

My uncle always assumed that we could do whatever he asked us to do. It didn't matter how difficult or impossible it seemed to me, the assumption was that if Uncle Verland asked me to do something, I could do it. He anticipated we boys could do all that he asked. That helped us not to be hampered too much by doubt or fear. My first driving lesson is an illustration of that technique. I suppose I was about thirteen or fourteen. My uncle seated me behind the wheel of the pickup, gave me the key, and said, "This is the clutch; this is the brake; this is the gas. Here's first gear; here's second; here's third. Put one foot on the clutch and the other foot on the brake. Turn the key on. When you pull your foot off the brake and put it on the gas, you pull your foot off the clutch at the same time, and away we go." That was my first driving lesson.

We drove down the road and he promptly fell asleep, because my uncle could fall asleep anywhere, anytime. We would sometimes find him out on the range asleep, slumped over on his horse. During my lesson, however, he didn't teach me how to downshift and as we drove toward a bridge, I panicked. There was a tight hairpin turn before the bridge, which crossed a river. I did make the turn. However, I didn't quite miss a large boulder on the other side of the bridge and scraped the front fender of the truck. My uncle didn't say much. He wasn't too critical, and the next day I was driving again.

The first time he put me on a horse I was about five. The horse ran away

I

with me. When Uncle Verland finally rode up and stopped my running mount, I scrambled off as fast as I could. But he threw me back on the horse, handed me the reins, and said, "You control the horse! You make him do what you want him to do!" Then he rode off.

I had to stack hay during the summer as well. My lesson on stacking hay was brief: "Keep the corners and the sides perpendicular, tromp down the center, and make a nice point at the top." After that he handed me a pitchfork, boosted me up onto the stack, and walked back to his tractor.

Maybe the most nervous time I ever experienced working for my uncle was the day he handed me the reins of a team of workhorses and told me to drive the wagon down the canyon on a very narrow road that dropped off into the river on one side. I remember feeling borderline terror as I first took the reins, but he assumed I could do it, and I assumed that since he told me I could do it, I could do it. That calmed me down some. I remember hugging the wall of the mountain, watching that dropoff down to the river about ten inches away from the outside wheel. This was the way he raised us.

Let me apply my uncle's lessons on a little higher level with issues much more critical than stacking hay or handling a team. We believe in a Father in Heaven who is raising not just boys, but who is raising gods. Should we not feel, in our relationship with our Father in Heaven, in his desire to exalt us, the same way I felt about my uncle? If God asks us to do something, we can do it, even though it may appear to be impossible. And sometimes it looks nearly impossible to live up to the expectations we sense or perceive God asks of us.

"Lord, If It Be Thou"

There is a wonderful story in the scriptures to which we may turn for inspiration in facing difficult challenges. It is that brief moment when Peter walked on the water of Galilee. It is his attitude as demonstrated on that occasion that is striking to me. It carries a most remarkable lesson. The story, as recorded by Matthew, begins when the disciples see the Savior walking toward them on the surface of the lake: "And when the disciples saw him walking on the sea . . ." (Matthew 14:26). Try to picture that moment. The first time I went to Israel, we traveled across the Sea of Galilee during the day. In future trips we went out at night, because this story takes place at night, and being on the Sea of Galilee at night is very different from being there in sunlight.

All the artist renditions I've seen of that night's experience have Christ lit up like a lightbulb, in a manner of speaking, while he walked toward the Apostles' boat, but I don't think he would have been lit up like a lightbulb. We can picture the winds and the waves in the depths of night—suddenly, out of the night's obscurity, a dark figure approaches, steadily moving across the surface of the water. Of course we would be frightened. We could not see the comforting face of Jesus, just a shape moving toward us in the darkness. "And when the disciples saw him . . . they were troubled, saying, It is a spirit; and they cried out for fear. But straightway Jesus spake unto them, saying, Be of good cheer; it is I; be not afraid. And Peter answered him and said, Lord, if it be thou, bid me come unto thee on the water. And he said, Come. And when Peter was come down out of the ship, he walked on the water, to go to Jesus" (Matthew 14:26–29).

Here we sense a wonderful attitude arising from Peter's fears. I assume his motivation was, "I desire to do everything my Master does—even the impossible!" I've often wondered what the Savior's face looked like when Peter said, "If it's really you, ask me to walk on the water." Do you think that the Savior looked disappointed? Do you think he thought, "Oh, for heaven's sake, Peter, I guess you'll have to learn the hard way"? I don't. I picture the Savior smiling, pleased at Peter's desire, at that soul-lifting motivation—if my Master does this, I want to do it too. I think he was more than satisfied with Peter's accompanying attitude, which I assume was, "If my Master can do this, and he invites me to do it, if he bids or asks me to do it, I can do it. I can walk on water too. I can do what no man has ever done before. I can do even the impossible." This theme is such an important lesson for us to learn here on earth that it is repeated a number of times in scripture.

I Can Do All Things

Another example is Nephi's conversation with his brothers when he was asked to build a boat. The brothers said: "Our brother is a fool, for he thinketh that he can build a ship; yea, and he also thinketh that he can cross these great waters." Nephi replies, "They did not believe that I could build a ship; neither would they believe that I was instructed of the Lord. And . . . they did rejoice over me, saying: We knew that ye could not construct a ship, for we knew that ye were lacking in judgment; wherefore, thou canst not accomplish so great a work" (1 Nephi 17:17–19). Notice Nephi's response to their delighted skepticism. "And I said unto them: If God had commanded me to do all things I could do them. If he should command me that I should say unto this water, be thou earth, it should be earth; and if I should say it, it would be done" (1 Nephi 17:50).

I think the formula we should use when God seems to ask us to walk on water, which even today is an expression for doing the impossible, can be expressed briefly and simply: The Savior can do it, and since he can do it, I want to do it, because I want to do everything he can do. I want to obey and love and forgive and pray just as he did. If he asks me to do it, I can do it!

There are many times in our lives when it seems like the Lord asks us to walk on water, or at least there are times when we might be tempted to say, "Lord you might as well ask me to walk on water as to do that, because I don't think I can do it." The scriptures contain walk-on-water phrases that are applicable to all of us. For instance, "What manner of men ought ye to be? Verily I say unto you, even as I am" (3 Nephi 27:27). When I read those words I think, "I want to do this, Lord, but to be exactly like you—that's impossible. Yet, if you can walk pleasingly before our Father, and you ask me to do it, I must be able to do it. I will not be discouraged with myself, but keep trying." Maybe the greatest walk-on-water command of all is: "Be ye therefore perfect, even as your Father which is in heaven is perfect" (Matthew 5:48). Again, we are tempted to say, "You might as well ask me to walk on water, Lord, as to ask me to be perfect." Here is another command that poses walk-on-water challenges: "Let virtue garnish thy thoughts unceasingly" (D&C 121:45). On and on we can pull phrases out of the scriptures that are difficult, walk-on-water kinds of commands.

There are other aspects of life we might consider, short of full scriptural exhortation. Here are a few that I have seen in my own life or in the lives of others. We are often asked to do the following:

- Reject and resist every temptation, just as Christ did.

- Overcome crippling habits and addictions.

- Change our very character, our personality, our desires, our lifestyle, and our very thought patterns.

- Conquer fear.

- Fulfill and master God-given talents.

- Accept and develop a difficult—even an unwanted—calling.

- Consecrate all of our time, all of our talents, all that we have, and all that we ever will have, to the Lord's work and kingdom.

- Let go of the traditions of past prejudice, anger, and hate.

- Forgive the unforgivable.

- Love the unlovable.

- Maintain faith in a God of goodness in the face of the vast inconsistencies, trials, and unfairnesses of life.

- Learn to trust a God who allows incredible suffering and allows men to be cruel and inhumane to one another.

- Endure crushing disappointment or betrayal.

- Rise from a suffocating, oppressive, or abusive environment.

- Live chaste in thought and deed in an immoral, sexually exploitive world.

- Mend broken, deeply wounded relationships.

- Sacrifice our most precious things.

- Rejoice and be of good cheer in the midst of pain and unfulfilled longings.

I could go on and on. Everyone probably has walk-on-water moments of life, times when you want very badly to do what you feel God is encouraging you to do—what you see he could do and did—but feel that it simply is impossible. Let us never forget, if he asks us to do it, the assumption is that we can do it. We must believe we can do the things he asks us. I think it is interesting to ponder that the sign Peter specifically asked for, in order to know that the dark shape on the water really was the Savior, was to do what Christ himself was doing—the impossible—just as if Peter thought, *No one else would ask me to do that. It must be my God.*

"WHEREFORE DIDST THOU DOUBT?"

Now, in fairness, one might say, "But Peter failed." There is some comfort to me in that. He did fail. But let us return to the story: "When he saw the wind boisterous, he was afraid; and beginning to sink, he cried, saying, Lord, save me. And immediately Jesus stretched forth his hand, and caught him, and said unto him, O thou of little faith, wherefore didst thou doubt? And when they were come into the ship, the wind ceased" (Matthew 14:30–32).

Three ideas seem to stand out in this description—*little faith, afraid,* and *doubt.* I ask myself, afraid of what or whom? Doubted what or whom? Little faith in what or whom? Did Peter doubt the Savior, or his gracious invitation to come to him on the water? Was he afraid that his desire was not proper? Or did he doubt himself and his own ability to do it? I sense it was this last—our challenge in life is to learn to have faith in ourselves, to conquer doubts regarding our ability, to conquer the fear that we will fail to do what we're asked to do, even to the extent of totally perfecting ourselves.

How do we do that? May I suggest a half-dozen things the scriptures offer that have been very helpful to me, that the Spirit whispers to me, when I face those walk-on-water moments of life, desiring to do, but fearing, and doubting, and feeling my faith draining away.

"Look, Learn, Listen, Walk"

First: Remember the three *L*s! In the Doctrine and Covenants, there are three words that all begin with the letter *L* that instruct us what we are supposed to do with the multiple examples the Savior's life presents. Remember it was the very example, the very image of Jesus walking across the surface of the Sea of Galilee that gave Peter the motivation and the desire to do likewise. In Doctrine and Covenants 6 the Savior says, "Fear not to do good, my sons, for whatsoever ye sow, that shall ye also reap; . . . Therefore, fear not, little flock; do good. . . . Perform with soberness the work which I have commanded you" (D&C 6:33–35). Then he gives us the first *L*: "*Look* unto me in every thought; doubt not, fear not" (D&C 6:36; emphasis added). It seems to me that the Savior is teaching that the very act of looking at him in every thought helps to conquer the doubts and the fears. "Look unto me in every thought!"

In Doctrine and Covenants 19 we get the other two *L*s. Speaking to Martin Harris, the Lord says, "*Learn* of me." There is the second *L*. The third *L* immediately follows: "*Listen* to my words; *walk* in the meekness of my Spirit, and you shall have peace in me" (D&C 19:23; emphasis added). Here we have a wonderful formula which will move us forward in life and conquer fears, doubts, and little faith. Jesus instructs us to *look* unto him in every thought, *learn* of him, *listen* to his words, and then *walk,* as best we can, as he walked.

Here are a few examples of how this can work in day-to-day life. Have you ever been impatient with a child? You don't seem to have enough time for all you need to do and a child asks for attention. "I just don't have the patience to deal with this child now," you might think. My granddaughter comes to our house and she wants to play "My Little Pony." She has every little pony that you could imagine and has all kinds of little circuses they can perform in. Sometimes she likes Grandpa to play with her. Perhaps this particular time I'm impatient. I want to sit down and read or watch TV. I don't want to play "My Little Pony." Then the Lord says, *Look unto me in that thought, in your impatience and irritation. Learn of me. Listen to my words: "Suffer the little children to come unto me, and forbid them not: for of such is the kingdom of God" (Mark 10:14). Now walk in the meekness of my Spirit.* Somehow, looking at that example, hearing those words, I soften, and the desire and ability to turn the news off and sit down and pull out the ponies and play becomes much easier.

Do you ever struggle with a commandment that you have difficulty obeying? Maybe it is worse than just difficult; you don't want to obey it. We wrestle in our desires, in our spirits. Then the Lord says, *Look unto me in that thought. Learn of me. Listen to my words: "Father, if it be possible, let this cup pass from me: nevertheless not as I will, but as thou wilt" (Matthew 26:39). Now walk in the meekness of my Spirit as best you can.* Once again, somehow, with that example in mind, with his words meekly singing in my ears, it is much easier to obey.

Perhaps someone has offended us or has done something against us. We've been hurt. We're bitter. We're angry. Yet we know we need to forgive. We sense the Lord urging us to do so. Then we pray, "Lord, to ask me to forgive under the circumstances, you might as well ask me to walk on water. I can't do it. I want to but I can't force the pain out of my heart." And he says, *I understand. Look unto me in that thought, in that challenge, in those pains. Learn of me. Listen to my words: "Father, forgive them; for they know not what they do" (Luke 23:34). Now walk in the meekness of my Spirit.* We could go on and on and on. In the scriptures there is an example in the Savior's life for almost every challenge, every disappointment, every frustration, every need, and every impossible walk-on-water request. I can look and learn and listen and then walk. When we're asked to walk on water, let us remember the three *L*s. There is strength and inspiration in them.

The Fleeces of the Lord

Second, God will give us fleeces. Look for fleeces! Ask for them! Anticipate them! Sometimes he will give us fleeces even when we don't ask because he understands human nature and human insecurities. From the story of Gideon and the Midianites in the Old Testament I have coined the expression "the fleeces of the Lord." To introduce it, we will discuss another story from the New Testament, one involving the Savior and an anxious fearful father. We can all relate to this father's anguished expression. He had a son who needed to be healed. He had asked the Apostles to do it, but they failed. This was a blow to this father's budding faith. Jesus was not present, but when he arrived later, the father approached him with his son and his request for intercession.

He has suffered a blow to his faith. He comes to the Savior in a state of desperation and asks, "If thou canst do any thing, have compassion on us, and help us" (Mark 9:22). Jesus turns his words around using his own doubtful *if:* "If thou canst believe," he responds, "all things are possible to him that believeth. And straightway the father of the child cried out, and said with tears, Lord, I believe; help thou mine unbelief" (Mark 9:23–24). Have you ever cried out that way? I believe. I know what you want me to do, what you expect of me. I want to do it, but it just seems so hard, so impossible. I believe. Help my unbelief. I need a fleece. I need something to encourage my belief, to sustain it, to prompt its saving faith.

In Judges we learn of a wonderful young man named Gideon. Gideon, like Peter, is easy to relate to because he is wonderfully human. We are introduced to him while he is hiding from the Midianites, threshing wheat. The Lord addresses him, saying, "The Lord is with thee, thou mighty man of valour" (Judges 6:12). I can visualize Gideon looking around and saying, *Are you talking to me? A mighty man of valor? I'm not one of those.*

Gideon replies, "Oh my Lord, if the Lord be with us, why then is all this befallen us?" They have been almost constantly raided by the Midianites. He continues, "And where be all his miracles which our fathers told us of?" (Judges 6:13).

"And the Lord looked upon him, and said,"—notice the assumption that Gideon can do it—"Go in this thy might, and thou shalt save Israel from the hand of the Midianites." I can almost see the doubt in Gideon's face. The Lord adds, "Have not I sent thee?" (Judges 6:14).

When my daughter was preparing for her mission, she had worked with some students from Taiwan in a summer program and had listened to them speaking Chinese. She came home one day and said "Chinese has to be the hardest language in the world to learn how to speak. That is the last language I hope I ever have to speak." Can you predict the outcome? You have to be careful when you say those types of things, lest the Lord is listening. When her mission call arrived, she was called to Taiwan. She felt like Gideon: *I am not a mighty woman of language ability.* We sat down and looked at this wonderful story in Judges and I said to her, "You have to look at it just like Gideon did. I think the Lord would say to you, *The Lord is with thee. Have not I sent thee? If I call you and I've sent you, I know you can do it.*" And she did!

Gideon still isn't convinced. "Oh my Lord," he asks, "wherewith shall I save Israel? behold, my family is poor in Manasseh, and I am the least in my father's house" (Judges 6:15). The first thing the Lord asks Gideon to do is to tear down the altar of Baal. He is afraid to do it in the daylight, so he destroys the altar in the middle of the night when nobody will see. As I said, he is easy to relate to—who among us wouldn't think of doing just that? Eventually Gideon does gather an army and prepares to go against the Midianites, but when he sees their numbers he doesn't feel like a mighty man of valor, and even though the Lord is with him and sent him, he needs a "fleece." He needs confirmation. He needs strengthening. He needs assurance beyond what he has already received. And the Lord responds.

"And Gideon said unto God, If thou wilt save Israel by mine hand, as thou hast said, Behold, I will put a fleece of wool in the [threshing] floor; and if the dew be on the fleece only, and it be dry upon all the earth beside, then shall I know that thou wilt save Israel by mine hand, as thou hast said. And it was so: for he rose up early on the morrow, and thrust the fleece together, and wringed the dew out of the fleece, a bowl full of water" (Judges 6:36–38).

That should be enough, one would think. But Gideon is human, just as all of us are. Sometimes in the walking-on-water experiences of our lives we may say, "Lord, could I have two fleeces?"

"And Gideon said unto God, Let not thine anger be hot against me [in other words, don't get upset, I know I should be satisfied with one fleece but . . .], and I will speak but this once: let me prove, I pray thee, but this once with the fleece; let it now be dry only upon the fleece, and upon all the ground let there be dew. And God did so that night: for it was dry upon the fleece only, and there was dew on all the ground" (Judges 6:39–40).

All of this might sound like seeking for signs, which is something the scriptures are rather harsh against. However, there is a difference between sign-seeking and fleece-asking. Sign-seeking says, "I'm not going to do it unless you give me a sign." Its foundation is usually doubt and opposition. When we ask for fleeces, we want to do what the Lord's asking. We intend to do it. We are going to do it. We have hope. We have faith that he has asked us to do it. We just need encouragement. We just need a little help. "I believe," we cry, "help thou mine unbelief." God is very good in granting that to us.

Shortly after receiving his two fleeces, Gideon is told by the Lord that he has too many soldiers. His ranks were reduced by the Lord to three hundred, based upon the manner in which they drank from the spring at Harod. Gideon had already promised the Lord when he received his second fleece that he would not ask again, but he had only three hundred men and his enemies were as numerous as grasshoppers. I think God knew Gideon intimately and so he mercifully asks, "Would you like another fleece?" Without Gideon even asking, the Lord offers him an additional confidence-building fleece. *It is time for battle, but if you're afraid, go down to the host and you'll hear something which will give you the courage you need.* And so Gideon climbs down to the edge of the Midianites' camp, where he hears a man recount a dream with its accompanying interpretation and realizes he will truly scatter the Midianite army (see Judges 7:13–15).

"Come over into Macedonia, and Help Us"

Let me give you an example in my own life of the mercy of fleeces. A number of years ago I was on the religion faculty at Brigham Young University. When I accepted the full-time position I assumed that I was going to teach at BYU forever, at least until retirement. This was an end-of-your-career move. Where would I go after having accepted an invitation to teach at the Church's flagship institution? The year before they asked me to join the faculty, I had taught one year at the institute adjacent to the University of Utah. I loved it. It was a wonderful year. I could not have been happier. I loved the students. I loved the environment. I loved the university. I loved the other instructors. Of all the places I had ever worked in the Church Educational System, the institute adjacent to the University of Utah felt most like home. There was a comfort zone there that fit me uniquely. I distinctly remember walking into the institute building the very first time and saying, "This feels like home."

A year later, the offer from BYU came. It was too hard to turn down for a number of personal reasons, so I went to BYU and joined the faculty and taught in Provo for four years. I received a call one day from the placement director at the Church Educational System who said, "Mike, there's an opening at the institute adjacent to the University of Utah. We'd like you to consider taking it and returning to your former assignment."

My first reaction was, "Well no, I'm at BYU. I'm at the end of the road. I'm at the flagship. Why would I do that?" Yet something inside of me said, "Don't answer just yet. Think it over."

So I said, "Could I have until Monday [the call came on a Friday] to give you an answer?"

He said, "Yes, by all means. You take all the time you need and call me next week."

I prayed and fasted and did all the things we always do when we're trying to make a big decision. One evening that weekend while I was praying, the Lord very clearly spoke only two words to me. He simply said, "Go home." I knew what he meant. He was referring to that feeling I had when I first walked into the institute adjacent to the University of Utah. "Go home." It was as clear and solid an answer as any I had ever received, but it was such a difficult decision. Everyone was encouraging me to do just the opposite and wondering why I would even entertain the thought of returning to the University of Utah.

I went to the Jordan River Utah Temple. As I sat in the chapel waiting for the session, I picked up the Bible, held it in front of me with both hands, and thought, *Lord, I know I have already received a clear answer, but I really need a fleece. I need to know this is truly what I should do, what you want me to do, and what is best for me to do. I need a fleece.* I suppose this could be looked on as a presumptuous thing, or even a silly thing, but I was hoping I'd get an immediate fleece by turning to an unavoidably clear verse in the scriptures that would validate my decision. I assume most of us have done this. We pick up our scriptures, open them, and anticipate that the answer is going to be right there on the page in front of us. In a way it's like saying, "Father in Heaven, give me an answer right now." I don't do it very often, but I was full of anxiety and hoped God would respond to me as he had to Gideon.

I opened the Bible to Acts 16. I looked at the top of the page and I thought, "Well, that didn't work." I had been teaching about the book of Acts and the life of Paul, and I knew that Acts 16 was his second missionary journey. I couldn't imagine there was anything there that could help me. I was just about to close the book. Sometimes if it doesn't work the first time we say, "I'll give you a second chance, Lord." But before I closed the book, my eye caught the very first verse on that page. This is what I read. You tell me if, in his kindness and graciousness and his mercy, knowing this was a difficult thing for me, the Lord gave me a fleece:

"After they were come to Mysia, they assayed to go unto Bithynia [I even noticed that Bithynia had the letters *B* and *Y* in it. Probably not significant, but I couldn't help seeing the irony]: but the Spirit suffered them not. And they passing by Mysia came down to Troas. And a vision appeared to Paul in the night; There stood a man of Macedonia, and prayed him, saying, *Come over into Macedonia, and help us.* And after he had seen the vision, *immediately we endeavoured to go into Macedonia, assuredly gathering that the Lord had called us for to preach the gospel unto them.* Therefore loosing from Troas, we came with a straight course to Samothracia, and the next day to Neapolis; and from thence to Philippi, which is the chief city of that part of Macedonia" (Acts 16:7–12; emphasis added).

Did I receive my needed fleece? When I saw Philippi mentioned, I realized how powerful the fleece I'd been given was, because I knew that Philippi was one of Paul's favorite cities. The Philippians were so good to him. Their relationship with Paul had a number of unique features. The Epistle to the Philippians is one of the sweetest of all the epistles and a personal favorite of mine. This was God's way of saying to me, "The University of Utah will be your Philippi." He gave me my fleece.

A final thought on fleeces. All of the truths and principles of the gospel, as taught in the scriptures, are delicately balanced. We must always remember that our very human need to find reassurance or validation or courage to face walking-on-water challenges is not an invitation to engage in subtle sign-seeking. It is, rather, a desire to interpret God's will correctly, to advance in the manner he wishes, and to increase our confidence—not so much in him or in his commands, but in ourselves and in our ability to read spiritual promptings properly.

Sometimes, as in the case of Peter on the Sea of Galilee, the situation may not have anything to do with the will of the Lord. It may be instigated by our own desires to which the Lord is finely tuned and anxious to both know and fulfill. We should not attempt to uncompromisingly dictate or demand how, where, or when the Lord provides the needed fleece. Each situation will define those parameters.

Neither must we be afraid that our requests for a fleece will be seen as a lack of faith or a sign of weakness or that the Lord will perceive it as sign-seeking. We cannot reduce the gospel to simple formulas that define all behavior. Even a cursory reading of the scriptures reveals that, though we often try or earnestly wish that we could. The only hope I can offer in finding the right balance is this thought: When I desire a fleece in my own life, if I can sincerely say to the Lord, "Father, it is not a matter of seeing with the eyes before I move forward or of comprehending with the mind (though understanding would be helpful), but one of feeling with the heart. I'm not trying to do an end run around faith, but there is comfort in feeling the water drip from my hands." Having offered these thoughts to the Lord, I wring the fleece with hope, anticipation, and ultimately gratitude.

EAGLE'S WINGS

Third, God often gives us eagle's wings to carry us over the surface of the water we're trying to walk upon. He increases our strength, our faith, our courage, our wisdom, our ability to forgive, our love, our willpower, or whatever is needed. Let us look at a verse in Isaiah that speaks of the lifting empowerment of eagle's wings.

Before doing so, I want to return to the story in Matthew and again visualize Peter walking on the water. He did do it for a while, didn't he? Yet after his initial success we read, "When he saw the wind boisterous, he was afraid; and beginning to sink . . ." How deep do you picture him? I always like to use my imagination and visualize events in the scriptures. Do you see him knee-deep? Waist-deep? Neck-deep? How deep is "beginning to sink"?

"Beginning to sink, he cried, saying, Lord, save me. And immediately Jesus stretched forth his hand." In my own mental image of this moment, Peter doesn't sink too deep in the water before the Savior immediately reaches out and catches him. Then Jesus, standing next to him as they together walk on the water, says, "O thou of little faith, wherefore didst thou doubt?" (Matthew 14:30–31). Do you imagine he said that to him while Peter was still halfway in the water? I don't picture it that way. I believe he lifted him up, and after he steadied Peter next to him, strengthened him, and upheld him, he asked the question.

How do you imagine their return to the ship? They must have taken a few steps to get back to the ship, because the next verse says, "When they were come into the ship, the wind ceased" (Matthew 14:32). That seems to suggest there was at least a little distance they had to cover together. Do you imagine Jesus had to drag him through the water? Did the Savior hook Peter's hand on the side of the boat and say, "Climb back in?" I don't picture it that way. Jesus reached out to him, caught him, steadied him, and lifted him up. Then, with the Savior by his side, Peter walked again on the water back to the ship.

We have promises literally throughout the scriptures that the Savior will help us, God will help us, and the Holy Spirit will help us. In Isaiah, the Lord promises, "I the Lord thy God will hold thy right hand, saying unto thee, Fear not; I will help thee" (Isaiah 41:13). And his help is wonderful. My favorite description of God anywhere in scripture is found in Isaiah 40. It is a poetic image, but it is simply a beautiful one.

Isaiah paints a picture of a majestic and powerful God, the God we all worship, a God "who hath measured the waters in the hollow of his hand" (Isaiah 40:12). Can you picture that? The Father we worship can encompass the oceans in his cupped and upturned hand! He can hold the Pacific Ocean right there in his palm. It is a beautiful, poetic image.

Isaiah continues, "And meted out heaven with the span . . ." Our God can measure all the heavens between his thumb and little finger, which constituted a span—a measure similar to the English foot. "And comprehended the dust of the earth in a measure . . ." A measure was roughly a few gallons, a small bushel basket. God can hold all the dust of the earth in a little container. "And weighed the mountains in scales, and the hills in a balance" (Isaiah 40:12). Can you see with your poet's eye the Lord grasping a little handheld scale? He is going to put the Himalayas, or the Rockies, or the Alps in the dish and tell us how much they weigh. "Who hath directed the Spirit of the Lord, or being his counsellor hath taught him?" Isaiah asks (Isaiah 40:13). The Lord doesn't need anyone to counsel or teach him. "Behold, the nations are as a drop of a bucket, and are counted as the small dust of the balance" (Isaiah 40:15). Can we imagine? Here is China, Russia, Brazil, Australia—just specks of dust on the balances that he can blow away with a whisper.

Isaiah asks some questions next: "Have ye not known? have ye not heard? hath it not been told you from the beginning? have ye not understood from the foundations of the earth? It is he that sitteth upon the circle of the earth" (Isaiah 40:21–22). Here is an image to contemplate. Can we see the horizon off in the distance? The Lord is sitting there on the edge of the world, contemplating the heavens above him, a benign presence in the midst of eternity. God, Isaiah assures us, "stretcheth out the heavens as a curtain, and spreadeth them out as a tent to dwell in." We are invited to "lift up [our] eyes on high" and contemplate the wonders of the galaxy (Isaiah 40:22, 26). At night we often ponder the stars. "Behold who hath created these things, that bringeth out their host by number:

he calleth them all by names by the greatness of his might, for that he is strong in power; not one faileth" (Isaiah 40:26). He knows the names of all those stars. He holds all of them in their orbits.

And this God, who holds the ocean in the palm of his hand, measures the heavens with the span of his thumb and little finger, weighs mountains in scales, and sits on the horizon enveloped by the tent of the universe, calling the stars by name—this God is the God that you and I casually talked to this morning in the intimate conversation of prayer. There is something wonderfully humbling about the dignity that that thought bestows on us. It is this God who promises, "I the Lord thy God will hold thy right hand, . . . Fear not; I will help thee" (Isaiah 41:13).

It is in the context of that cosmic drama of universal majesty that Isaiah records these words about the Lord: "He giveth power to the faint; and to them that have no might he increaseth strength. Even the youths shall faint and be weary, and the young men shall utterly fall: But they that wait upon the Lord [that is, hope or anticipate help from God] shall renew their strength; they shall mount up with wings as eagles; they shall run, and not be weary; and they shall walk, and not faint" (Isaiah 40:29–31).

Sometimes I look at this verse and wonder if maybe the order of movement should be reversed. The actions are descending from highest to lowest. Would it not be better if the listing went lowest to highest? "They shall walk and not faint. They shall run and not be weary." It takes more energy to run than walk, doesn't it? "They shall mount up with wings as eagles." Now they are flying. Walk, run, fly. I'll renew your strength in ever-increasing amounts as the need arises. Yet the more I think about it, I suppose it is better that it starts from highest to lowest— flying, running, walking—as if the Lord is saying, "I will more than renew your strength. I will give you more than the faith, the love, the courage, the forgiveness, the talents, the willpower, whatever it is that you feel you need. I will renew your strength from your highest needs to even your simplest ones."

The theme that God will increase what we have, making it sufficient for whatever need we have, is so important that we see it taught again and again and again in the scriptures. When Jesus fed the five thousand, all of his disciples were focused on the need—on the hunger of five thousand men, women, and children. The Savior wanted them to focus on what they had—the five loaves and two fishes (see Matthew 14:15–21). He can increase what we have to fill the hungers of the moment. So often in my life I focus on the five thousand and not on the five. The Savior asks them what they have, just as he asks us to bring whatever we do have to him. He then blesses what they have (and what we have) and makes it sufficient. Yet the story does not end there—twelve baskets of fragments are left over. He gives us sufficient for our needs and beyond. Always in this genre of stories you get more than you need. You are allowed to gather up the fragments of his abundant blessings and power to use in future times of need. This happened after they had already eaten as much as they wanted and were filled. So it is in our own lives.

In 2 Kings, we meet a woman who is facing a creditor who threatens to take her two sons to fulfill the debt. She hurries to Elisha for help, and Elisha asks her, "What hast thou in the house?" (2 Kings 4:2). The question is critical. God always asks us to bring what we have. Peter had a "little faith"—not enough for an extended walk across the face of the Sea of Galilee—but he had to bring that little faith. He didn't have enough, but he brought what he had. "What hast thou in the house?" Elisha asked the widow, and she answered, "Thine handmaid hath not any thing in the house, save a pot of oil" (2 Kings 4:2). *I don't have enough for the need,* she thought. *What I do have is not "any thing" that could even begin to face this crisis.* Elisha told her to borrow empty vessels of many kinds from all her neighbors and shut the door and then start pouring the oil out. "So she went from him, and shut the door upon her and upon her sons. . . . And it came to pass, when the vessels were full, that she said unto her son, Bring me yet a vessel. And he said unto her, There is not a vessel more. And the oil stayed. Then she came and told [Elisha]. And he said, Go, sell the oil, and pay thy debt, and live thou and thy children of the rest" (2 Kings 4:5–7).

In this story we find all the elements in the feeding of the five thousand. We find them also in the feeding of the four thousand (see Matthew 15:32–38) and in the barrel of meal and cruse of oil that Elijah multiplies for the widow he meets at the gate (see 1 Kings 17:8–16). There was enough oil for the needs of the widow in 2 Kings 4 and beyond. There was enough meal and oil to feed the widow at the gate through the famine. Time and time again we read in the scriptures of people who have needs that are not sufficiently met. Is this not a fairly clear assessment of the human condition? The Lord asks us to bring what we have. How can he ask for more? He is not unjust! He will bless what we have, multiply it, make it sufficient for the need, and always—*always*—beyond. God strengthens his children. He gives them wings as eagles so they can fly. Not only run, not only walk, but fly.

LET DOWN THE NETS

Fourth, when it seems like I am trying to walk on water, the Spirit sometimes whispers, "Let down the nets." This spiritual encouragement comes from another story about Peter. The Savior is in Capernaum and is crowded by followers, so he enters Peter's boat and pushes off from the shore to give him some room to teach. When he is finished, he turns to Peter: "Now when he had left speaking, he said unto Simon, Launch out into the deep, and let down your nets for a draught [for a catch]. And Simon answering said unto him, Master, we have toiled all the night, and have taken nothing" (Luke 5:4–5). When I read this passage, I always put a little pause at this moment. Perhaps, Peter is thinking of the reasons—good reasons—why he shouldn't do something at this particular time. He is the fisherman and the fishing is done for the day, but it is the Savior asking. Occasionally, I think like Peter when I face a difficult thing. I sometimes respond: "I already tried and I failed, so why try again?" But in that pause, I see the Savior just looking at Peter, even smiling, and eventually Peter answers, "Nevertheless at thy word I will let down the net. And when they had this done, they inclosed a great multitude of fishes: and their net brake" (Luke 5:5–6). There are times we simply have to "nevertheless let down the net." In spite of all our own expertise and reasoning the proper response is one of "nevertheless."

When we face challenging things, even things which we have already attempted and failed, it may be difficult to return to the task. We can personally arrive at many reasons why we shouldn't try again, but because the Lord asks us, we let down the net. We may fail again and again and again, but each time we must say "nevertheless . . . I will let down the net." Maybe the very grace that Christ gives us is discovered in our ability to keep trying in the face of repeated disappointments.

C. S. Lewis once said, "I believe that if a million chances were likely to do good, they would be given."[1] We simply must continue to let down the nets. What if Alma had not gone back to Ammonihah? (See Alma 8.) I'm sure he could have thought of many good reasons why he shouldn't go back. They had rejected him; they had spat upon him; they obviously didn't want to listen to his message. But he went back. He faced a "nevertheless" moment and responded just as Peter did. Down went the nets, and he caught Amulek and Zeezrom.

I recall just such a moment in my own life while serving a mission in France. My companion and I had just finished thoroughly tracting an area. I found myself in that same area, working with the zone leader and some members. There was a little building with maybe a dozen apartments in it. We had tracted it out the previous week. The Spirit said, "Tract out that building again." Well, I argued, saying in so many words, "Master, we have toiled all the night [at that building] and have taken nothing." Pause. "Nevertheless at thy word I will let down the net [again in that building]." You know the outcome. This is one of those "last-door missionary stories." It wasn't the last door, actually. It was the second-to-the-last door. We found a wonderful man who joined the Church two weeks later with his wife. A few weeks later his brother joined the Church. His

sister joined the Church. I received a letter a few years ago from that family telling me how many of their children had been on missions, how many had been
married in the temple, how many grandchildren were in the mission field at that
time. What if I had not let down the nets again? There are times when we must
try and try and try again. Let down the nets!

WILL THE REAL THOMAS PLEASE STAND UP!

Fifth, we must learn to see as we are seen, and to know as we are known.
That is a promise the scriptures give to us—that one day we will see as we are
seen and know as we are known. I read that very, very positively. I sense that
the Lord is saying, "Mike, you don't know yourself as well as I do. You don't see
yourself as I see you." And he always sees us at our most competent.

If we return again to the same story in Luke where Peter lets down the nets,
we find some additional interesting details: "And they beckoned unto their part-
ners, which were in the other ship, that they should come and help them. And
they came, and filled both the ships, so that they began to sink" (Luke 5:7).
There is a certain truth in this story I really love, and it's this: God tends to ask
us to leave when our nets are full. Have you ever noticed that? Why did he work
this fill-the-nets miracle? I think it may be to teach us that one of the walk-on-
water, impossible things he might ask us to do is to leave when the nets are full.
Let me illustrate. The nets may be full when a boy has an athletic scholarship to
his dream college and the Lord's call for a mission is extended. It may be when
a girl is asked to the prom by the coolest guy in the high school, but she is only
fifteen and a half years old. It may be when we have a houseful of wonderful
grandchildren and the Lord says, "I'd like you to serve a mission as a couple." It
may be when we have everything to live for that cancer or something else calls us
home. God tends to call us when the nets are full.

Continuing on with the narrative, we read: "When Simon Peter saw it, he
fell down at Jesus' knees, saying, Depart from me; for I am a sinful man, O
Lord" (Luke 5:8). Peter saw himself as a sinful man, not worthy of Christ's presence. "And Jesus said unto Simon, Fear not; from henceforth thou shalt catch
men" (Luke 5:10). I like Matthew's version of that call a little better. "Follow
me, and I will make you fishers of men" (Matthew 4:19). Peter saw himself as a
sinful man. Jesus saw him as a fisher of men, an Apostle, and one worthy of his
intimate friendship.

We are taught the same truth in the calling of the Apostle Paul. After his
experience on the road to Damascus, Paul was waiting for Ananias to come and
to give him back his sight. "And there was a certain disciple at Damascus, named
Ananias; and to him said the Lord in a vision, Ananias. And he said, Behold, I

am here, Lord. And the Lord said unto him, Arise, and go into the street which is called Straight, and enquire in the house of Judas for one called Saul, of Tarsus: for, behold, he prayeth. . . . Then Ananias answered, Lord, I have heard by many of this man, how much evil he hath done to thy saints at Jerusalem: And here he hath authority from the chief priests to bind all that call on thy name" (Acts 9:10–11, 13–14). How did Ananias see Paul? He saw him as a persecuting problem. "But the Lord said unto him, Go thy way: for he is a chosen vessel unto me" (Acts 9:15). What was Paul? A persecuting problem or a chosen vessel? God saw his potential. He always sees our potential.

My favorite see-as-we-are-seen and know-as-we-are-known (or learning-to-see-ourselves-at-our-best) story is the story of Thomas. How would any group in our church, or any Christian church, fill in the following blank: _____ Thomas? They would say "Doubting Thomas." We remember Thomas at one of his worst moments. After asking the first question I like to ask people a follow-up: "Do any of you know of another story about Thomas in the New Testament?" I rarely get a response to that question. But there is another story about Thomas in the New Testament. In it we see him differently. Mary and Martha have sent word to Jesus that Lazarus, their brother, is sick. Jesus knows from the beginning he is going to raise Lazarus from the dead. Their home is in Bethany, just over the Mount of Olives, close to Jerusalem and danger from the Jewish authorities. "His disciples say unto him, Master, the Jews of late sought to stone thee; and goest thou thither again?" (John 11:8). When they realize that the Savior truly is intent on returning to Bethany, even though they fear for his life, Thomas shows his true colors. "Then said Thomas . . . unto his fellow-disciples, Let us also go, that we may die with him" (John 11:16). Is the true Thomas, the real Thomas, the one we call "Doubting Thomas," or should we change it to "Devoted Thomas"? "Sacrificing Thomas"? "Willing-to-die-for-Jesus Thomas"? I think the real Thomas is Thomas at his best. The real Paul was the chosen vessel. The real Peter was the fisher of men. One day we will see as we are seen and know as we are known.

THE HARD SAYINGS

Sixth, there is one last idea I want to share that helps me when I face a walk-on-water moment. It is a realization that gives me courage to move forward even without much assurance. This idea comes from a question Peter asked at a critical juncture in his relationship with Jesus. He said: "To whom shall we go?" (John 6:68). There are times when we realize there isn't any other choice. This expression comes from a story in John 6. Jesus has just fed the five thousand; he has walked on water during the night; and he arrives at the synagogue in Capernaum. The disciples are there, many of his followers are there, and he teaches them the bread of life discourse. In that discourse he essentially says to the Jewish nation, "I cannot be the kind of a God you want me to be. I did not come to solve all your physical problems. I came to solve spiritual problems. You must accept me as my Father wants me to be, not as you want me to be" (see John 6:26–59). This is very difficult for many of the disciples—not just the curious listeners, but also the believing disciples. We then read this rather poignant sentence: "Many therefore of his disciples, when they had heard this, said, This is an hard saying; who can hear it?" (John 6:60).

All of us face what we can call "hard sayings." They come at different times and in different ways. We don't need to judge one another in these matters. Your hard saying may not be hard for me, and mine may not be difficult for you, but there are many "hard sayings" we run into in life. Some come directly from God and some are delivered to us by the vicissitudes of mortality. One way or the other we wonder how God can ask this of us, or why he would allow it. Is it not impossible? We simply can't do it! It's a hard saying.

"When Jesus knew in himself that his disciples murmured at it, he said unto them, Doth this offend you? . . . From that time many of his disciples went back, and walked no more with him" (John 6:61, 66). You can see that moment in the synagogue in Capernaum. There is complete silence as the disciples—not the Twelve, but the other followers—slowly file out and leave the Savior. He has asked too hard a thing of them. They can't do it. Then in a very poignant moment in the Savior's life, he turned to the Twelve and said, "Will ye also go away? Then Simon Peter answered him, Lord, to whom shall we go? thou hast the words of eternal life. And we believe and are sure that thou art that Christ, the Son of the living God" (John 6:67–69).

Are there not times in your life when you simply have to say, "Where would I go? I really don't have any choice. It may be a hard saying, but what do I do? The gospel is true. The commandments are real. The Savior is my Lord." That idea is taught again and again in a number of different ways.

In the Book of Mormon the three days of darkness teach this very relevant truth. Notice that when Mormon describes those days, he doesn't emphasize so much that it's dark, he emphasizes that there is no light. Four times in his description he stresses the complete absence of light. We read, "And there could be no light, because of the darkness, neither candles, neither torches; neither could there be fire kindled with their fine and exceedingly dry wood, so that there could not be any light at all" (3 Nephi 8:21). He states it twice in the above sentence. He then adds, "And there was not any light seen, neither fire, nor glimmer, neither the sun, nor the moon, nor the stars, for so great were the mists of darkness which were upon the face of the land. And it came to pass that it did last for the space of three days that there was no light seen" (3 Nephi 8:22–23). He mentions it two more times in this sentence to equal four times in total. We receive the impression that we're really supposed to understand that there is no other source of light anywhere. Out of that darkness Christ introduced himself by saying, "I am the light and the life of the world" (3 Nephi 9:18). The implication is that there is no other light!

There are a lot of "I am" statements made by the Savior throughout the scriptures. Jesus compares himself, for instance, to bread, a vine, a shepherd, the way, the truth, the life, a rock, a nail, living water, and so on. "I am the bread of life," he tells us (John 6:35).

Sometimes we respond by saying, in so many words, "I'm sure you bring nutritious bread, but there are other breads I'd like to eat whose flavors are more to my liking. I'm going to go and eat that other bread."

And he answers, "You don't understand. There is no other bread. I am the bread of life." He is "the way" (John 14:6).

Once again we may respond, "Your way is probably very good, Lord, and I'd love to walk it, but it is a hard way sometimes, a bit too steep in places. I'm going to walk this other way." He gently replies, "You don't understand. There is no other way. I am the way. I am the light. I am the truth."

There Is No Other Stream

In *The Silver Chair,* one of the Chronicles of Narnia series, C. S. Lewis writes of an exchange between a girl named Jill and the great lion Aslan, who represents the Savior in those books. She is very thirsty. As she walks through a forest she comes into a little clearing where she sees a stream. She breaks into the clearing, heading for the stream, and then sees a great lion sitting by the bank and freezes in fear.

"She knew at once that [the lion] had seen her, for its eyes looked straight into hers for a moment and then turned away. . . . 'If you're thirsty you may drink.'"

For a moment, Jill is confused as to the source of the voice, then realizes it is coming from Aslan. The voice renews its invitation.

"'Are you not thirsty?' said the Lion."

"'I'm dying of thirst,' said Jill."

"'Then drink,' said the Lion."

The voice was not like a man's voice but "deeper, wilder, and stronger, a sort of heavy golden voice."

Jill responds to this second invitation by saying, "'May I? Could I? Would you mind going away while I do?' said Jill. The lion answered this only by a look and a very low growl. And as Jill gazed at its motionless bulk, she realized that she might as well have asked the whole mountain to move aside for her convenience. The delicious rippling noise of the stream was driving her nearly frantic.

"'Will you promise not to—do anything to me, if I do come?' said Jill.

"'I make no promise,' said the Lion.

"Jill was so thirsty now that, without noticing it, she had come a step nearer.

"'*Do* you eat girls?' she said.

"'I have swallowed up girls and boys, women and men, kings and emperors, cities and realms,' said the Lion. It didn't say this as if it were boasting, nor as if it were sorry, nor as if it were angry. It just said it.

"'I daren't come and drink,' said Jill.

"'Then you will die of thirst,' said the Lion.

"'Oh dear!' said Jill, coming a step nearer. 'I suppose I must go and look for another stream then.'"

Now you can tell me what the Lion's going to say, can't you?

"'There is no other stream,' said the Lion. It never occurred to Jill to disbelieve the Lion. No one who had seen his . . . face could do that."[2]

There is no other way! To whom shall we go? There is no other light! There is no other bread. There is no other water! He is the living water. If we understand this, even though we may face the hard sayings, even though life's challenges or the Lord's counsels are difficult, we can succeed.

"SILVER AND GOLD HAVE I NONE"

It is often helpful to ask ourselves if we're attempting to walk on the wrong sea, or to walk on water the Savior has not asked us to walk on, or to attempt an impossible act of our own making. This is only a warning thought we may need occasionally. Often we want to do the impossible, particularly as it relates to others. We would like to give life, to restore health, to create testimony, to take away someone's pain, to fix a marriage or to create one for someone, to bring happiness, to end sorrow. Often we feel these longings for our children and they can unintentionally create a certain guilt, a certain subtle anxiety, because we want so much to bring blessings to other people's lives and we can't always do that. In those moments when I'm trying to do the impossible that, perhaps, God hasn't asked me to do, or I have no means or ability to do, I have to remind myself of the "silver and gold" principle.

In Acts 3, as Peter and John entered the temple to pray, "A certain man lame from his mother's womb was carried, whom they laid daily at the gate of the temple which is called Beautiful, to ask alms of them that entered into the temple; who seeing Peter and John about to go into the temple asked an alms. And Peter, fastening his eyes upon him with John, said, Look on us. And he gave heed unto them, expecting to receive something of them. Then Peter said, Silver and gold have I none; but such as I have give I thee: In the name of Jesus Christ of Nazareth rise up and walk" (Acts 3:2–6).

There are many times, particularly with my own children, in my own situation, sometimes with students, when I would love to supply for them what they need, what they want, or to bring some happiness into their life, but I can't. And I have to say, as Peter did, "Silver and gold have I none." This, however, doesn't mean I haven't something to give. "Such as I have give I thee." I can only give what I have. I'd love to provide a husband for a daughter, a baby for another daughter who would love very much to be a mother and is not able to have a child. I deeply desire to create health for a wife and a testimony for a beloved friend. I would love to place forgiveness into the heart of another friend riddled with bitterness. None of those things do I have the power to do independently. But that doesn't mean I can't do something. There are times in our lives we must say, "Silver and gold have I none. Such as I have give I thee."

I have learned through my own experiences that occasionally we demand of life what it really cannot give. There is a verse in Doctrine and Covenants 101 that I have fought all of my life. I probably still fight it. Sometimes I want total fulfillment in this world, splendid and encompassing happiness in this very realm, and yet as the Savior said to the Saints in the midst of the Missouri persecutions, "Fear not even unto death; for in this world your joy is not full, but in me your joy is full" (D&C 101:36). I have fought that truth most of my life. I want joy to be full in this world somehow, but that is an impossibility. That is water we're not asked to walk on, finding total fulfillment and satisfaction in this life. That doesn't mean there isn't joy in life. There is joy in life, and happiness, and great reason to be glad. We're encouraged constantly to be of good cheer, but only in the Savior is our joy full. Not in this world.

"LOVEST THOU ME?"

May I add one more *L* to the three *Ls*? What is the most powerful agent in replacing doubt and fear? I believe that agent is love. Shortly after the Resurrection, the Savior asked Peter to do a very difficult thing. Jesus took him aside, walked with him along the shore of the Sea of Galilee, and said, "Verily, verily, I say unto thee, When thou wast young, thou girdedst thyself, and walkedst whither thou wouldest: but when thou shalt be old, thou shalt stretch forth thy hands, and another shall gird thee, and carry thee whither thou wouldest not. This spake he, signifying by what death he should glorify God. And when he had spoken this, he saith unto him, Follow me" (John 21:18–19).

He had asked Peter to follow him earlier, also on the shore of Galilee, in being a teacher of the gospel. Now he was asking him to follow him even in his death, even in the manner of his death. This seems to me to be so fitting for the Peter who manifested in his life the attitude, "I want to do everything my Master did!" His life would terminate in like manner. How difficult that would have been for Peter. He would live the rest of his life knowing that when the end finally came, not only would he die for the Savior, but he would be crucified as Christ had been. I suppose Peter must have been a little bit shocked when the Savior said that to him. Again, as at his first call to follow the Master, I hear a little pause before those last words, "Follow me." Jesus tells Peter he will die a similar death, and pauses to let it sink in, and then those last two words, "Follow me." Will you, Peter, follow me even in my death?

What would give Peter the ability to do that? To live, knowing what lay ahead for him? I think we find the answer in the conversation that immediately precedes that sobering announcement. It is a famous conversation:

"So when they had dined, Jesus saith to Simon Peter, Simon, son of Jonas, lovest thou me more than these? He saith unto him, Yea, Lord; thou knowest that I love thee. He saith unto him, Feed my lambs. He saith to him again the second time, Simon, son of Jonas, lovest thou me? He saith unto him, Yea, Lord; thou knowest that I love thee. He saith unto him, Feed my sheep. He saith unto him the third time, Simon, son of Jonas, lovest thou me? Peter was grieved because he said unto him the third time, Lovest thou me? And he said unto him, Lord, thou knowest all things; thou knowest that I love thee. Jesus saith unto him, Feed my sheep" (John 21:15–17).

It is the love of the Lord and the love of his lambs that gives Peter strength and courage. "If you love me, Peter, and I know that you do, then follow me. Even in this last, great, impossible walk-on-water act I have asked of you. Give your life as a final testimony for both me and my lambs." It is this same love that the Savior himself felt that enabled him to endure Gethsemane and Calvary. Of all the impossible things that were ever done in the history of the world, of all the walk-on-water-difficult, heart-tearing things to face, surely the Savior's own sacrifice is unequaled. When faced with the reality of this sacrifice, Jesus himself pleaded with the Father that he would not have to go through it. Yet he did it. What power enabled him to accomplish it? It was his love. John introduced the last hours of the Savior's life with these words. "Now before the feast of the passover, when Jesus knew that his hour was come that he should depart out of this world unto the Father, having loved his own which were in the world, he loved them unto the end" (John 13:1–2). It is love that gives us the power to walk on water. We look unto Christ in every thought. We learn of him. We listen to his words. We love. Then we step off the boat onto the surface of the water and walk.

OF MICE AND MAZES

I would like to share a story as a small illustration of the power of love in helping us do impossible things. When I was in the eighth grade, I entered the school's science fair contest. I decided that I would test the intelligence of guinea pigs, rats, and mice to find out which species was smartest. (In case you want to know, the rat is the smartest of the three.) I built a large and complex maze, and I trained the animals to go through it. I timed them and ran graphs and charts comparing their learning speed. After they had learned to race through the maze to the food at the other end, I placed metal plates that gave the animals a tiny electric shock to see if they could change their route and find the end using a different way. It was great fun. I actually won the school science fair project. It was amazing to me, and I had an opportunity to represent my grade in the California regional science fair.

A couple of weeks before the final competition was to be held at the regional level, the mouse grew ill. He was sneezing. Have you ever heard a mouse sneeze? It's a dreadful, dreadful sound if you're an eighth grader with a science fair project to defend. I begged my mother to let me bring the mouse into the house. She said, because she hates mice, "All right, son, bring him in, but promise me that the mouse will stay safe. I don't want him loose in the house." I promised quickly enough. I brought the mouse into the house, put him in a shoe box, and locked it in the bathroom—not a smart thing to do. In the morning there was a lovely little hole chewed in the bottom of the shoe box and no mouse. I sneaked around my bedroom and into the hall, quietly trying to find the mouse. I could not find him. I finally had to go into the kitchen where my mother was preparing breakfast and break the tragic news to her that we had a mouse loose in the house. That was not one of my more triumphant moments.

I stayed home from school that day and the next searching the house, desperately hunting for my mouse. My mother said, "You will find that creature." I found everything anyone had ever lost since the pre-mortal life. I just couldn't find the mouse. For a few days we experienced the mystery of the flashing mouse. We would be watching TV and he'd go scurrying across the carpet behind the bookcase. Everyone would scream and we'd try to surround him, but we couldn't catch him. Finally, when there were just a few days before the science fair project, I noticed a different attitude in my mother. She began to realize what I knew from the beginning: If I didn't have that mouse to run through that maze, my hopes of doing anything at the regional science fair were pretty much dashed.

One night as she was sleeping—she had a long bedspread that draped over the bed—the mouse climbed up her bedspread, right onto the pillow next to her head. She woke up and could hear something on the pillow. Terrified, she began to slowly reach over to try and turn on the light. She did get the light turned on, but her movement and the sudden light scared the mouse and he ran right across her head into her hair. She sat upright and pulled at him, throwing him onto the middle of the bed. Can you picture this scene? There sits the mouse, right in the middle of the bed, watching and waiting for a brief second. He starts to move toward the edge. My mother's mind went through the following thought process: *There's the mouse! My son needs that mouse. But I hate mice! My son needs that mouse.* Without even thinking, just reacting on her love for me, she reached out and scooped him up in her hands. Then she realized what she had done. But rather than let him go, she began to shake her hands back and forth so the mouse couldn't stop and bite her. She rushed through the house, yelling for me, trying to turn on lights with her elbows, all the time continuing to shake her hands. I was deep in sleep, but finally woke up with all the commotion. She said, "Mike, I've got the mouse! I've got the mouse!"

I said, "Where is it? Where is it?"

"Right here," she responded, shaking her hands in front of my face. Then, with relief, she dropped it on the bed. I got ready to pounce, but I didn't need to because the poor little fellow looked like he had been on a three-week bender— he could hardly walk straight. I did pick up the mouse, returned him to his cage, and a few days later he was able to run the maze for the judges at the regional science fair. However, he never quite walked the same way through the maze again.

The memory of that story makes me laugh. It is a very simple story, but I realized from that day forth that my mother really loved me and that her love for me enabled her to do something impossible for her, or at least something extremely difficult. It is our love for each other and for our Heavenly Parents and for the Savior that enables us to do all the difficult, impossible, walk-on-water things.

Mustard Seed and Mountains

There is a scripture in Matthew which for years and years I read literally and always felt guilty regarding my lack of faith. It is the "mustard seed/moving mountains" verse. I felt dejected by that verse because I knew I didn't have enough faith to move a mountain. I've since realized in my study of the scriptures that a verse isn't a whole lot of good if its application is so infinitesimal. This usually signals to me that I am reading it too literally or that I am misunderstanding it. There are so few people who are ever going to need enough faith to move a real mountain that if the Savior's statement to that effect is meant to be read literally, the verse is irrelevant. I don't think the Lord deals in irrelevancy; there must be more to it than that. If I read it on a figurative level, however, it suddenly strikes me with great power. These are the Savior's words: "Verily I say unto you, If ye have faith as a grain of mustard seed, ye shall say unto this mountain, Remove hence to yonder place; and it shall remove; and nothing shall be impossible unto you." (Matthew 17:20). The mountain symbolizes every impossible, walk-on-water challenge, commandment, difficulty, trial, hope, or action life may bring to us. We can overcome every obstacle that stands in the way of our progression. The mountains will move with just a little faith. That faith must be not only in God, but also in ourselves.

May we doubt not. May we fear not. May we, like Peter, carry always in our hearts the desire to do what our Master does. May we know that if *he* does it—no matter how difficult, no matter how impossible—if *he* does it, and he asks us to do it, even to the extent of being perfect, even to becoming a God, we can do it. May we say as Paul once did, "I can do all things through Christ which strengtheneth me" (Philippians 4:13).

Chapter Two

The Jesus We Need to Know

~

What Is It Like to Be a Latter-day Saint?

I was once asked by a good friend who is not a member of our church, "What is it like being a Mormon?" I thought about a verse, something that the Savior said, as I was considering how to answer that question. Jesus once gave mankind an invitation with these words, "Come unto me, all ye that labour and are heavy laden, and I will give you rest. Take my yoke upon you, and learn of me; for I am meek and lowly in heart: and ye shall find rest unto your souls. For my yoke is easy, and my burden is light" (Matthew 11:28–30). As we think about an answer to my friend's question, would our answer be that it is restful? It is easy? The burdens the gospel places on us are light? Is the life that we live, as Latter-day Saints, restful, easy, and light? Is that how we would answer?

I'm not sure that's the way most Latter-day Saints would answer that question—I didn't answer it that way. But that is the way I think the Savior would have us answer. If we know certain things about the Savior's character—not the Savior as a God or Redeemer or Creator, but the man himself and how he treated people—we come to better understand the three key words in his gracious invitation. He meant for life, as he desired us to live it, to be restful, easy, and light. I believe that as we strive to be more and more like the Savior, our lives will be more restful, easier, and lighter.

"Aslan, You're Bigger!"

A thought from the writings of C. S. Lewis gives us an interesting insight into our opportunity to learn about the Savior and what happens as our understanding of him grows. I emphasize that the Savior we are going to ponder is Christ as an individual. In *Prince Caspian*, the second in the Chronicles of

Narnia series, the children return to Narnia for their second visit. Lucy meets Aslan, who is the Christ figure in Lewis's Chronicles of Narnia, and the following exchange is shared:

"'Aslan, Aslan. Dear Aslan,' sobbed Lucy. 'At last.' . . .

"'Welcome, child,' he said.

"'Aslan,' said Lucy, 'you're bigger.'

"'That is because you are older, little one,' answered he.

"'Not because you are?'

"'I am not. But every year you grow, you will find me bigger.'"[1]

I think that is a profound insight into the Savior and his effect on us. For me at least, the more I've learned about him, the more I've read, the more I've pondered, the more I've tried to visualize his life, the greater he becomes to me. While there is not room to cover all of his perfections and characteristics and attributes—all the qualities I would love to cover—I would like to share some of those moments in his life that have been restful and burden-easing and light in my life in particular. I hope that it will be of value to you.

WHO TOUCHED ME?

Jesus as an individual, in his personal nature, accepted people. Because of his accepting nature, people came to him, even those who were sinful. Publicans, harlots, sinners, and others were drawn to him because they sensed in him acceptance in spite of their own frailties. Let me give you an example that I love. It is the story of the woman with the issue of blood. By weaving two of the accounts together, that of Mark and Luke, we receive a fuller understanding. I'll begin with Mark's account:

"A certain woman, which had an issue of blood twelve years, and had suffered many things of many physicians, and had spent all that she had, and was nothing bettered, but rather grew worse, when she had heard of Jesus, came in the press behind, and touched his garment. For she said, If I may touch but his clothes, I shall be whole. And straightway the fountain of her blood was dried up; and she felt in her body that she was healed of that plague. And Jesus, immediately knowing in himself that virtue [meaning strength] had gone out of him, turned him about in the press, and said, Who touched my clothes?" (Mark 5:25–30).

Why doesn't this woman come out of the crowd, raise her hand, and say, "I did, and I'm healed, thank you very much"? Turning to Luke's account of this episode, when Jesus asks, "Who touched me?" Luke adds, "When all denied" (Luke 8:45). The Savior was looking for her; he was trying to find her, but everyone—including the recipient of his virtue—denies. Jesus said, "Somebody hath touched me: for I perceive that virtue is gone out of me" (Luke 8:46). And in Mark's account, "And he looked round about to see her that had done this thing" (Mark 5:32).

Picture yourself in that crowd. You are the woman and Christ is looking for you. He's scanning everyone's faces. He wants to discover the person who pulled healing strength out of him. What are you thinking? "When the woman saw that she was not hid" (Luke 8:47)—the verb used is *hid*. She is hiding back in the crowd. Can you see her, looking nervously at the Savior, trying not to meet his eyes? Why is she hiding? Why doesn't she confess the miracle? I sense it is because she feels she has done something wrong. Her particular problem, an issue of blood, made her unclean under the law of Moses. She's had it twelve years; she's been unclean for twelve years. Leviticus details certain serious restrictions for one who had this ailment.

"He looked round about to see her that had done this thing" (Mark 5:32). Finally the time comes when Jesus finds whom he was searching for. Can you see that moment when their eyes met? He is looking at her, right into her eyes; she still tries to withdraw, but the Master now sees her. He knows, and she knows that he knows. We read, "But the woman fearing and trembling, knowing what was done in her, came and fell down before him, and told him all the truth. And he said unto her, Daughter, thy faith hath made thee whole; go in peace, and be whole of thy plague" (Mark 5:33–34).

Fearing and Trembling

Two words that have always resonated in my heart and have helped me in different moments of my life are the words *fearing* and *trembling*. Many times in our lives we may find ourselves before the Savior, before our Lord, fearing and trembling, thinking that we've done something with which he's not pleased. We maybe judge ourselves a little too harshly. We feel guilt when we need not.

I'll give you an example. I was teaching a class when President Ezra Taft Benson was the President of the Church. A woman raised her hand and said, "Brother Wilcox, could I ask you a personal question?"

I said, "Sure."

"We've been asked by President Benson to read the Book of Mormon," she continued. "I love the Book of Mormon; I've read it many times and I'm not arguing against the need to read it. We need to read it, but we're studying the New Testament this year in our Gospel Doctrine classes. I have never read the New Testament all the way through and so I've been reading the New Testament. I'm wondering—is it okay that I'm reading the New Testament instead of the Book of Mormon? Am I disobeying the prophet?" Then she said, "I should probably do both, but I have little children and my time is limited."

What do you think? If the Savior came into her ward on Sunday morning and looked around and said, "Somebody in this ward has been reading the New Testament instead of the Book of Mormon," what would she have done? She would have hid and said, "Oh, I hope he doesn't know it's me." There he is, looking at the faces of the congregation. He looks for her and finally their eyes meet. How would she come before him when she knew that he knew she was the one not reading the Book of Mormon? I assume she would have come "fearing and trembling." Do you have any fearing and trembling moments? But Jesus was accepting. Many times we fear and tremble because we feel we've done something wrong, but really, we are pleasing to him. We've done nothing wrong. We will find acceptance in him.

Years ago I was asked to go to the Caribbean to help start the Church Educational System there. We would be living in Haiti. I needed to get my French back in shape and I needed to learn Creole. At the time, I was the stake mission president. I tried to study and also do my church calling, but I couldn't do it all. My schedule was so tight that I went to my stake president and I asked to be released from my calling. He was understanding. He was gracious. He was good about it and he released me from my calling. But I felt terribly guilty about my request and wondered if it was okay to do what I'd done. What did God think about my asking to be released?

Picture me in church on the Sunday morning after I asked to be released. If the Savior had come into my ward that particular Sabbath and said, "Somebody here asked to be released from their calling. Who was it?" I would have hid, wouldn't I? And if he kept looking for and finally found me, how would I have approached him? Fearing and trembling. But I think the Savior would have said, "Be of good comfort. It's a good thing to serve as a stake mission president; it's also good to try and learn two languages so you can begin the Church Educational System in the Caribbean." I think we have fearing and trembling moments too much. Let us find comfort in the assurance that Jesus has an accepting personality that he extends to us constantly.

JESUS WEPT

Jesus felt the sorrows and the griefs of all people. When I say he felt them, I mean he *felt* them. He not only knew them and understood them, he felt them at a very deep level. An example or two: Mary and Martha asked the Savior to return to Bethany from east of the Jordan River because Lazarus, their brother, was sick. Jesus came up to Bethany, but it was dangerous for him. There was much hostility toward the Savior in Jerusalem at the time, and Bethany is just over the hill from Jerusalem. Mary and Martha both left the village to meet him because, by the time he arrived, Lazarus was already dead. Both of these women, whom the Savior loved, said the same thing to him, "Lord, if thou hadst been here, my brother had not died" (John 11:21, 32). "When Jesus therefore saw her [Mary] weeping, and the Jews also weeping which came with her, he groaned in the spirit, and was troubled" (John 11:33).

A window is opened into the Savior's soul with those words and that description: "He groaned in the spirit, and was troubled, and said, Where have ye laid him? They said unto him, Lord, come and see." We then read two words, the single shortest verse in scripture, two simple words, "Jesus wept." That is the verse! "Then said the Jews, Behold how he loved him! . . . Jesus therefore again groaning in himself cometh to the grave" (John 11:33–36, 38).

In Alma 7, Alma used six words or phrases to describe what Jesus wanted to know about the human experience and could only discover at the level he desired by going through it himself, or "according to the flesh," as Alma terms it. Jesus wanted to know, according to the flesh, these six experiences: pains, afflictions, temptations of every kind, sicknesses, infirmities, and death (see Alma 7:11–12). These words portray, we might say, life at its most challenging. The Savior knew life at its very best—laughter, joy, love, friendship—but he also knew life at the level of affliction, pain, sickness, and infirmity. In John 11, we see before him two women whom he loves, weeping.

The remarkable thing about the empathy contained in the words, "Jesus wept . . . [and] groan[ed] in himself" (John 11:35, 38) is that the Lord knew what he was going to do before he ever left the Jordan River to go up to Bethany. This was not going to be a miracle of spontaneous compassion like the raising of the widow of Nain's son. Jesus knew before departing for Bethany that he was going to raise Lazarus from the dead. This was to be a sign, a shadow or symbol, of his power over death. He knew that in a few minutes all those tears would be turned to joy and celebration and laughter, the kind that come after great grief is released, when the worst fears vanish in a single moment. He knew that within a few minutes those tears would be dry, but he still wept and he still groaned in himself at their sorrow. He not only understands and knows our sorrows, he feels them, and at a level that causes him to groan in himself and weep.

"HOLD ME NOT"

We see a similar situation on Resurrection morning when Mary Magdalene comes to the tomb. Because we plan things in the Church, it's typical to think that major events have been planned as well. The decision regarding who should

[handwritten margin note: He knew soon grief would be turned to joy, but he felt the sorrow anyway]

be the very first to see the resurrected Savior seems to fall into this category. There is something inside of me that likes to visualize a council in Heaven discussing who should be the first to see the resurrected Savior. A decision is made, and the council, surely including the Father, decides on Mary Magdalene. That the most appropriate person would be a woman has a graciousness, a gentleness, and a wisdom to it that is quite profound and wonderful. But there is another part of me that very much wants that visitation to be a spontaneous moment. I believe on a deeper level that it was a spontaneous moment. Let us look at that tiny slice of time that is so revealing of the Lord we worship.

It is Resurrection morning. Mary has been to the grave early, the stone is rolled away, and Jesus is gone. Mary runs to find John and Peter. The two disciples run back to the tomb, look in with wondering awe, and then walk away in reflection. But Mary stays at the tomb and looks again into the emptiness that once contained her Lord. That is a very human moment. She looks again to see if he is really gone. This time, however, the angels are there. "And they say unto her, Woman, why weepest thou? She saith unto them, Because they have taken away my Lord, and I know not where they have laid him. And when she had thus said, she turned herself back, and saw Jesus standing, and knew not that it was Jesus. Jesus saith unto her, Woman, why weepest thou? whom seekest thou? She, supposing him to be the gardener, saith unto him, Sir, if thou have borne him hence, tell me where thou hast laid him, and I will take him away. Jesus saith unto her, Mary" (John 20:13–16).

I've never been able to say "Mary" with the proper tenderness that I think the Savior used, but there was something in the way that he said her name that immediately told her that it was Jesus. "She turned herself, and saith unto him, Rabboni; which is to say, Master" (John 20:16). I've also never been able to say that word, *Rabboni,* with the proper tenderness and joy that I think she would have used at that moment.

I repeat that, perhaps, this appearance was a decided thing, a planned occurrence, but I hope that it was somehow not that formal. Let us reflect on this further. Jesus needs to ascend to his Father and report—in the most important personal priesthood interview ever—the Atonement, the Resurrection, and the initiation of the preaching of the gospel in the spirit world. That is a fairly significant conversation he is about to have, but a woman is weeping, and it is not in his nature, his personality, to leave without comforting her. So he remains just long enough to wipe away her tears and fill her with joy.

Joseph Smith made a profound change in his translation of this story. He only changes one word in this story. It is a good change; it matches the earlier

Greek. Here is the difference: "Jesus saith unto her, Hold me not" (JST, John 20:17) instead of "Touch me not" (John 20:17).

"Hold me not; for I am not yet ascended to my Father: but go to my brethren, and say unto them, I ascend unto my Father, and your Father; and to my God, and your God" (JST, John 20:17). "Hold me not"—I assume they embraced, and that she touched his feet, his hands, his side. We read in one of the other gospels that the other women held him by the feet (see Matthew 28:9). "Hold me not," meaning, "Don't detain me, Mary. I have to go to my Father," almost as if, had she wished, she could have detained him as the Nephites did in 3 Nephi 17:5. There, they look at Jesus longingly, wishing he would remain with them a little longer. He doesn't look at his watch and say, "I've got a full agenda today. I've got to go visit the lost tribes." He says, "You want me to stay—I will stay."

"Hold me not." Jesus was a person who felt our pains. More than just knowing and understanding them, he felt them and he responded to them. After all, he knew them "according to the flesh" (Alma 7:12).

EXTREME STORIES

Jesus multiplies what little we have, what is insufficient for our needs, raising us to sufficiency and beyond. He understands those insufficiencies, and knows how to make weaknesses strengths. I will illustrate what I mean by this characteristic of our Lord. Before we examine some of the scriptural stories about the multiplication of things, let us understand an aspect of the scriptures. Sometimes there are principles in the scriptures that are so important that the Lord wants us to learn those truths intensely, so he will spread the idea in different places throughout the canon. He says, "I'm going to put one of these stories in the Old Testament. I'll put one in the Book of Mormon. I'll put a couple in the New Testament. I'll put one over here in the Doctrine and Covenants, because I want you to understand the importance and necessity of this life-enhancing truth." One of these life-enhancing truths, that is important to the Lord because it is critical for us, deals with the idea of human insufficiencies. "When you have insufficiencies, when you don't feel you have enough of whatever it is you need, I will multiply it."

Most scriptural stories are extreme stories. That is, they tend to push the limits of the continuum. They deal in extremes so that they can cover everything less than that story as well. Whatever God did for the men and women of the Bible (or the Book of Mormon) in a dramatic, major way, he will also do for you and me, but often the application is more spiritual or figurative. When I was younger, I used to wish to see great miracles. I wished I could see the Red Sea split and fire called down from Heaven and the blind made to see and lepers healed. I never witnessed anything even close to those great events and I wondered why they weren't still happening. It took me quite a while, and some Biblical maturity, to realize they are still happening. They just happen on a spiritual level. Those dramatic stories like the splitting of the Red Sea, for example, are the Savior's way of saying, and the Father's way of saying, "Whenever there are barriers that bar your way from progressing, I will make a path for you so you can move forward." I've seen God split the Red Sea in my life and others' lives many times.

A leper came to Jesus and said to him, "If thou wilt, thou canst make me clean. And Jesus, moved with compassion, put forth his hand, and touched him, and saith unto him, I will; be thou clean" (Mark 1:40–41). You and I also come to Jesus with our sins, our spiritual leprosies, and say to him, "Master, if thou wilt, thou canst make me clean." Does he not reach out and touch us and say, "I will; be thou clean"?

All these great, miraculous stories we read need to be understood and applied in the manner that has meaning for us. What God did for them, he will do for us. With that background, let us examine stories of insufficiency.

TWELVE BASKETS

Twice during his ministry, Jesus fed many people from a little bit of bread. There is a pattern in the stories of feeding the five thousand and the four thousand. Here is the basic pattern—as always, when reading the scriptures, place yourself in the story:

First, you have a lack, an insufficiency. You don't have enough of something. In this case, it is bread.

Second, you go to someone for help—to God, to the Savior, to a prophet such as Elijah. You take your problem and ask for aid.

The third point is critical: You are always asked to bring with you what you have, to stop focusing so much on what you lack and see instead what you have. It is only in Mark's account of feeding the five thousand and the four thousand that we see this invaluable insight. The other gospels leave that very important point out, though it is in the Old Testament stories of this genre.

In Mark's account we read, "He answered and said unto [his disciples], Give ye them to eat. And they say unto him, Shall we go and buy two hundred pennyworth of bread, and give them to eat? [There is the insufficiency.] He saith unto them, How many loaves have ye? go and see. And when they knew, they say, Five, and two fishes" (Mark 6:37–38).

In the account of the feeding of the four thousand we read, "His disciples answered him, From whence can a man satisfy these men with bread here in the wilderness? And he asked them, How many loaves have ye? And they said, Seven" (Mark 8:4–5).

Third, you're always asked what you have and are expected to provide it.

Fourth, God multiplies what you have brought and makes it sufficient for your need.

Fifth, because God is gracious and good, his character is such that you always get beyond your need. He multiplies to sufficiency and beyond. The Apostles take up twelve baskets of remaining bread after the feeding of the five thousand. They take up seven baskets after the feeding of the four thousand.

POUR OUT

One of my favorite and perhaps one of the clearest examples of this principle is found in the Old Testament in the book of Second Kings. Watch for the pattern; look for our five points: "Now there cried a certain woman of the wives of the sons of the prophets unto Elisha, saying, Thy servant my husband is dead; and thou knowest that thy servant did fear the Lord: and the creditor is come to take unto him my two sons to be bondmen" (2 Kings 4:1).

She's got a problem—not enough to satisfy her creditors. "Elisha said unto her, What shall I do for thee? tell me, what hast thou in the house? And she said, Thine handmaid hath not any thing in the house, save a pot of oil. Then he said, Go, borrow thee vessels abroad of all thy neighbours, even empty vessels; borrow not a few" (2 Kings 4:2–3).

Notice how common, how human, her response is: I don't have anything. I have a pot of oil, but what can that do? But, with trust and faith she borrows vessels from all the neighbors. She brings them into her room and shuts the door and then—I love these words—"she poured out" (2 Kings 4:5). What she had, she poured out, and every vessel was filled. "Then she came and told the man of God. And he said, Go, sell the oil, and pay thy debt, and live thou and thy children of the rest" (2 Kings 4:7). God will fill our insufficiencies and leave us "the rest."

Sometimes we come to the Lord and say, "Lord, I don't have enough wisdom for this problem. I don't have it. I need wisdom."

Our idea is, "Will you give me the wisdom I lack?'" We expect him to supply what we don't have, but usually he says, "What *do* you have? Bring me what wisdom and experience you have. I'll multiply it, make it sufficient, and give you beyond." Maybe we don't have enough emotional strength or spiritual strength. Maybe we're dealing with a troubled child or have a problem in our marriage. Maybe we have a calling that is beyond our ability, we don't have sufficient talents. But if we will bring him what we have, he will multiply it and make it sufficient and beyond.

IN THE SYCAMORE TREE

It was inherent in Jesus' character to be sensitive to the lonely, to the marginalized. I call these "the people in the sycamore tree." One of my favorite stories, even as a child, was the story of Zacchaeus, who climbed a sycamore tree to see Jesus pass through Jericho. There are some words in this story that are marvelous as we apply them to how we interact with other people. We find the story in Luke. "And Jesus entered and passed through Jericho. And, behold, there was a man named Zacchaeus, which was the chief among the publicans, and he was rich. And he sought to see Jesus who he was; and could not for the press, because he was little of stature" (Luke 19:1–3).

Let's take those two little phrases and explore them—*for the press* and *little of stature*. Now, I know that "little of stature" means he was physically short, but we will broaden it. "For the press" means that because of all the people along the front of the road who are interested mainly in themselves, Zacchaeus can't see Jesus. Occasionally, the front-of-the-road people, the press, are not too sensitive to those in the sycamore tree, those who are little of stature. As Jesus walks through Jericho, everyone wants to see him. They crowd together, leaving Zacchaeus behind the front line. Why didn't somebody in the press turn and say, "Zacchaeus, come and stand next to me and we'll see Jesus together"? Well, they didn't like him. He was different. He was little of stature, not only physically, but also socially. In their eyes, he was of no great importance; he had an occupation that was odious to them—he was a publican.

Many things make people little of stature in our eyes. For instance, racial differences too often make others little of stature. Those whom we consider minorities are far too frequently kept back behind the lines, not up in the press with the more important and acceptable people. C. S. Lewis called the front-line spectators "the Inner Ring."[2] They are the beautiful people. Will they have time to notice, to help the lonely, the marginalized, the little-of-stature? There are also people who are of little stature because of physical differences. They may be too tall, too overweight, too short. Maybe economic differences make them climb the sycamore tree—they're not in the right class. Maybe they have personality quirks. Perhaps they are a touch obnoxious. There are Zacchaeuses in every ward in the Church. They haunt the ground behind the press. Let us continue with Luke's account and see what Jesus does.

"[Zacchaeus] ran . . . and climbed up into a sycamore tree to see him: for he was to pass that way" (Luke 19:4). There he was, alone in his tree. Do you know any sycamore-tree people? Little of stature? Alone? Marginalized? Unimportant? Behind the press? Of all the people in Jericho that morning, who do you think Jesus is going to spend the day with?

"When Jesus came to the place, he looked up, and saw him, and said unto him, Zacchaeus, make haste, and come down; for to day I must abide at thy house. And he made haste, and came down, and received him joyfully" (Luke 19:5–6). Jesus was sensitive to the lonely, the marginalized, the little of stature, the people in the sycamore tree—those who couldn't get through the press.

I had a very good friend when I was in college who, when the big dance of the year came up, asked a girl who was not in the press of beautiful girls. If ever there was a young lady who lived in the sycamore tree, it was her. Nobody else would have taken her to that dance, and yet he asked her. He bought her flowers. He rented a limousine. He took her to dinner. He went the whole ten yards, much to the amazement of almost everybody else. I asked him why he did that and his reply was, "She needed to go to the dance and no one else would take her." There are Zacchaeusettes and Zacchaeuses who need to be invited out of the tree and into the press. They need to feel welcome and befriended. Jesus was ever sensitive to them.

He Went to Another Village

Jesus was not confrontational. He was not combative. He was not defensive. He did not persecute. Luke recounted a story concerning an episode with the Samaritans. We must, before reflecting upon this story, remember there was deep animosity on the part of the Jews toward the Samaritans, and that enmity was reflected back toward the Jews. We read in the Gospels of an earlier encounter between Jesus and the Samaritan woman at the well, but there he charms and captivates her into listening to him. He wondrously and skillfully removes all her defenses. The other story about Samaritans concerns a rather hostile and defensive attitude displayed by James and John.

"And it came to pass, when the time was come that he should be received up, he stedfastly set his face to go to Jerusalem, and sent messengers before his face: and they went, and entered into a village of the Samaritans, to make ready for him. And they did not receive him, because his face was as though he would go to Jerusalem" (Luke 9:51–53).

A large part of the argument between the Samaritans and the Jews centered on the proper place to worship. The Samaritans had their holy mountain and the Jews had the temple in Jerusalem. In the previous verse, the Samaritans are essentially saying, "If you're going to go worship in Jerusalem, we don't even want to see you." His disciples James and John saw this. They were indignant. "You can't treat Jesus that way!" It's clear they didn't like the Samaritans anyway.

"They said, Lord, wilt thou that we command fire to come down from heaven, and consume them, even as Elias did? But he turned, and rebuked them, and said, Ye know not what manner of spirit ye are of. For the Son of man is not come to destroy men's lives, but to save them. And they went to another village" (Luke 9:54–56). I love that last phrase—"they went to another village."

How much pain, persecution, argument, debate, war, how many burnings at the stake, inquisitions, and excommunications would not have come to pass had Christianity really understood this part of the Savior's personality? "The Son of man is not come to destroy men's lives, but to save them." Too often religions—and this is true of all religions, not just of Christianity—disguise a lack of charity for their fellowman under a cloak of zeal towards God. I repeat: Jesus was not confrontational. He was not combative. He was not defensive. He did not persecute. Because he was not that way, he had the ability to draw all men to him. His response is instructional to any who would call down fire upon those who believe differently than they. He would go to another village. He would leave in peace and go to another village because he did not relish confrontation. That was the way he was. He won people to him.

"A Proper and Affectionate Manner"

Joseph Smith said something wonderful about this particular attitude. After having suffered years of persecution in his teenage years, notice the true spirit of Christ in the following words from the Prophet: "Being of very tender years, and persecuted by those who ought to have been my friends and to have treated me kindly, and if they supposed me to be deluded to have endeavored in a proper and affectionate manner to have reclaimed me—I was left . . ." (Joseph Smith–History 1:28). Notice those key words: *friends, kindly, proper, affectionate.* That's the true spirit of Christ—not persecuting, not defensive, not combative, not argumentative, not violent, not uncharitably zealous.

When Paul is introduced in the book of Acts, he's introduced with an interesting phrase. Think about how sad it is that these words, describing Saul of Tarsus, also, unfortunately, throughout the history of Christianity, describe it as well: "And Saul, yet breathing out threatenings and slaughter against the disciples of the Lord . . ." (Acts 9:1). How many times in the history of the world have people breathed out threatenings and slaughter against each other due to differences in their dogma or doctrine? Now let us by contrast examine the Savior's response to the threatening Saul. "As he journeyed, he came near Damascus: and suddenly there shined round about him a light from heaven: And he fell to the earth, and heard a voice saying unto him, Saul, Saul, why persecutest thou me?" (Acts 9:3–4). It is difficult to read these words with the proper tone. Imagine the most gentle and loving voice you can. Here is a man breathing out threatenings and slaughter, persecuting, and disguising a lack of love for his fellow man under a cloak of zeal for God. Yet the Lord says, "Saul, Saul, why persecutest thou me? And he said, Who art thou, Lord? And the Lord said, I am Jesus whom thou persecutest" (Acts 9:4–5).

I can't read those words in a tender enough voice. I just can't get there. Jesus would change Saul to Paul with a voice of love and tenderness, and Paul would change the world. With that tender question, Christ would change Saul from threatenings and slaughter on the road to Damascus, to Paul, the man who would write 1 Corinthians 13, that magnificent definition of charity.

I've had the opportunity of traveling throughout the world. It's a great blessing to me and I'm very grateful for it. I've noticed as an American Christian and a Latter-day Saint that people get defensive in many places in the world where I go. I can see, figuratively speaking, their fists going up—not ready to fight, particularly, but I see that they have a distrustful and defensive attitude because I'm of a different faith and come from a different country. I've noticed, however, that if I talk about the positive, good things in their culture, religions, heroes, poetry, and art, something begins to happen. I watch those same faces soften. They warm up because they realize somebody else favors their culture and has found good things in their religion, in their poetry, in their art, and in their history. They relax, conversations are initiated, and they become wonderful friends. Too often we're defensive and combative; the Savior was not that way.

I think the greatest compliment I ever received came in the Orient when my wife and I took a group to China. I had been teaching Chinese religion and culture. At the end of the tour I said goodbye to our guide, whose name was Bing. I said to him at the airport, "Bing, I just love your country and your people. I have learned so much from its history. The philosophy and literature that has come out of China has enriched my life and I want to thank you as a representative of the Chinese people for making me a better person." I was sincere, for I truly feel that way. He reached out and patted my heart as he quietly said, "Chinese, Chinese." That is what we want to try and do with everyone—not call down fire, not threaten, not slaughter, but somehow, in those oppositions that we sometimes face, be able to remove prejudice and anger with the disarming voice of tenderness that Jesus used with Paul.

NEVERTHELESS

We receive a similar idea in a story related by Matthew, the one about the coin in the fish's mouth. Jesus avoided giving offense when he could. He did not insist on his rights. So we read this little story: "When they were come to Capernaum, they that received tribute money came to Peter, and said, Doth not your master pay tribute?" (Matthew 17:24).

The tribute money went to the temple and the temple was Jesus' own house, so technically, he didn't have to pay tribute to himself. Peter, however, answers, "Yes." Peter sometimes felt the need to be defensive about the Savior. "And when he was come into the house, Jesus prevented him, saying, What thinkest thou, Simon? of whom do the kings of the earth take custom or tribute? of their own children, or of strangers? Peter saith unto him, Of strangers. Jesus saith unto him, Then are the children free" (Matthew 17:25–26).

What is Jesus telling Peter? "I don't have to do this; this is not necessary." And then the great lesson: "Notwithstanding, lest we should offend them, go thou to the sea, and cast an hook, and take up the fish that first cometh up; and when thou hast opened his mouth, thou shalt find a piece of money: that take, and give unto them for me and thee" (Matthew 17:27).

Wouldn't it be nice to pay our taxes that way? I think the power of this story lies in the word: "notwithstanding." If we can avoid offense, let's avoid it. That could be in the simplest of things, such as driving down the freeway. Sometimes I don't give the other driver the lane when he wants it. Do you do that? My personality changes when I get behind a wheel of a car. It's terrible! Have you ever noticed how driving, politics, and sporting events can just change your whole frame of reality? Too often I think, "I have the right of way. Get out of my lane. Who do you think you are?" The Savior would probably say, "Give them the lane, notwithstanding." How wonderful it would be if, when there is a mess in the house, we would say, "I didn't make it, but I'll clean it up anyway." Jesus was not concerned about rights. He avoided giving offense when he could. We hear many strident voices today crying out "Rights! Rights! Rights!" Too many people invite confrontation and argument with an insistence that could not care less what other people think or feel. Who cares if offense is given? What they want is their own and often in the most trivial of matters.

"AS THOUGH HE HEARD THEM NOT"

Jesus was not judgmental in the negative way that the word has come to embody. He simply did not wish to judge. He said so in the gospel of John: "I judge no man" (John 8:15). He took no pleasure in other people's sins and weaknesses. He was not critical. He rejoiced not in iniquity, as Paul says of the Christlike love we call charity (see 1 Corinthians 13:6). We sense this particularly in the story of the woman taken in adultery, also found in John 8. This poor woman was dragged out in front of the multitude and her most shameful sin proclaimed openly. It is far beyond just an embarrassing moment; they have made this woman's sins public before the purest of men.

"The scribes and Pharisees," we read, "brought unto him a woman taken in adultery; and when they had set her in the midst, they say unto him, Master, this woman was taken in adultery, in the very act. Now Moses in the law commanded us, that such should be stoned: but what sayest thou?" (John 8:3–5).

Notice how Jesus responds to this: "But Jesus stooped down, and with his finger wrote on the ground, as though he heard them not" (John 8:6). What is he saying by this action? "I don't want to be involved in this. I'm giving you the chance to just go away. I have no desire to revel, exult, or have my curiosity satisfied or titillated with the sins of others." There is a world of discomfort we sense in the Savior in those few words, "as though he heard them not." He did not wish to judge. Remember, he follows this disagreeable moment with the announcement, "I judge no man."

How wonderful would it be if, when somebody came to me or you with some gossip or story, we stooped down to write on the ground as though we "heard them not." It is sad that there is something within the human soul—it's in me; I wish it weren't—that we take pleasure sometimes in hearing of other people's weaknesses and sins. There are whole newspapers, whole segments of the media, dedicated to that very purpose. Watch the nightly news and you will see this human desire to dwell on, to probe into the sins and the weaknesses of others. Would it not be better if, in a metaphorical way, the next time somebody came to us and said, "Did you hear what so and so did?" we stooped down and wrote on the ground as if we heard them not? We don't want to judge. We don't want to condemn. We don't want to hear about other people's weaknesses and sins. We rejoice not in iniquity but rejoice in the truth.

I sometimes try to stand outside myself and observe my own behavior. I look at what I chose to read in the newspaper. I can't read everything, but what stories drew my attention? If our mind and then our eyes go to the salacious stories, to those stories so popular with the press rather than other types of reporting, perhaps we should feel a little shame. Have we failed a test somehow? Let us continue with the story in John. The accusers won't let Jesus off the hook.

"When they continued asking him, he lifted up himself, and said unto them, He that is without sin among you, let him first cast a stone at her" (John 8:7). He seems to be saying, if you are going to judge, judge yourself: "And again he stooped down, and wrote on the ground" (John 8:8). I don't think he even wanted to judge those who brought her, but he certainly turned their thoughts inward. Later, after the accusers leave, he says to her, "Where are those thine accusers? hath no man condemned thee? She said, No man, Lord. And Jesus said unto her, Neither do I condemn thee: go, and sin no more" (John 8:10–11). All that is important is the abandonment of the past in the hopeful behaviors and promises of the future.

The Joseph Smith Translation adds this interesting phrase: "And the woman glorified God from that hour, and believed on his name" (JST, John 8:11). Condemnation often brings alienation and deepens movement into sin. His was an invitation out of sin because he didn't dwell on it. There was no stinging condemnation in his voice, perhaps not even the hint of disappointment, just pure and open forgiveness.

He Wist Not Who It Was

Jesus did not draw unnecessary attention to himself. He was not concerned about center stage. He sought the Father's glory. He didn't play what I call the "Watch me, Daddy" game. We all play that game in some way or another. It is human nature to do so. When my children were little and they would do something wonderful, they would say, "Watch me, Daddy! Watch me! Watch me, Daddy!" Do your children do that? "Watch me, Daddy!" And I would clap my hands and say, "Oh, wonderful! How good!" As we grow older, we can't play that game quite so openly and with such childlike innocence, but some people even into old age still play "Watch me, Daddy." They do things to draw attention to themselves. They want to be the center. They want the praise of men. Those whom we sometimes call celebrities, from movie stars to athletes, are very good at it. I am occasionally embarrassed for them. The Savior was not that kind of person. He didn't play "Watch me, Daddy." When he invited others to come to him or to listen to his words, the total focus was on the glory of the Father and the happiness and welfare of those who listened and followed him.

An example may help bring this personality trait of the Savior home. Remember the man who was at the pool of Bethesda, waiting for the angel to trouble the waters? The first man into the pool would be healed, it was believed. At the edge of the pool there is a man, "which had an infirmity thirty and eight years. When Jesus saw him lie, and knew that he had been now a long time in that case, he saith unto him, Wilt thou be made whole? The impotent man answered him, Sir, I have no man, when the water is troubled, to put me into the pool: but while I am coming, another steppeth down before me. Jesus saith unto him, Rise, take up thy bed, and walk" (John 5:5–8).

How long would it take for somebody to rise, take up their bed, and walk? Not very long—twenty, thirty seconds at most—but in that time Jesus had disappeared. Later, as the man is carrying his bed, he is confronted. It's the Sabbath, and the Jews stop him, saying, "It's not lawful to carry your bed on the Sabbath day."

And he says, in his defense, "Well, the person who healed me told me to take it up and walk."

They respond, "Who was he? Who told you to take up your bed and walk? Who healed you?" (see John 5:8–12).

"And he that was healed wist not who it was: for Jesus had conveyed himself away, a multitude being in that place" (John 5:13).

Jesus often said to people, "Don't tell anyone I healed you." He didn't stand around and say, "My name is Jesus. Would you please go tell everyone what I did for you?" The man at the pool didn't even know who he was.

One of the greatest examples of this character trait was William Tyndale. He is one of my great heroes, for he gave us our religious language as it was incorporated into the King James Bible. The translators of the King James Bible drew a great deal on William Tyndale's work. He published his first New Testament in 1526 without his name on it. He smuggled it into England from the Continent, but he didn't put his name on it. When he was asked why, he responded, and I am paraphrasing, "The Savior told me not to let my left hand know what my right hand doeth but to do good for the sheer sake of doing good. I just want people to have the stories of the scriptures in English. They don't need to know that I was the translator."

TAUGHT BY THE CHILDREN

We see another example of this aspect of Christ's personality in 3 Nephi. Who did Jesus teach the deepest, most powerful truths to in his visit to the Nephites and the Lamanites after the destruction following his death? The high priests group? The Relief Society? The Young Women? The elders quorum? We read, "It came to pass that he did teach and minister unto the children of the multitude of whom hath been spoken, and he did loose their tongues, and they did speak unto their fathers great and marvelous things, even greater than he had revealed unto the people; and he loosed their tongues that they could utter" (3 Nephi 26:14).

Who received the deepest, most profound and beautiful, the greatest teachings of Christ to the multitudes gathered at Bountiful? The junior Primary! Then the junior Primary taught their parents. There is a lesson in humility in that! As a Gospel Doctrine teacher who sometimes team-teaches with another person, that is remarkable to me. If you have ever team-taught a class, did you do what I do?

I look ahead and see if I get the good stuff. Do you do that? I say, "Oh darn, that chapter falls on his week. I want to teach that chapter. That's a good chapter." And sometimes I think, "Oh, this isn't very interesting. He can have that lesson." Who did Jesus allow to teach the great stuff? Not even himself! He let little children teach the greatest of all truths to their astonished parents.

WHEN THE SOUL IS TROUBLED

When Jesus was burdened with heaviness, sorrow, or care he turned outward to give solace to others. It is one of the greatest elements of the last hours of his life. Immediately preceding the last hours of his life he said something interesting. Notice his thoughts as he approached the defining moments of his life: "Now is my soul troubled." Keep that word in mind, *troubled*. He is moving into his last hours, and his soul is troubled. "And what shall I say? Father, save me from this hour: but for this cause came I unto this hour" (John 12:27). That verse is a window into his soul. He is troubled as he faces those last painful moments of his life.

Picture him sitting at the Last Supper. He looks around at the faces of his disciples. What does he know as he looks at these men? He knows Judas has already betrayed him. He knows Peter will deny him three times before the morning light. He knows that all the other Apostles will leave him. He knows that within hours, the whole weight of the suffering and sins of the world will descend upon him in Gethsemane. He knows he will be scourged and crucified. If ever there was a man in the history of the world who needed someone to comfort him because his heart was troubled, it would have been Jesus at that time.

We read once again of the troubled state of his heart as he sits with this knowledge on his mind. "When Jesus had thus said, he was troubled in spirit, and testified, and said, Verily, verily, I say unto you, that one of you shall betray me" (John 13:21). It pained him deeply that Judas would betray him. I think if he could have he would have saved Judas from himself even then. He certainly did not call this man as an Apostle thinking he needed a betrayer and that Judas would fit the bill. He loved this man. But he is troubled again as the heaviness of the hour begins to settle upon him. Yet as we read the account of the Last Supper and the last moments of Christ's life, who comforts whom? Remember our key word is *troubled*. Some of the most beautiful statements from the Last Supper are the following, but we have to read them knowing that Jesus' own soul was troubled. "Let not your heart be troubled," he told them. "Ye believe in God, believe also in me. In my Father's house are many mansions: if it were not so, I would have told you. I go to prepare a place for you. And if I go and prepare a place for you, I will come again, and receive you unto myself; that where I am, there ye may be also" (John 14:1–3).

These words are so familiar that most could quote them from memory. They are some of the most beautiful statements Christ ever made, but he made them when he himself was heavy and troubled. Later Jesus said, "Peace I leave with you, my peace I give unto you: not as the world giveth, give I unto you. Let not your heart be troubled, neither let it be afraid" (John 14:27).

Moments later he says, "These things I have spoken unto you, that in me ye might have peace. In the world ye shall have tribulation: but be of good cheer; I have overcome the world" (John 16:33).

They depart for Gethsemane where he prays prior to his solitary moments with the Father. He is now minutes from the full atoning weight. It is already starting to descend upon him. We know this because he tells his disciples as he arrives at the garden of Gethsemane that he is heavy and amazed. Christ himself is astonished at the agony of suffering that is beginning to settle upon him as his understanding of human misery becomes intense. He now prays. Who does he pray for?

"I have manifested thy name unto the men which thou gavest me out of the world: . . . I pray for them: I pray not for the world, but for them which thou hast given me; for they are thine. . . . And now I am no more in the world, but these are in the world, and I come to thee. Holy Father, keep through thine own name those whom thou hast given me, that they may be one, as we are. . . . I pray not that thou shouldest take them out of the world, but that thou shouldest keep them from the evil. . . . And for their sakes I sanctify myself. . . . Father, I will that they also, whom thou hast given me, be with me where I am; . . . I have declared unto them thy name, and will declare it: that the love wherewith thou hast loved me may be in them, and I in them" (John 17:6, 9, 11, 15, 19, 24, 26).

That's a magnificently beautiful prayer, but it's not for himself. He's not saying, "Father, help me, strengthen me, I'm going to go through this awful agony." He is praying for others. He looked outward throughout that prayer.

On the very cross itself, who was he concerned about? Look at those famous statements from the cross. One of the first concerned assigning his disciple John to care for his mother: "Woman, behold thy son! . . . Behold thy mother!" (John 19:26–27). "To day shalt thou be with me in paradise" (Luke 23:43) was directed to those crucified with him. "Father, forgive them; for they know not what they do" (Luke 23:34) showed his concern even for his very persecutors and tormentors. He forgave them in the very act. It is one thing to forgive when the sin is over and the initial pain is gone; it is another to forgive at the very moment you are sinned against. He was always turned outward. Always outward, outward,

outward! In this there is a great lesson for us all. In our own times of grief, when we are troubled and need solace, we can look outward toward those who are also troubled and give them solace.

WHO IS THE GREATEST?

Jesus had a secure sense of himself that was not dependent upon an outward posture of dignity. He never felt too great to serve in the lowliest of tasks. The disciples argued about who was the greatest. In the way of the world, the greatest are those who are served by the most. You and I have probably had leaders who felt that the people existed to serve them. That is the worldly way, but the great leaders, the true leaders, understand that they are there to serve others. The disciples had a great deal of trouble coming to grips with that particular idea. They argued often about who was the greatest.

Once when they were walking along the way, Jesus asked them, "What was it that ye disputed among yourselves by the way? But they held their peace: for by the way they had disputed among themselves, who should be the greatest" (Mark 9:33–34).

They knew this would not be acceptable to the Lord and they didn't want to tell him that they were arguing about who would be the greatest in the coming kingdom. "And he sat down, and called the twelve, and saith unto them, If any man desire to be first, the same shall be last. . . . And he took a child, and set him in the midst of them" (Mark 9:35–36). He took a child because, in our existence here, the closest thing to what Christ is like is a little child. He used the little child because the little child best demonstrated the qualities of his own soul.

This was a difficult lesson, so contrary to human nature that the Apostles were still arguing about who was the greatest and who should have preference in his kingdom at the Last Supper itself! I suppose at that event it may have had something to do with who would sit closest to Christ. In order to demonstrate this powerful ideal, the truth and necessity of serving other people in all things—that no task of service is too menial, too undignified for the greatest of us all—"He riseth from supper, and laid aside his garments; and took a towel, and girded himself. After that he poureth water into a bason, and began to wash the disciples' feet, and to wipe them with the towel wherewith he was girded" (John 13:4–5).

This was the most menial of tasks. He explained his actions when he was finished, "Ye call me Master and Lord: and ye say well; for so I am. If I then, your Lord and Master, have washed your feet; ye also ought to wash one another's feet. For I have given you an example, that ye should do as I have done to you" (John 13:13–15).

"The servant is not greater than his lord [in other words, if I can do it, you can do it]; neither he that is sent greater than he that sent him. If ye know these things, happy are ye if ye do them" (John 13:16–17).

What is the natural consequence of realizing there is nothing so menial, so tedious, or so undignified that I can't do it as an act of service? The result of thinking that way, Jesus taught, is joy.

"Not of the Fulness at First"

Almost always when I look at the life of the Savior I realize that I am a long way from being like him in just about every quality of his personality. I am not all those things discussed in this chapter. I'd like to be. I'd like to pay attention more to the Zacchaeuses in my life. I would like to be willing to serve in even the most unimportant of tasks. I would like to be less judgmental and more turned outward. I would like to do all the things that we've talked about today better than I do them, and so it is important that we know that Jesus developed grace for grace. He understands that we must do so also. While we strive to imitate him he is patient and longsuffering. He will not be discouraged in our failures. He is not critical.

In Doctrine and Covenants 93, the Lord wants us to understand that the Savior developed into what he was, and so he emphasizes one phrase:

"I, John, saw that he received not of the fulness at the first, but received grace for grace; and he received not of the fulness at first, but continued from grace to grace, until he received a fulness; and thus he was called the Son of God, because he received not of the fulness at the first" (D&C 93:12–14). That's three in three verses—"grace for grace."

Can you see how much God has emphasized that particular idea? Jesus grew; he developed over the span of his life. All the qualities—and we have touched on just a few that the Savior had—he magnified, developed, and grew in those first thirty years of his life. If it took Jesus thirty years of development and growth from grace to grace to arrive at the point where he was ready to begin his mission, what does that mean for us? D&C 93 teaches that at his baptism John testified, "he received a fulness of the glory of the Father" (D&C 93:16). If it took Jesus thirty years ascending grace for grace, it is going to take Mike Wilcox three hundred or more. In D&C 78, the Lord says, "Verily, verily, I say unto you, ye are little children, and ye have not as yet understood how great blessings the Father hath in his own hands and prepared for you; and ye cannot bear all things now; nevertheless, be of good cheer, for I will lead you along. The kingdom is yours and the blessings thereof are yours, and the riches of eternity are yours" (D&C 78:17–18). We'll get there. You're going to make it. We'll go slowly, patiently. The kingdom is ours. He will help us. He will see us to the end.

MY LINES AREN'T STRAIGHT LIKE YOURS

A number of years ago I was working on a lesson from the Book of Mormon. When I prepare a lesson, I underline various verses with blue and red pencils, highlighting here and there and adding comments in the margins. I was lying on the bed with a page open. My son, about five or six years of age at the time, was playing with his trucks. He saw what I was doing, dropped his truck, ran into his bedroom, and picked up his own copy of the Book of Mormon. He crawled up on the bed with me, opened his book, and borrowed my pencils to color in his book. My children used to say, "Dad colors in his scriptures, so we get to color in ours."

When I work on a lesson I can get deeply absorbed with what I'm doing and not always be aware of everything that's going on around me. Though I was aware that my son was marking his scriptures as I was marking mine, I wasn't looking at what he was doing. About half an hour later when I was done with my lesson, I looked up to see his book. He had duplicated my page. Every word I had underlined, he had underlined. Every word I had highlighted, he had highlighted with the same colors that I had.

I had written a quote by Brigham Young in the margin, "How the Devil will play with a man who so worships gain."[3] My son had tried to write that same phrase, but it was too much for his little hand to write, so he just wrote, "How the devil." He got the "d" backwards so it read, "How the bevil."

As he saw me scrutinizing his book and looking at each duplication—and I was amazed at how closely he matched my book—he reacted in a way I had not anticipated. By the way, my son was exemplifying true worship. True worship is imitation, is it not? I looked at him and his little lips started to quiver and his eyes started to tear up and I said to him, "Oh, McKay, what's the matter?"

And he said, "My lines aren't straight like yours, Dad."

He thought I was looking at his book with a critical eye, judging because his lines weren't straight. As I study the life of the Savior, what he did, how he forgave, how he treated others, his relationship with his Father, I try to imitate him. Yet I fail frequently to get it right. Sometimes I look up and I'm afraid he is looking down at my crooked lines. I'm ready to break into tears and say, "My lines aren't straight like yours, Lord." Do you understand that feeling?

However, do you think that as a father I cared if my son's lines were straight? He will get the lines straight in time. You and I will get our lines straight too. We'll become everything that he was, all the qualities we've discussed here that we admire so much in him and that we're not yet as good at as he is. We'll get there. We'll get those and every other thing we try to emulate from him right in time. In the meanwhile, he isn't a chastening God. He doesn't sigh in frustration. Isaiah wrote of him, "He shall not cry, nor lift up, nor cause his voice to be heard in the street. A bruised reed shall he not break" (Isaiah 42:2–3).

I love that. He won't rail at you, bawl you out, or be critical. There are times in our lives when we will feel like a little bruised reed. Reeds are cylinders; when you bruise them, they become very weak and can barely stand straight. That is a beautiful image of how we feel from time to time. We're bruised reeds and the tiniest critical remark will break us. Yet he says, "I don't break a bruised reed." He is not judgmental. He understands that we must grow from grace to grace. He will be patient with us. He is not critical with us in those matters.

Why does he feel this way, why is he so patient and un-condemning and hopeful for us all? What is his great motivating power? I conclude with one final quality that I admire so much in the Savior. If we understand this quality, our lives are going to be easier and more restful, and our burdens will be lighter.

The Ultimate Characteristic

Jesus was always motivated by love in all his relationships. It was simply love that carried him through life. You see it in a number of different places. We read, "Now Jesus loved Martha, and her sister, and Lazarus" (John 11:5). John was called "the Beloved." The rich young ruler, of whom we are often critical, is introduced in Mark's account with the words, "Jesus beholding him loved him" (Mark 10:21). At the Last Supper, Jesus said, "A new commandment I give unto you, That ye love one another; as I have loved you" (John 13:34). John introduced the last part of Jesus' life with the words, "having loved his own which were in the world, he loved them unto the end" (John 13:1).

When I was a student at Brigham Young University and was engaged, I was so head-over-heels with Laura Chipman that I can't imagine anybody being deeper in love than I was. I was totally enamored with that young woman. I had a professor named Arthur Henry King who taught Shakespeare. He was a great man. He was an English educator and he taught using the English system—small classes, very personal. Sometimes he'd bring a little group of students to his home and he would read poetry to us and ask us to read what we had written. It was a wonderful educational experience. I was there once with Laurie; we were engaged, in love. He looked at me and said, "Do you know what the greatest discovery of life is? It's the knowledge that the woman you love loves you." He added, "That will change you. That will have a profound impact on your life." I believe that with all my heart.

I have since come to understand there is an even more profound lesson. It is that the God I love loves me. That too will change you. The Lord's words to us in Isaiah are very beautiful and comforting. "Fear not: for I have redeemed thee, I have called thee by thy name; thou art mine. When thou passest through the waters, I will be with thee; and . . . when thou walkest through the fire, thou shalt not be burned; . . . for I am the Lord thy God . . . thy Saviour: . . . thou wast precious in my sight . . . and I have loved thee (Isaiah 43:1–4). Understanding that love, being motivated by that love, will change us all.

I enjoy reading the works of a poet named Maya Angelou. She had a very rough life. She was sexually assaulted as a little girl; I think at about age seven. She didn't speak, except to her brother, for five years after that experience. Finally, as a young woman, she began to tell her story. She has a penetrating and finely tuned intellect. She learned to speak again by studying poetry, but her belief in God was gone because of the challenges and pain in her life. I suppose she was mad at God as sometimes happens when life is cruel.

She tells of an experience that changed her. These are her words: "One of my earliest memories of Mamma, of my grandmother, is a glimpse of a tall cinnamon-colored woman with a deep, soft voice, standing thousands of feet up in the air on nothing visible. That incredible vision was a result of what my imagination would do each time Mamma drew herself up to her full six feet, clasped her hands behind her back, looked up into a distant sky, and said, 'I will step out on the word of God.' . . .

"I could see her flung into space, moons at her feet and stars at her head, comets swirling around her. . . . I grew up knowing that the word of God had power.

"In my twenties in San Francisco I became a sophisticate and an acting agnostic. . . . One day [my] teacher, Frederick Wilkerson, asked me to read to him. I was twenty-four, very erudite, very worldly. He asked that I read . . . a section which ended with these words: 'God loves me.' I read the piece and closed the book, and the teacher said, 'Read it again.' . . . 'God loves me.' He said, 'Again.' After about the seventh repetition I began to sense there might be truth in the statement, that there was a possibility that God really did love me. Me, Maya Angelou. I suddenly began to cry at the grandness of it all. I knew that if God loved me, then I could do wonderful things, I could try great things. . . .

"That knowledge humbles me, melts my bones, closes my ears, makes my teeth rock [and] it liberates me. I am a big bird winging over high mountains, down into serene valleys. I am ripples of waves on silver seas. I'm a spring leaf trembling in anticipation."[4]

I don't measure up to all the things that Christ is that we've discussed. I doubt you do either. I would like to measure up, but knowing that you and I are precious to him, that he loves us, will give us the motivation and power to become one day all that he wants us to be.

Epiphany in the Elm Tree

The first real testimony I had of Jesus came when I was a little boy about seven years old. I was sitting in a sacrament meeting with my mother who had a beautiful singing voice. The sacrament hymn that day was "More Holiness Give Me." Normally I wasn't too interested in sacrament meeting. I was wanting to get back home, to *The Wonderful World of Disney* and the Ponderosa ranch on *Bonanza,* so I fidgeted through sacrament meeting. But for some reason as I listened to my mother sing "More Holiness Give Me," the words of the hymn began to fill an empty place in my heart that was reserved only for sacred and special things. Nothing had ever touched that spot in my heart before, but those words went in and touched that spot. When she came to the line, "More longing for home," I was filled with an intense homesickness for a place—but more for a Being, for two Beings. Then I heard the last line, "More, Savior, like thee," and I knew somehow that the secret to my returning to that place and to those beings that I longed for was to be "More, Savior, like thee."[5] In my little-boy heart, I wanted to be like him. I went home that afternoon to the elm tree that grew in our front yard. I climbed up into it and sat there in the leaves and I quietly sang that song over and over again to myself. I so dearly wanted to go home. I wanted to be like Jesus so that I could go home.

Sometimes we stand back and look at ourselves through our memories. I stand back now so many years later and I look at that little boy in the tree—it's almost as if it wasn't me, that little boy. There are times I wish I was still a little boy, seven years old, just starting out trying to be like Jesus, no failures, just wanting to go home, trying to be like him. Then I hear the Savior say to me, "I still see the little boy in the tree. Keep trying. You'll make it home."

May our burdens be light. The next time somebody says to you or me, "What's it like being a Latter-day Saint?" may we reply, "It is restful. It is easy. Our burdens are light because of what we know about the Savior we worship."

CHAPTER THREE

OF LIONS, DRAGONS, AND TURKISH DELIGHT

C. S. Lewis for Latter-day Saints

A BOY FROM BELFAST

Perhaps an introduction would be helpful before beginning a study of some of C. S. Lewis's thoughts that resonate with Latter-day Saints. C. S. Lewis spent his youth in Ireland and had some unpleasant experiences in the English educational system before a private tutor he called "The Great Knock" taught him how to think. Oxford came next and became his home for the majority of his life. In his youth, he shed his religion with some relief and became a sometime atheist. "I maintained that God did not exist," he said. "I was also very angry with God for not existing. I was equally angry with Him for creating a world."[1] But God knew his potential and pursued him relentlessly, as Lewis himself asserted. In time, influenced by his Christian friends (J. R. R. Tolkien among them), and after a struggle, C. S. Lewis accepted the realities of Christianity and became its greatest defender.

His warmth and humane understanding of the personalities, the character, and the attributes of God the Father and His Son Jesus Christ, and his honest insight into the human condition and how the teachings of Christ speak with such mercy and compassion to that condition have endeared C. S. Lewis to Christians of all denominations. We all claim a share in him. He attended the Anglican Church because, as he put it, "I thought one ought to 'fly one's flag' by some unmistakable overt sign."[2] But the words he wrote and spoke bridge many divides. Though as Latter-day Saints we may not find agreement and clarification on all points of doctrine in C. S. Lewis's writings, his penetrating accuracy on so many fronts resonates within us as it resonates within the hearts of Christians everywhere. I discovered Lewis when I came across his story about a busload of sinners from hell making a visit to heaven. One of them had a red lizard on his shoulder that eventually turned into a beautiful stallion—but more of that later.

I was hooked immediately, and from that time forward, devoured every book Lewis ever wrote. With that brief introduction, let us begin with a foundation principle of Lewis's writing—that of longing.

As a small boy in Belfast, Ireland, Lewis often looked out his nursery window at a low line of hills in the distance. "They were not very far off," he said, "but they were, to children, quite unattainable. They taught me longing."[3] This was a longing for something he could not understand, or discover how to reach the unknown thing or person or place he longed for. That longing and its realization and fulfillment became, as he later said, "the central story of my life."[4] He would in time discover what it was he yearned for and how to reach that destination. In those discoveries, he would change not only himself, but deeply influence and strengthen the Christian world. His given name was Clive Staples Lewis, but his friends all called him Jack. When he was very little, he decided Clive was not a suitable name for a boy to have. He called himself "Jacksie," and everyone for the rest of his life knew him as Jack.

As we discuss C. S. Lewis and the great impact he had, I want to let him do the talking—not me—so that you get a flavor and a sense for this great man and his theology, especially how that theology dovetails into and helps us understand our own theology. There are things that Lewis taught that reverberate with all Christians, certainly, but in some instances particularly with us as Latter-day Saints. Almost all Christian groups claim him, so there must be something about him that appealed to everyone, from the Roman Catholics to the Jehovah's Witnesses and to you and me as Latter-day Saints.

The Destination

I would like to preface some of Lewis's writings by appealing to yet another Lewis, Lewis Carroll, also a great British writer of children's literature. In *Alice in Wonderland,* when Alice meets the Cheshire Cat, there is an interesting little conversation between them that has some profound ideas in it.

"'Would you tell me, please, which way I ought to go from here?'

"'That depends a good deal on where you want to get to,' said the Cat.

"'I don't much care where—' said Alice.

"'Then it doesn't matter which way you go,' said the Cat.

"'—so long as I get *somewhere*,' Alice added as an explanation.

"'Oh, you're sure to do that,' said the Cat, 'if you only walk long enough.'"[5]

The idea of destinations and roads fascinated Lewis Carroll, as it fascinated C. S. Lewis. It seems obvious to us that it is critical that we know where we're going and that we know the road that will get us there. Many people are like Alice—they're lost in a different, sometimes frightening, world. And they don't know where they're going. They don't have a destination and so they take any road and they end up, as we might say, anywhere.

I had the opportunity—the great fortune—to study Lewis for my Ph.D. dissertation. For over three years I just studied Lewis's writing. I read everything he wrote. Something of which I became convinced by the end of my studies was that Lewis knew the ultimate destination of Christianity—the destination that one would reach if one made correct choices. He also knew the road that would get us there, and he knew that the journey and the destination both involved a great deal of joy and happiness. He titled his autobiography with a phrase from Wordsworth—*Surprised by Joy.* By "surprised," he meant surprised by both the amount and the quality of joy God wishes us to have.

"As Happy as I Mean You to Be"

You are probably familiar with C. S. Lewis's series of children's books, the Chronicles of Narnia. Walden Media has begun an ambitious project to film the entire series, beginning with *The Lion, the Witch and the Wardrobe.* In the seventh and last book of the Chronicles of Narnia, titled *The Last Battle,* Lewis described man's destination. (For those who are not aware of the Chronicles of Narnia, Narnia is an imaginary world that children enter through a wardrobe, or a picture, a gate, a doorway. There they meet Aslan, the great lion, the Lord of Narnia, who is a symbol for Christ. Everything we read and learn and hear about Aslan should lead us to think: *This is really the Savior that Lewis is teaching me about.*) At the end of the great Last Battle, the children have a final conversation with Aslan. They have just watched the destruction of the Narnia they had come to love, as the giant, Time, reached up and grabbed the sun, squeezing it into blackness. A great flood of water washes over all of Narnia. As they turn around and look behind the door through which they have witnessed the end of Narnia, they realize that the real Narnia—the eternal Narnia—still exists, even better than it was before. Even in their dawning joy, they aren't as happy as Aslan thinks they should be. He says, "You do not yet look so happy as I mean you to be." I think that is a statement the Savior often makes to us in our lives now. "You do not yet look so happy as I mean you to be." Lucy, one of the children, replies, "'We're so afraid of being sent away, Aslan. And you have sent us back into our own world so often.'

"'No fear of that,' said Aslan. . . . 'The term is over: the holidays have begun. The dream is ended: this is the morning.'"[6]

Something to keep in mind is just how much Lewis hated school. That may be why I like Lewis so much—I simply hated school growing up. Kindergarten was okay. In a perfect world, we would go from kindergarten right into college.

Lewis had such poor experiences at school that he nicknamed one "Belsen," after the Nazi concentration camp. That might give you an idea how he felt about school. When Aslan promises, "'the term is over: the holidays have begun,'" you can almost feel the sense of June joy that Lewis meant:

"'The term is over: the holidays have begun. The dream is ended: this is the morning.'

"And as He spoke He no longer looked to them like a lion; but the things that began to happen after that were so great and beautiful that I cannot write them. And for us this is the end of all the stories, and we can most truly say that they all lived happily ever after. But for them it was only the beginning of the real story. All their life in this world and all their adventures in Narnia had only been the cover and the title page: now at last they were beginning Chapter One of the Great Story which no one on earth has read: which goes on forever: in which every chapter is better than the one before."7

"A New Kind of Man"

What we want to understand as we look at Lewis's theology in its application to our Latter-day Saint perspective is "Chapter One of the Great Story." In over a third of the sections of the Doctrine and Covenants, we are told to be happy, to be of good cheer, to rejoice, to be glad. Obviously God intends us to be joyful. What does "Chapter One of the Great Story" consist of? What constitutes the joy? Lewis felt that the purpose of Christianity, of the scriptures—really, of anything God does with his children—is not just to produce better men or to help us live a good life. There is a specific end, a precise destination we are heading toward, and that end will generate a tremendous amount of joy. He wrote, "In setting up 'a good life' as our final goal, we have missed the very point of our existence."8 And what is the point? Lewis answers: "God became man to turn creatures into sons: not simply to produce better men of the old kind but to produce a new kind of man."9

What was this new kind of man? As Latter-day Saints, you and I would say "Gods." That is the destiny toward which we are heading. Lewis, in large measure, would agree.

"[Christ] is going to make good His words. If we let Him—for we can prevent Him, if we choose—He will make the feeblest and filthiest of us into a god or goddess, a dazzling, radiant, immortal creature, pulsating all through with such energy and joy and wisdom and love as we cannot now imagine, a bright stainless mirror which reflects back to God perfectly."10 In *The Screwtape Letters,* Lewis wrote, "[God] wanted to make Saints; gods; things like Himself."11 From *The Great Divorce* the same assertion is made: "The Lord said we were gods. How long could ye bear to look (without Time's lens) on the greatness of your own soul and the eternal reality of her choice?"[12] In a letter to a woman who inquired about a character in one of Lewis's science fiction novels, Lewis replied, "In reality every real Christian is really called upon in some measure to *enact* Christ."[13]

Lewis wrote a series of three science fiction novels. In *Perelandra,* the king of another world—not Christ, but an inhabitant of another planet—is described this way: "It was that face which no man can say he does not know. You might ask how it was possible to look upon it and not to commit idolatry, not to mistake it for that of which it was the likeness. For the resemblance was, in its own fashion, infinite, so that almost you could wonder at finding no sorrows in his brow and no wounds in his hands and feet."[14]

Picture a wagon wheel with spokes radiating from the hub at the center that holds them together. Without the hub, the spokes are useless. They will all fall apart. It's the hub that holds them together and gives them meaning. In a sense, as you look at Lewis's theology, his belief in the ultimate destination is the hub and every other aspect of Christianity is meaningless without that hub to hold it together. The divine destination toward which we are headed is the central purpose of Christianity and the mortar that holds scripture together. Understandably, Lewis writes, "In the same way the Church exists for nothing else but to draw men into Christ, to make them little Christs. If they are not doing that, all the cathedrals, clergy, missions, sermons, even the Bible itself, are simply a waste of time. God became Man for no other purpose. It is even doubtful, you know, whether the whole universe was created for any other purpose."[15]

JOSEPH SMITH'S DEEPER INSIGHT

Sometimes it amazes me as I read Lewis how closely he came to Joseph Smith. Yet, the Prophet Joseph seems to always take one step further, deeper into the light of truth. Joseph Smith once said, "Thy mind, O man! if thou wilt lead a soul unto salvation [and I have to believe Lewis led a lot of souls to salvation], must stretch as high as the utmost heavens . . . and the broad expanse of eternity."[16] As you think about what Lewis was teaching, you can see his mind stretching out and expanding. As we read in the Pearl of Great Price, "This is my work and my glory—to bring to pass the immortality and eternal life of man" (Moses 1:39). God said that to Moses after he had revealed to Moses that he has created "worlds without number" (Moses 1:33). In essence, the Lord said to Moses, "I made worlds without number in the past. I am making worlds without number now and I'm going to go right on making worlds without number on into eternity. I like my job, and I'm going to keep on doing it. The whole focus of my job is man and to allow man to enjoy life the way I enjoy it." Somehow, in his own manner, Lewis came to understand that mind-expanding truth.

It seems that celestial happiness consists of seeking, ensuring, and promoting the happiness of others—helping all of God's children feel the same joy and live the same life that God and Christ live. Lewis wrote, "[Christ] really *does* want to fill the universe with a lot of . . . little replicas of Himself—creatures whose life . . . will be qualitatively like His own, not because He has absorbed them but because their wills freely conform to His."[17]

Lewis never got to the point where he asked the next logical question, or at least he never wrote about or discussed that question. Joseph Smith asked it, though. The next sensible question is: If we're going to be little Christs, if we're going to be like God, if we're going to pulsate and radiate with the same joy as God, what will we do? Lewis's answer was, essentially, "We'll be happy." Yet the conclusion of godhood as the ultimate destination of Christianity asks the question: What will one do in that state of existence? And it was Joseph Smith who took that next step. He helped us reason thusly: "If I have the joy of a god, and the light and the radiance of a god, if I am a god, *I must therefore do what a god does!*" One cannot escape the logic of this conclusion. I repeat: Joseph Smith is always amazing to me, especially as I read Lewis and contemplate his conclusions and then read Joseph Smith and watch him take that next step, that doctrinal leap to eternal increase and the creation of worlds, and God's children not only becoming like him, but doing what he does!

"The Galaxies as an Old Tale"

If we are going to be gods, it must mean that the individual is critical. Lewis affirmed this over and over again. Everyone has infinite worth—that was the practical ramification, for Lewis, of that doctrine. If that is our destiny, then every single individual has infinite worth. The Doctrine and Covenants says, "Remember the worth of souls is great in the sight of God" (D&C 18:10), then qualifies that worth by saying one soul is worth the Atonement. That's infinite worth. A soul is worth a lifetime of a man's labor! That's a finite value, but we can at least begin to get our mind around the concept. Lewis also understood the great value of the soul. As he wrote:

"If Christianity is true, then the individual is not only more important but incomparably more important, for he is everlasting and the life of a state or a civilisation, compared with his, is only a moment."[18] The significance of each individual is greater than that of a state or of a civilization.

As a teacher of Renaissance and medieval literature at both Oxford and Cambridge, Lewis knew the value of, for instance, Shakespeare and Jonson, as well as other masters of English literature. But how do Shakespeare's writings compare to each one of us? In an essay titled "Christianity in Literature," Lewis wrote, "The Christian knows from the outset that the salvation of a single soul is more important than the production or preservation of all the epics and tragedies in the world."[19] From a lover of *King Lear, Hamlet, Romeo and Juliet,* and other "epics and tragedies," that is a profound statement. "There will come a time," he wrote in an essay titled "Membership," "when every culture, every institution, every nation, the human race, all biological life is extinct and every one of us is still alive. Immortality is promised to us, not to these generalities. It was not for societies or states that Christ died, but for men. [I particularly like this next phrase:] We are assured of our eternal self-identity and shall live to remember the galaxies as an old tale."[20]

You and I as individuals—not as a group, but as individuals—are worth more than states, civilizations, cultures, institutions, arts, nations, and the great literary epics and tragedies. When Lewis was at Oxford, he gave a talk called "The Weight of Glory" at St. Mary's Church. That expression, "the weight of glory," comes from Paul's writings. Paul spoke of an "exceeding and eternal weight of glory" (2 Corinthians 4:17). Joseph Smith used that phrase as a definition of godhood (see D&C 132:16). Both Lewis and Joseph Smith drew on that phrase from Paul and expanded it. In the Oxford speech, Lewis states the value of the individual better than anywhere else I have read:

"The load, or weight, or burden of my neighbour's glory should be laid daily on my back. . . . It is a serious thing to live in a society of possible gods and goddesses, to remember that the dullest and most uninteresting person you could talk to may one day be a creature which, if you saw it now, you would be strongly tempted to worship, or else a horror and a corruption such as you now meet, if at all, only in a nightmare. All day long we are, in some degree, helping each other to one or other of these destinations. It is in the light of these overwhelming possibilities, it is with the awe and circumspection proper to them, that we should conduct all our dealings with one another, all friendships, all loves, all play, all politics. There are no *ordinary* people. You have never talked to a mere mortal. Nations, cultures, arts, civilizations—these are mortal, and their life is to ours as the life of a gnat. But it is immortals whom we joke with, work with, marry, snub, and exploit—immortal horrors or everlasting splendours. . . . Next to the Blessed Sacrament itself, your neighbor is the holiest object presented to your senses."[21]

LOOK!

May I add a personal reflection? When I first started teaching, two young men in my seminary class sat at the back of the room whose goal in life, it seemed to me, was to make my life miserable. I was not much older than these two young men. They both played on the high school football team. They were bigger than I was and, I must admit, I was intimidated. If you let high school students know you're even a little intimidated by them, they will take advantage of it, and these two boys took advantage of my insecurity. I had an interesting dream one night about these two boys. To be honest, I didn't like them. If I had a good lesson prepared, I would pray that God would smite them with the flu so they wouldn't wreck for it me. They never seemed to get sick. They were the healthiest young men the Lord ever put on earth. But one night I had a dream about them. It is always interesting to explore the symbolism our minds create for us with the help of the Spirit.

I dreamed I was in prison with these two boys. We were filthy and walking back and forth in the exercise yard outside of the prison cells. There was mud everywhere. We were dressed in rags and they were covered with mud. There wasn't a beautiful or lovely thing anywhere, just concrete walls and mud. The boys were walking on either side of me. I remember feeling uncomfortable to be in that environment and to be with that company. Then a light from an unknown source wrapped itself around us and flowed through us. It filled me with great joy and great glory and great warmth and great beauty. But it did more than this—it began to lift us out of the mud, higher and higher into the air. I looked down—I never stopped looking down until the very last moments of the dream. From the moment the light wrapped itself around us and began to lift us up, I never stopped looking down. I was aware that these two boys were being lifted with me in the air, but I was fascinated by watching the earth receding as we were lifted higher. Soon the prison shrunk until we could see beyond the walls to the green countryside on the outside. Our prison kept shrinking as we went higher and higher; the light increased, and with its increase the joy intensified. It felt as if the light went right through me—that if I looked behind me, I would see no shadows. It was that kind of a light.

Soon the prison was so small I couldn't even see it. It had become a tiny brown dot in a great, beautiful countryside of green. We kept lifting higher and higher until all the distinct features of the countryside disappeared. In time, the edges of the continent came into view. The east and west coastlines diminished. I was looking down at America, and yet all the while the light kept getting greater and greater. It was proving to be so powerful that it almost hurt. I thought to myself, *I can't bear much more of this glory.* Then the edges of the world came into view, a vast circular horizon set against the heavens. Then the world receded into the distance, becoming smaller and smaller as farther into heaven we went, until finally the earth was just a pinpoint in a great sea of light. Finally, it just disappeared. When that happened I looked up for the very first time. In front of me was a beautiful city made out of crystal. As the light flowed through every angle and corner of it, it was split into all the colors of the rainbow. It was simply glorious.

A great open gate led into the city, and a Being walked out of this gate dressed in white. The light radiated from Him in great flooding waves. I thought, *This is the source of the light whose joy was so overwhelming!* He approached us, and when He arrived at a point just a few feet in front of us, He stopped and looked carefully at the three of us. We were silent in His presence. Then this great celestial Being said a single word, but He said it with great intensity. He said, "Look!"

I looked at Him. Who else could one look at in that situation? He smiled and shook His head, then repeated His invitation a second time, but with even greater eagerness. I sensed that it would give Him great joy for me to see what He desired me to look at. He said, "Look!"

I looked at Him more intensely, trying to focus all my attention on His face. He shook His head again, still smiling, and once again offered His invitation. However, this time He pointed straight at the three of us and said in a tone of tenderness, "Look!"

I thought, "He wants me to look at myself." So I looked down. Then I looked at the two boys on either side of me. The rags and the filth were gone; we were dressed in white as He was. But more important, and what He wanted us to see, was that the light was flowing from us in the same intensity that it was flowing from Him.

I think that experience describes as well as I can what Lewis was teaching: All people—even those we don't like, even those two boys at the back of my classroom—who reach their full potential will be just as radiant and glorious as Christ himself. Therefore we have the same quality of light that every celestial being has and that our Father in Heaven and his Son have. And that will create tremendous joy for you and me. That takes time; it doesn't happen at once.

"Do Not Dare Not to Dare"

Lewis helps us look at ourselves and at each other through time's great lens. "Remember," he said, "we Christians think man lives for ever. Therefore, what really matters is those little marks . . . on the central, inside part of the soul which are going to turn it, in the long run, into a heavenly . . . creature."[22] Knowing our destination, we receive profound motivation to walk the road that will get us there, though the road isn't always easy to walk. If we're going to be pure as Christ is pure, if we're going to radiate the light that he radiates, if we're going to be a god as he is a God, changes must come. They will often undoubtedly be painful, as Lewis believed, because I think they were painful in his own life. But joy, it must be remembered, was the final outcome—joy even in the challenge of pain and change. Lewis felt that we dare not shy away from the changes.

In one of the Chronicles of Narnia there is a wonderful little exchange between Aslan and two talking horses. We find this conversation in a book called *The Horse and His Boy.* That is the right title—the horse owns the boy, not the other way around. One of the horses struggles with pride. His name is Bree; the mare's name is Hwin. At the end of the story these two horses come face to face with Aslan.

"'Please,' [Hwin] said, 'you're so beautiful. You may eat me if you like. I'd sooner be eaten by you than fed by anyone else.'"

Isn't that a beautiful concept of Christ? To rather be swallowed up in him than fed by any other source. The conversation continues:

"'Dearest daughter,' said Aslan, planting a lion's kiss on her twitching, velvet nose, 'I knew you would not be long in coming to me. Joy shall be yours.'

"Then he lifted his head and spoke in a louder voice:

"'Now, Bree,' he said, 'you poor, proud frightened Horse, draw near. Nearer still, my son. Do not dare not to dare.'"[23] What a wonderful challenge: "Do not dare not to dare." Sometimes it will be difficult to approach the Lord, knowing the changes he will ask us to make. We are not the kind of being that Christ is. But knowing that we can ultimately reach the dignity of his divine nature will help us pass through the necessary changes.

T. S. Eliot wrote a poem titled "The Waste Land." Therein he speaks of the type of daring Bree is invited to try, namely: "The awful daring of a moment's surrender / Which an age of prudence can never retract."[24] This type of surrender demands of us all that we have and are. And *that* is the daring that will be required of us to meet God's expectations.

THERE IS NO OTHER STREAM

There's a wonderful little moment in the Chronicles of Narnia that expands our understanding of this aspect of Lewis's theology. In *The Silver Chair,* a young girl named Jill arrives in Narnia for the first time and meets Aslan, the great lion. Jill is very thirsty. She can hear running water in the distance and moves toward the sound of the water. This is the living water Christ offers to us all. Yet when she sees Aslan sitting by the stream, not knowing much about him, she is hesitant to quench her thirst. He invites her to drink from his stream but she wishes to know something about him first.

"'Will you promise not to—do anything to me, if I do come?' said Jill."[25] Sometimes that is what we say to Jesus. He says, "Come!"

We reply, "I want to, but please don't hurt me."

How does Aslan respond to Jill's need for assurance?

"'I make no promise,' said the Lion.

"Jill was so thirsty now that, without noticing it, she had come a step nearer.

"'*Do* you eat girls?' she said.

"'I have swallowed up girls and boys, women and men, kings and emperors, cities and realms,' said the Lion. It didn't say this as if it were boasting, nor as if it were sorry, nor as if it were angry. It just said it.

"'I daren't come and drink,' said Jill.

"'Then you will die of thirst,' said the Lion.

"'Oh dear!' said Jill, coming another step nearer. 'I suppose I must go and look for another stream then.'"

Would you care to guess what the Lion will say next?

"'There is no other stream,' said the Lion."[26]

We drink the living water or we die spiritually. We dare not, not to dare. We must approach and endure (for *endure* is sometimes the only word that adequately describes what we are in for) through the remaking. Lewis felt we needed to be new creatures. Christ was the first example of this new creature. He said Christ's role was "not that of a prodigy but of a pioneer. He is the first of His kind; He will not be the last."[27] Many of us will follow him.

"STRONG, RADIANT, WISE, BEAUTIFUL, AND DRENCHED IN JOY"

There is a beautiful exchange in a children's book called *The Wind in the Willows.* Lewis liked this particular exchange. Kenneth Grahame, like many British writers of children's literature, put spiritual truths into his writing. I do not say they all did it intentionally, but those truths were in them and therefore came out in what they wrote. There is a story in the book about a lost otter. As you read it, you sense it is really the story of the lost sheep, only this time the good shepherd is not Christ. Christ's role, in this story, is occupied by the Greek god of forest animals—the god Pan, who plays such enchanting music on his pipes. Rat and Mole are searching for the otter and hear the call of the pipes. Following the music they enter a flowery enclosure along the river and there they find both the baby otter and the god Pan, who is caring for him. As we read, we feel about Pan the same way we feel about Aslan in Lewis's children's stories. He is a type of Christ. Rat and Mole enter his presence and Grahame writes, "And still, as [Mole] looked, he lived; and still, as he lived, he wondered.

"'Rat!' he found breath to whisper, shaking. 'Are you afraid?'

"'Afraid?' murmured the Rat, his eyes shining with unutterable love. 'Afraid! Of *Him?* O, never, never! And yet—and yet—O, Mole, I am afraid!'"[28] That is probably how we will all approach the giver of the living water, he who will anticipate great changes in us. Only our faith—and above all, our love for him— will be sufficient, for we do not dare not to dare.

Lewis wrote an essay titled "Rabbit or Man." In the essay, the rabbit is all the things that make us unhappy, all the elements of what King Benjamin called "the natural man" (Mosiah 3:19). What Christ will do is remove all the "natural" things that make us so unhappy in order to let us experience a fulness of joy. "We are to be re-made," Lewis commented. "All the rabbit in us is to disappear—the worried, conscientious, ethical rabbit as well as the cowardly and sensual rabbit. We shall bleed and squeal as the handfuls of fur come out; and then, surprisingly, we shall find underneath it all a thing we have never yet imagined: a real Man, an ageless god, a son of God, strong, radiant, wise, beautiful, and drenched in joy."[29] I sincerely do love that last phrase and the idea behind it: "drenched in joy."

REMOVING THE LIZARD

Sometimes Lewis used different images for what we call the "natural man" or the old man of sin that needs to be removed—what he calls "the rabbit" in the previous quotation. My first introduction to Lewis came when I was invited by a friend to read *The Great Divorce*. In that book, the rabbit—the thing that we have to get rid of because it prevents us from having joy—was a lizard sitting on the shoulder of an inhabitant of hell who was visiting heaven. Briefly, *The Great Divorce* is a story about a busload of sinners from hell who drive to heaven. (Lewis had a great imagination.) All of the people on the bus have problems. When they get to heaven they see a chain of mountains in the distance. A legion of angels travel over the mountains to greet them, and they give the busload of sinners a choice. First of all, the angels tell the sinners that they aren't in heaven proper. Where they are is a kind of heavenly suburb—the real heaven is on the other side of the mountains. However, they can stay where they are; they don't have to go back to hell. They can even progress over the mountains into the highest, most central part of heaven. They simply have to give up their most precious possession.

As *The Great Divorce* continues, no one can give up that possession except one man. The sinners all get back on the bus and go back to hell, unable to give up what is most precious to them. The one man who does stay has a lizard sitting on his shoulder. It is red and ugly and it talks to him. He talks to the lizard also. An angel approaches this strange pair and asks (I am paraphrasing), "Do you want to stay?"

"Oh, I don't want to go back to hell."

"Well then, you will have to give up your most precious possession. What is it?"

With some degree of chagrin the man answers, "It's the lizard. He has been with me for the longest time. I've raised him from a little lizardette" (or whatever it is we call baby lizards).

"Well, you'll have to kill it." There follows an immense struggle between the man and the angel and the lizard. He can't bring himself to tear the lizard off his shoulder. The lizard keeps trying to talk him out of it, saying, "They don't really mean it. They don't really want you in deep heaven. You'll always be a lesser inhabitant."

The angel counters every argument of the lizard until finally, in a great and difficult moment, the man, with the help of the angel, reaches up and grabs the lizard, who clings to him so tightly that the man is afraid that if he pulls the lizard off, it will take some of him with it. After much hesitation and rationalization, the man in desperation agrees to the painful removal of the lizard. He and the angel pull the lizard off and throw it to the ground. The man then collapses in pain. Then something wonderful happens. The angel touches the man, heals him, lifts him up, and he rises, young and virile and powerful. Together they watch the lizard, who writhes and changes and transforms into a beautiful stallion, which he rides triumphantly over the mountains into heaven. He truly gave up his most precious thing.[30]

What does that lizard symbolize? It symbolizes his sins; in this case, a particular sin the man had constantly struggled with. What is our most precious possession? If, by definition, our most precious possession is that which we keep at the expense of all other things, sadly, our sins are our most precious possessions. Lewis believed that the door to hell was locked from the inside. God does not lock you in. You go there of your own free will, largely because you cannot remove your lizards. Man is not condemned for his sins; he is condemned only if he will not leave them.

THE TALE OF THE DRAGON

In *The Voyage of the Dawn Treader*, another of the Chronicles of Narnia, the lizard, the rabbit fur, that which holds us back from receiving joy, is represented by a dragon. In this book, Lewis tells us how we get the lizards on our backs. We are introduced to a young boy named Eustace. His name sounds like "Useless" because that's what he is, at least at the beginning of the story. He's a nasty little kid who complains about everything. He is Lewis's symbol for all of us who need the change that Christ offers. The *Dawn Treader* is a ship that sails from island to island, reminiscent in some ways of Homer's *Odyssey*. There is a shipwreck and the *Dawn Treader* needs repairs. But Eustace doesn't want to help, so he wanders off on his own to get out of work and also to get away from other characters in the story for whom he has developed a certain dislike. As he climbs down the slope of a mountain, he sees an opening in the trees, which leads to a cave and a pool of water and evidence of fire. While watching the cave, he freezes when he hears a noise. At that moment, a great dragon comes out of the cave, obviously in pain. The dragon walks over to the pool, drinks, and then collapses.

Eustace doesn't know if the dragon is dead or alive because, as Lewis says, he'd read all the wrong books and didn't know anything about dragons. Finally, timidly, he walks out from his hiding place and discovers that the dragon is dead. It begins to rain and he rushes into the cave. There he finds what is in all dragons' caves. If you have (unlike Eustace) read the right books, you know what is in a dragon's cave—treasure, mounds of treasure. He revels in the treasure, plotting how he can get it back to Narnia and how he will live with such wealth. His thoughts are selfish and mean. He can live like a king! These and other evil thoughts dominate his mind and eventually make him tired. He makes a bed in the treasure and goes to sleep, but just before he goes to sleep, he places a golden ring upon his arm.

When he awakes, the sun has set. It is dark; the moon is shining at the entrance to the cave. Ahead of him he sees two jets of steam. *Oh, no!* he thinks, *the dragon has a mate and it's returned.* He holds his breath. But when he holds his breath, the steam stops. When he lets it out again slowly, trying not to draw attention to himself, the steam issues forth in a straight, steady jet. He reaches to his left, feeling for the wall to sneak out of the cave. Yet as he reaches out his hand, he sees a great dragon claw come into view. He freezes. The claw freezes. He lowers his hand. The claw lowers. He thinks the dragon is to the left of him. He reaches out his right hand. As he does, another great claw comes into view. He freezes. The claw freezes. He drops his hand. The claw drops. He thinks the dragon must be above him, its paws around him, mimicking his every move.

He decides that the only possible way to escape is to make a run for it. Maybe he can get to the pool. He jumps up and runs, but as he does, he notices a biting, pinching pain in his arm where he put the gold ring earlier. Strange that it would feel so tight now. He also notices he's running on all fours. A great noise erupts from the cave as gold and jewels scatter. Finally, when he arrives at the reflection pool, as he reaches his head over the water, there in the moonlight he sees the ugly face of a dragon looking up at him. What a horrible discovery! The jets of steam were his own breath! The claw on the left was his claw! The claw on the right was his claw! He has become a dragon!

Lewis writes, "Sleeping on a dragon's hoard with greedy, dragonish thoughts in his heart, he had become a dragon himself. That explained everything."[31] We might paraphrase this lesson thus: "Sitting in the world's cave on worldly treasure, thinking worldly thoughts, we become like the world." And by opposition: "Sitting in God's cave on God's treasure, thinking Godly thoughts, we become like God."

There is always hope. Aslan will not let him remain a dragon. Eustace goes through a period of internal change, a type of repentance. He lets the other children know that he is really Eustace, and with his great strength he helps in repairing the ship. After a time of penitence and sorrow, one night he sees a great lion pacing in the moonlight, calling to him. Though he feels a sense of fear, the beckoning Lion is impossible to resist, and he follows. In time they arrive at the top of a mountain where a garden is located. In the garden is a beautiful pool of water. Eustace had never been able to remove the golden ring from his arm. It pinches and bites and cuts him. He thinks if he could just bathe it in the water, maybe it would help.

Peeling Back the Dragon Skin

Perhaps the ring can symbolize one's conscience, which fits very well when you're a little boy, but hurts and bites and cuts when you're a dragon. Eustace moves toward the pool and Aslan tells him he can bathe in his pool, but he must first undress. Eustace does not understand what that means, but finally realizes that dragons are like snakes, and maybe he is being asked to remove a layer of outer skin. He claws and scratches and pulls a layer off and throws it into the moonlight. Then he steps toward the pool for his bath. When he sees his ugly dragon foot, he realizes he is not yet ready for the pool. He scratches and pulls off another layer of dragon skin. He does this a third time, but senses he is still unfit for Aslan's beautiful pool. The great Lion is still waiting.

Finally Eustace is in despair. Aslan says, "You will have to let me undress you." He lies on his back and Aslan's claws tear and cut through the dragon skin to the little boy inside. The tearing and pulling is so deep that it goes into his heart. Eustace explains the experience: "And when he began pulling the skin off, it hurt worse than anything I've ever felt. The only thing that made me able to bear it was just the pleasure of feeling the stuff peel off. . . . Well, he pulled the beastly stuff right off—just as I thought I'd done it myself the other three times, only they hadn't hurt—and there it was lying on the grass: only ever so much thicker, and darker, and more knobbly-looking than the others had been. And there was I as smooth and soft as a peeled switch and smaller than I had been."[32] Then with velvet paws, Aslan picks him up and places him in the water, healing him, clothing him, and finally sends him back to the other characters in the story.

Eustace's observation that the layers of dragon skin he had peeled off himself did not hurt is an important idea for Lewis. Sometimes we go to the Savior and we want to get healed or helped in some little thing that is troubling us. We feel the pinch of our conscience. Something in our lives no longer fits comfortably. Maybe we are watching the wrong sort of movies. We scratch and peel and throw that bad habit at the Lord's feet and say, "Is that enough?" We know in our hearts it is not. Maybe we're irritable. Maybe we get angry. Maybe we gossip. Maybe we have a little problem with the Word of Wisdom or tithing. Maybe we waste time. We continue to peel off layers and lay them down. But the whole dragon skin has got to come off. The lizard has to be removed. All the rabbit hair has to be pulled out because those are all the things that make us unhappy and hinder our growth toward godhood.

"I Will Give You Myself"

Lewis taught these same principles straight up, without fantasy, but not without metaphor—metaphor was his natural environment. Let us see in plainer terms what he means by pulling out the rabbit fur, or taking the lizard off our shoulders, or peeling off the dragon skin. In *Mere Christianity* he said: "We take as starting point our ordinary self with its various desires and interests. We then admit that something else—call it 'morality' or 'decent behaviour' or 'the good of society'—has claims on this self: claims which interfere with its own desires. What we mean by 'being good' is giving in to those claims. Some of the things the ordinary self wanted to do turn out to be what we call 'wrong': well, we must give them up. Other things, which the self did not want to do, turn out to be what we call 'right': well, we shall have to do them. But we are hoping all the time that when all the demands have been met, the poor natural self will still have some chance, and some time, to get on with its own life and do what it likes. . . . As long as we are thinking that way, one or other of two results is likely to follow. Either we will give up trying to be good, or else we become very unhappy indeed."[33]

It might be helpful here to know that Lewis was raised Christian, but the constant effort to be good was so great that it finally drove him to atheism, or at best agnosticism or apathy. In his very first Christian book, *The Pilgrim's*

Regress, he called church leaders "the Stewards." God was "the Landlord," and the commandments were the "rule card." He felt he could not live them all. The protagonist in this book was Lewis himself. It was an early attempt to write an autobiographical account of his development. He describes the way he views his responsibilities: "He would wake one morning full of fear, and take down his card and read it—the front of it—and determine that today he would really begin to keep the rules. And for that day he would, but the strain was intolerable. He used to comfort himself by saying, It will get more easy as I go on. Tomorrow it will be easier. But tomorrow was always harder."[34] Because he could not live all the Christian commandments, because in his perception God was not a loving being, a being who desired our happiness, his fear of "the Landlord" and the burden of the rules, in time, drove Lewis to abandon his faith with relief. Later, J. R. R. Tolkien and other friends would bring him back. When Lewis writes we may "give up trying to be good, or else we will become very unhappy indeed," that's exactly what happened to him.

The next idea from Lewis's *Mere Christianity* is this: "Make no mistake: if you are really going to try to meet all the demands made on the natural self, it will not have enough left over to live on. The more you obey your conscience, the more your conscience will demand of you. And your natural self, which is thus being starved and hampered and worried at every turn, will get angrier and angrier."[35]

There are some interesting paradoxes in the scriptures. Jesus says we should let our light shine, but also that we shouldn't let our left hand know what our right hand is doing. That is a paradox! He says, "My yoke is easy, and my burden is light" (Matthew 11:30), but he also tells us to pick up our cross (see Mark 8:34; Luke 9:23). Is the burden easy or heavy? Is it a heavy cross or an easy yoke? Lewis answered these paradoxes thus: "The Christian way is different: harder, and easier. Christ says 'Give me All. I don't want so much of your time and so much of your money and so much of your work: I want You. I have not come to torment your natural self, but to kill it. No half-measures are any good. I don't want to cut off a branch here and a branch there, I want to have the whole tree down. I don't want to drill the tooth, or crown it, or stop it, but to have it out. Hand over the whole natural self, all the desires which you think innocent as well as the ones you think wicked—the whole outfit. I will give you a new self instead. In fact, I will give you Myself: my own will shall become yours.'"[36]

"The Whole of Christianity"

In the Doctrine and Covenants there are three beautifully powerful but simple words that begin with the letter *L* that our Savior offers by way of invitation to us. I call them the "Three Ls": "*Look* unto me in every thought" (D&C 6:36; emphasis added). "*Learn* of me, and *listen* to my words" (D&C 19:23; emphasis added). Look! Learn! Listen! Then we are told what we should do next: "*Walk* in the meekness of my Spirit" (D&C 19:23; emphasis added). We immerse ourselves in the gospels, in Christ, in what he did, and then we try to do what he did. That was Lewis's goal. That is the way we tear the dragon skin off, pull the lizard off our shoulders, and pull the rabbit fur out.

Notice the following encouragement by C. S. Lewis: "When He said, 'Be perfect,' He meant it. He meant we must go in for the full treatment. It is hard; but the sort of compromise we are all hankering after is harder—in fact, it is impossible. It may be hard for an egg to turn into a bird: it would be a jolly sight harder for it to learn to fly while remaining an egg. We are like eggs at present. And you cannot go on indefinitely being just an ordinary, decent egg. We must be hatched or go bad. . . . This is the whole of Christianity. There is nothing else."[37]

COUNTING THE COST

There is a wonderful parable told by Jesus about building a tower. It teaches that we are supposed to count the cost of discipleship as we begin to follow Christ. One should not start the construction of a tower unless we intend to finish it or people will mock us. The Savior ended that parable by saying, "So likewise, whosoever he be of you that forsaketh not all that he hath, he cannot be my disciple" (Luke 14:33). The building of the tower—the cost of discipleship— requires the forsaking of all that we have, not necessarily in a material sense, but spiritually. It means our thoughts, our attitudes, our words, our feelings, everything that would not fit perfectly with Christ's life must be gone. All the dragon skin! All the rabbit fur! All the lizards perched on our shoulders!

"'Make no mistake,' [Christ] says, 'if you let me, I will make you perfect. The moment you put yourself in My hands, that is what you are in for. Nothing less, or other, than that. You have free will, and if you choose, you can push Me away. But if you do not push Me away, understand that I am going to see this job through. Whatever suffering it may cost you in your earthly life, whatever inconceivable purification it may cost you after death, whatever it costs Me, I will never rest, nor let you rest, until you are literally perfect—until my Father can say without reservation that He is well pleased with you, as He said He was well pleased with me. This I can do and will do. But I will not do anything less.'"[38] Lewis then quotes George MacDonald, who once said, "'God is easy to please, but hard to satisfy.'"[39]

Taking his cue from that thought, Lewis teaches: "On the one hand, God's demand for perfection need not discourage you in the least in your present attempts to be good, or even in your present failures. Each time you fall He will pick you up again. And He knows perfectly well that your own efforts are never going to bring you anywhere near perfection. On the other hand, you must realise from the outset that the goal towards which He is beginning to guide you is absolute perfection; and no power in the whole universe, except you yourself, can prevent Him from taking you to that goal."[40]

"The command *Be ye perfect* is not idealistic gas. Nor is it a command to do the impossible. He is going to make us into creatures that can obey that command. He said (in the Bible) that we were 'gods' and He is going to make good His words. If we let Him—for we can prevent Him, if we choose."[41]

So the fur will come out, the dragon skin peeled off, the lizards gone, the tooth out, the branch cut off, all the different resolutions that Lewis described in this daily battle with the self, because all of those things are what bring us unhappiness. Lewis knew that the business of God was joy. "There is no other way to the happiness for which we were made," he said.[42] "When we want to be something other than the thing God wants us to be, we must be wanting what, in fact, will not make us happy."[43]

DIVINE HOMESICKNESS

This brings us back to the longing that Lewis felt as a boy looking at the hills beyond Belfast. Because our journey, our transformation, is hard, we need encouragement along the way. Lewis feels that this longing supplies that encouragement. He uses a diversity of expressions for this longing—a yearning for a place or a thing or a relationship that nothing on earth could satisfy. He once described the soul as "but a hollow which God fills."[44] I love that description. The longing, the ache, is a desire to satisfy this emptiness. It is the realization that there is nothing on earth that could bring one the fulness of joy for which you and I were created. It was a type of an "earnest," an idea Paul used in his epistles. He spoke to the early Saints about the "earnest" that the Holy Spirit bestowed. God "hath . . . given [us] the earnest of the Spirit," he wrote to the Corinthians (2 Corinthians 1:22). And the Ephesians were reminded that they had received "the earnest of our inheritance" (Ephesians 1:14). In large monetary transactions, like buying a house, earnest money is what you pay up front to assure the seller that more is coming. It is usually a small amount, compared to the latter installment. Lewis feels that this longing, this divine homesickness, this ache of joy that he felt from time to time, is the "earnest" of which Paul wrote. It is God promising us that all will be worth the effort—the joy will be more than ample reward for the death of the lizard and the tearing off of the dragon skin. The

Lord assures us that he will give us from time to time little bright spots of God-light to keep us moving—a foretaste of the great joy that one day we will receive.

Here is a selection from the Chronicles of Narnia: "Aslan threw up his shaggy head, opened his mouth, and uttered a long, single note; not very loud, but full of power. Polly's heart jumped in her body when she heard it. She felt sure that it was a call, and that anyone who heard that call would want to obey it and (what's more) would be able to obey it, however many worlds and ages lay between."[45] This joy, this longing, this divine homesickness, this Blue Flower, this *Sehnsucht,* this inkling, this spilled religion—Lewis had all kinds of words for it—this "earnest" of the promised joy that would come exists to teach us that there is a far greater happiness designed for us than any we can imagine on earth. We should then be more willing to let go, when necessary, of the "Turkish delights"—the world with all its temporal tastes. Only this inward planted homesickness is strong enough to help us endure our dragon skin being torn off and our lizard removed. We will come to understand in the intensity of the longing that smaller, worldly pleasures are not worth giving up that eternal pleasure and joy.

"Tantalizing Glimpses"

If we are honest with ourselves, we will admit that we are not entirely at home here on earth, but are strangers, pilgrims, seeking a happiness we can't find on our own. The longing penetrates our hearts and gives us glimpses of an eternal world. We read in Isaiah, "Since the beginning of the world men have not heard, nor perceived by the ear, neither hath the eye seen, O God, beside thee, what he hath prepared for him that waiteth for him" (Isaiah 64:4).

"'This is my real country,'" one of the characters in Narnia says. "'This is the land I have been looking for all my life, though I never knew it till now.'"[46] "In speaking of this desire for our own far-off country," Lewis wrote, "which we find in ourselves even now, I feel a certain shyness. . . . I am trying to rip open the inconsolable secret in each one of you. . . . Apparently, then, our lifelong nostalgia, our longing to be reunited with something in the universe from which we now feel cut off, to be on the inside of some door which we have always seen from the outside, is no mere . . . fancy, but the truest index of our real situation."[47]

"The experience," he wrote in another place, "is one of intense longing. . . . yet the mere wanting is felt to be somehow a delight. . . . This hunger is better than any other fullness; this poverty better than all other wealth."[48] "That something which you were born desiring, and which, beneath the flux of other desires and in all the momentary silences between the louder passions, night and day, year by year, from childhood to old age, you are looking for, watching for, listening for."[49] "If a man diligently followed this desire . . . he must come out at last into the clear knowledge that the human soul was made to enjoy some object that is never fully given—nay cannot even be imagined as given—in our present . . . experience."[50] "Most people, if they had really learned to look into their own hearts," discover that they "want acutely, something that cannot be had in this world."[51] "I find myself wondering whether, in our heart of hearts, we have ever desired anything else. . . . All the things that have ever deeply possessed your soul have been but hints of it—tantalising glimpses, promises never quite fulfilled, echoes that died away just as they caught your ear. . . . Beyond all possibility of doubt you would say 'Here at last is the thing I was made for.'"[52]

I have deliberately quoted Lewis from several sources to show how prevalent this idea was in his writings. Perhaps you have felt this longing? These are moments when the celestial breeze floats open the veil and we feel it fan our faces. When I was married in the Cardston Alberta Temple I felt that breeze as it opened the veil just a bit and refreshed me with celestial glory. I'll never forget that moment. I can't describe it. For years I wondered, *How do I describe that moment, the feeling, and the warmth that came as I knelt there?* I think God allowed a single ray of celestial glory to hit the altar where we knelt, but I could never put it into words. One day, however, I found that Lewis had described it for me. Perhaps you too have felt these celestial breezes somewhere, sometime, that said to you, "This really isn't home, and no happiness here can approach the happiness that will be there."

The passage that expressed what I could only remember but never vocalize is from *The Magician's Nephew,* another of the Chronicles of Narnia, when the children say goodbye to Aslan at the conclusion of the book. "Such a sweetness and power rolled about them and over them and entered them that they felt they had never really been happy or wise or good, or even alive and awake, before. And the memory of that moment stayed with them always, so that as long as they both lived, if ever they were sad or afraid or angry, the thought of all that golden goodness, and the feeling that it was still there, quite close, just round some corner or just behind some door, would come back and make them sure, deep down inside, that all was well."[53]

A MEMORY WITHIN THE LONGING

The quality of this longing has something of remembrance in it. Lewis's theology never posited a premortal existence as did Wordsworth in his oft-quoted poem, "Ode: Intimations of Immortality": "Our birth is but a sleep and a forgetting."[54] Wordsworth apparently arrived at the point where he truly believed in a premortal existence. Here again we see Joseph Smith going a step further. But some of Lewis's writings suggest that this longing, this homesickness, supposes a previous life. In a poem he wrote—he did write poetry—we read of "vanished knowledge . . . a music that resembled / Some earlier music / That men are born remembering."[55]

At the end of *The Screwtape Letters* Lewis writes, "that central music in every pure experience which had always just evaded memory was now at last recovered."[56] In another poem he writes of ancient "memory" that "reaches us. We know more than bones can teach. / . . . Before we're born we have heard it."[57] In one of his science fiction novels, Lewis writes of "a sense of great masses moving at visionary speeds, of giants dancing, of eternal sorrows eternally consoled, of he knew not what and yet what he had always known, awoke in him with the very first bars of the deep-mouthed dirge, and bowed down his spirit as if the gate of heaven had opened before him."[58]

In another of Lewis's science fiction novels, one of the characters hears and speaks of "the cord of longing which . . . seemed to him at that moment to have been fastened long, long before . . . long before the earliest times that memory could recover in his childhood, before birth, before the birth of man himself, before the origins of time. It was sharp, sweet, wild, and holy, all in one."[59] So the longing is not for something we have never had, a happiness we have never before enjoyed, but for something we once had and lost, and need, and want to return to.

LONGING FOR A PLACE OR A PERSON?

This longing, this joy, this divine homesickness, this spilled religion, these patches of God-light—I love all the phrases that Lewis has for it—is not just for a far-off country or place, but for a being, a relationship that occupies the very center of that country. We are longing for our Father. We are longing for his Son. And we knew them both. Their imprint on our memory is in large measure responsible for our longings. In *The Magician's Nephew,* Aslan greets a cabby who has been brought into Narnia: "'Son,' said Aslan to the Cabby, 'I have known you long. Do you know me?'

"'Well, no, sir,' said the Cabby, 'Leastways not in an ordinary manner of speaking. Yet I feel somehow, if I may make so free, as 'ow we've met before.'

"'It is well,' said the Lion. 'You know better than you think you know, and you shall live to know me better yet.'"[60]

There is a wonderful exchange in *Prince Caspian,* the second in the Chronicles of Narnia series, between Aslan and Lucy. Lucy is the youngest of the children who first discovered Narnia in the book *The Lion, The Witch and the Wardrobe.* When she returns and sees Aslan they have a wonderful reunion. "'Aslan,' said Lucy, 'you're bigger.'

"'That is because you are older, little one,' answered he.

"'Not because you are?'

"'I am not. But every year you grow, you will find me bigger.'"[61] What a beautiful thought about our relationship with Christ. We know him. We remember him. But the more we know, the older we become, the bigger, the grander, the more magnificent he becomes.

In *The Voyage of the Dawn Treader,* Lucy discovers a magician's book of spells. While turning its pages one of the spells reads, "For the refreshment of the spirit." Captivated, Lucy begins to read the story contained in the spell. As she reads, she feels an intense homesickness, not for a place, but for a Being, and the story of that Being's life and sacrifice. Notice how Lewis weaves into his narrative the great elements of the story of Christ, including our hunger for a renewed association with him.

"On the next page she came to a spell 'for the refreshment of the spirit.' The pictures were fewer here but very beautiful. And what Lucy found herself reading was more like a story than a spell. It went on for three pages and before she had read to the bottom of the page she had forgotten that she was reading at all. She was living in the story as if it were real, and all the pictures were real too. When she had got to the third page and come to the end, she said, 'That is the loveliest story I've ever read or ever shall read in my whole life. Oh, I wish I could have gone on reading it for ten years. At least I'll read it over again.'" The book wouldn't let her turn back the pages, so Lucy tried to lock it in her memory. "'I must remember it. Let's see . . . it was about . . . about . . . oh dear, it's all fading away again. . . . It was about a cup and a sword and a tree and a green hill, I know that much. But I can't remember and what *shall* I do?'

"And she never could remember; and ever since that day what Lucy means by a good story is a story which reminds her of the forgotten story in the Magician's Book."[62]

Lewis believed that almost anything that ever touched us in literature, in art, or in life was but an echo or a shadow of the great story of which we are all a part. In *The Lion, the Witch and the Wardrobe,* the first time the children hear the very name of Aslan, a remarkable thing happens. The children have found the Beavers, one of whom informs them: "'They say Aslan is on the move—perhaps has already landed.'

"And now a very curious thing happened. None of the children knew who Aslan was any more than you do; but the moment the Beaver had spoken these words everyone felt quite different. Perhaps it has sometimes happened to you in a dream that someone says something which you don't understand but in the dream it feels as if it had some enormous meaning . . . a lovely meaning too lovely to put into words, which makes the dream so beautiful that you remember it all your life and are always wishing you could get into that dream again. It was like that now. At the name of Aslan each one of the children felt something jump in its inside. . . . Lucy got the feeling you have when you wake up in the morning and realize that it is the beginning of the holidays or the beginning of summer."[63] Again, we see through Lucy's reaction Lewis's visceral feelings about school, which as we have noted before included nicknaming one of the schools he attended "Belsen," after the concentration camp.[64]

"There I Have Another Name"

The main reason that Lewis wrote the Chronicles of Narnia was to help us, particularly children, love Christ. If we are going to be like Jesus, if we're going to go through the challenge of being de-dragonized, we must know what our Savior is like. Perhaps more important, we must love him. The love is already there, buried in the memory to be awakened. We have to respond to the gentle calls and spiritual music that touch the vibrant chords in the mind and heart. We must be grateful. We must be alert. We must not disregard the longing. Lewis created Aslan for the purpose of touching the love already in us. And you do love that Lion as you read about him. With each new book, love and appreciation increase. You love Aslan, and thus Christ, for his dignity, his wisdom, his pure goodness, his gentleness. Perhaps most of all you love him because he wants us to receive his love, to know him, and to share his happiness.

There is a beautiful moment in *The Horse and His Boy* when a young boy named Shasta is riding over a high mountain all alone on an old horse. It is foggy and misty and he can't see. He is feeling sorry for himself and lonely. Suddenly, as he rides along, he senses something walking beside him in the mist and the darkness. He is terrified. So he urges his steed on, but the old horse can't do more than plod along slowly. Even when he gets a little speed out of him, the thing in the darkness keeps pace with his every movement. Finally, in his fear he turns into the darkness and he asks, "Who are you?" And the answer he receives is, "One who has waited long for you to speak."[65] Shasta meets Aslan, tells him his sorrows, and finds comfort. This exchange is the fictional counterpart to the story of Lewis's life. God—Christ—walked beside him and waited, and waited, for him to talk to him; to call out in the darkness so the Divine Master could help Lewis find true happiness and receive joy. Lewis was surprised by that joy—not the harshness of the Landlord and the burden of the rules he feared as a child—but the joy and happiness the divine whisperings placed in his soul and in ours too.

Lewis described his conversion to Christianity this way: "You must picture me alone in that room in Magdalen, night after night, feeling, whenever my mind lifted even for a second from my work, the steady, unrelenting approach of Him whom I so earnestly desired not to meet. That which I greatly feared had at last come upon me. In the Trinity Term of 1929 I gave in, and admitted that God was God, and knelt and prayed: perhaps, that night, the most dejected and reluctant convert in all England. I did not then see what is now the most shining and obvious thing; the Divine humility which will accept a convert even on such terms. The Prodigal Son at least walked home on his own feet. But who can duly adore that Love which will open the high gates to a prodigal who is brought in kicking, struggling, resentful, and darting his eyes in every direction for a chance of escape? . . . The hardness of God is kinder than the softness of men, and His compulsion is our liberation."[66] We truly are surprised by joy.

In the last chapter of *The Voyage of the Dawn Treader,* the children are afraid that it is going to be quite a while before they can come back to Narnia. They wish their return to be sooner. In their final conversation with Aslan they hear distressing news. Lucy says: "'Will you tell us how to get into your country from our world?'

"'I shall be telling you all the time,' said Aslan. 'But I will not tell you how long or short the way will be; only that it lies across a river. But do not fear that, for I am the great Bridge Builder. And now come; I will open the door in the sky and send you to your own land.'

"'Please, Aslan,' said Lucy. 'Before we go, will you tell us when we can come back to Narnia again? Please. And oh, do, do, do make it soon.'

"'Dearest,' said Aslan very gently, 'you and your brother will never come back to Narnia.'

"'Oh, *Aslan!!*' said Edmund and Lucy both together in despairing voices.

"'You are too old, children,' said Aslan, 'and you must begin to come close to your own world now.'

"'It isn't Narnia, you know,' sobbed Lucy. 'It's *you.* We shan't meet *you* there. And how can we live, never meeting you?'

"'But you shall meet me, dear one,' said Aslan.

"'Are—are you there too, Sir?' said Edmund.

"'I am,' said Aslan, 'But there I have another name. You must learn to know me by that name. This was the very reason why you were brought to Narnia, that by knowing me here for a little, you may know me better there.'"[67]

Lewis had a profound love for Christ. How grateful we are for God's divine humility that brought that prodigal, kicking and screaming, into his kingdom. That same divine humility seeks us out also, and how grateful for us that it found C. S. Lewis who put into words, stories, and pictures of lions and dragons lessons that enrich our lives and enhance our own continual conversions. His great gift was to make concrete so many concepts and doctrines that seem, to us, hard to express.

Of Lions, Dragons, and Turkish Delight, Part 2

"THE SERIOUS BUSINESS OF HEAVEN"

Most of us, when we study an author or a writer or even a figure in scripture, will favor certain statements they made. These quotations resonate within us, catch our own beliefs, express what we feel, or speak to our souls in a unique manner. These statements seem to encapsulate everything that author stood for, believed in, and taught—the theme of their life. If I were to pick a theme for C. S. Lewis, it would be his phrase: "Joy is the serious business of Heaven."[68] I believe that is true—almost everything Lewis taught after his conversion to Christianity centered on that magnificent affirmation.

The six major elements of C. S. Lewis's philosophy dovetail very beautifully into Latter-day Saint philosophy and belief. Briefly, they are as follows:

1. God desires us to be, to use Lewis's words, "drenched in joy."[69] "Joy is the serious business of heaven."[70] The present as well as the eternal happiness of his creations is the focus of God's thoughts and actions.

2. *Joy* ultimately means to live life qualitatively as God lives it, to be, in effect, "a god or goddess,"—as Lewis described: "dazzling, radiant . . . pulsating all through with such energy and joy and wisdom and love."[71] This is our destiny, the goal which we seek. The accomplishment of that destination will require all our efforts and lay the foundation for all our hopes.

3. Because we can become like God, the individual is immeasurably important—more important than civilizations, cultures, arts, nations, whole worlds. We "shall live to remember the galaxies as an old tale," Lewis wrote.[72] We must learn to see ourselves and others in the light of that great shining truth.

4. The journey to become like God will necessitate great changes. We must be new creatures. Not just new kinds of men and women. The

lizards must come off. The dragon skin must be peeled back. "All the rabbit in us is to disappear."[73] This is sometimes painful and requires a great deal of effort, but it is something that we must not dare *not* to dare to do. It is only that which will bring us ultimate joy.

5. We are but a "hollow" that God wishes to fill, Lewis taught.[74] There is something empty in us that no earthly thing can satisfy. We come to earth with a longing, a divine homesickness. To use Paul's words, an "earnest" of future things (Philippians 1:20). We experience haunting memories that teach us that our deepest fulfillment and our greatest happiness lie elsewhere than this mortal existence. We belong to a far country, higher up and deeper in. The promise that this longing, this divine homesickness, this hollow can be filled to overflowing is the prime motivator for removing the dragon skin.

6. The longing which tells us of our eternal home, our far country, is also a desire for a relationship which lies at the center of the yearning. We want a person as well as a place. It is our Father in Heaven and his Son that we hunger for—as Lucy says to Aslan at the end of *The Voyage of the Dawn Treader,* "And how can we live, never meeting you?"[75]

"A Million Chances"

I repeat Lewis's phrase: "Joy is the serious business of heaven." It is so serious that every conceivable opportunity to obtain it will be allowed to us. Students of all ages have asked me, "Do you think we get a second chance?" How many have ever wondered that? Am I going to get a second chance? If I fail, but want to try again, is God going to let me? How many chances do I get? Do I get three? Do I get four? I always answer that question with a quote from Lewis taken from his book *The Problem of Pain.* I sincerely believe in the hope contained in its message. He said, "I believe that if a million chances were likely to do good, they would be given."[76]

So we are going to get all the chances that we can conceivably have, or that God can offer. In *The Great Divorce,* even those in hell are allowed in heaven and they can remain there if they desire to do so deeply enough, but they must be willing to make changes, to remove the lizard from their shoulders, to give up the dragon skin, or in other words, to abandon their most precious possessions. Lewis continues in *The Great Divorce:* "'Never fear. There are only two kinds of people in the end: those who say to God, "Thy will be done," and those to whom God says, in the end, "*Thy* will be done." All that are in Hell, choose it. Without that self-choice there could be no Hell. No soul that seriously and constantly desires joy will ever miss it. Those who seek find. To those who knock it is opened.'"[77]

Alma teaches us the very same thing, and Alma (the Younger) would know, wouldn't he? He was in the midst of hell and he wanted out. He asked and the Savior brought him out. And so Alma proclaims, "The one raised to happiness according to his desires of happiness, or good according to his desires of good; and the other to evil according to his desires of evil; . . . Now, the decrees of God are unalterable; therefore, the way is prepared that whosoever will may walk therein and be saved" (Alma 41:5, 8). Either our will *will* be done, or God's will *will* be done. And His will for us is joy.

"Turkish Delight"

If joy is the serious business of heaven, and if we all desire happiness, as Joseph Smith taught when he said, "Happiness is the object and design of our existence; and will be the end thereof, if we pursue the path that leads to it,"[78] then, with a million chances to do good, what is the problem? Our challenge is that we all like "Turkish delight" too much.

If you've read *The Lion, the Witch and the Wardrobe* or if you've watched one of the film versions, you will remember that Turkish delight is the treat that the White Witch gives to Edmund in order to turn him into a traitor. It was Lewis's symbol for the allurements of a fallen world—for sin. Turkish delight is a type of candy well-loved in the United Kingdom. Lewis felt children would understand its attractions. Edmund tastes the Witch's offering and it tempts him away from goodness, alienates him from the other children—even from the idea of Aslan—and draws him silently away. As you remember, Edmund does not enjoy the little meal of wholesome food offered in the Beavers' hut. Lewis writes: "[Edmund] had eaten his share of the dinner, but he hadn't really enjoyed it because he was thinking all the time about Turkish delight—and there's nothing that spoils the taste of good ordinary food half so much as the memory of bad magic food."[79]

Lewis's insight has value and is true in many areas of life. That is why the Lord tells us as parents to "bring up your children in light and truth" (D&C 93:40). If we do, they will naturally gravitate to light and truth; they will recognize goodness when it is presented before them. We all must learn to reject the Turkish delight that tempts us, realizing that if we eat too much of it, it may spoil the taste of other good, joyful things which God would have us feast upon. We may not only reject the good when it is offered, but reach a point where we cannot even recognize it when it is presented to us.

Lewis identified and spent a great deal of effort trying to describe in very plain terms the various types of Turkish delight that could spoil our appetite for true happiness and joy. He wrote whole books about it—*The Abolition of Man, The Problem of Pain, The Great Divorce*. And of course, his most famous creative work, and the book that really launched his career, *The Screwtape Letters*. (A brief note: *The Screwtape Letters* are a series of letters written from the point of view of a "senior devil," Screwtape, to his nephew, a "junior tempter" named Wormwood. Lewis's aim is to get us to think about what it is that derails us in our journey to Christ, a kind of "know thy enemy" tactic.)

Ironically, perhaps tragically, most of us are pretty good at enjoying Turkish delight, often at the expense of experiencing a deeper appreciation of real joy. There is a wonderful moment in *The Magician's Nephew* when Aslan—the Christ figure—wants to help one of the characters, but he cannot. With a sad resignation he tells them, "I cannot tell that to this old sinner, and I cannot comfort him either; he has made himself unable to hear my voice. If I spoke to him, he would hear only growlings and roarings." And then, Aslan speaks one of my favorite lines: "Oh, Adam's sons, how cleverly you defend yourselves against all that might do you good!"[80]

Let us look at some of the Turkish delight in the worldly box of candy that is often presented to us by the White Witch we call Lucifer. While I would love to discuss all the different deviations and wayward wanderings that Lewis warns us about, space will not permit. I would like to point out a few that he emphasized and that are particularly pertinent to our own day and age.

THE DISTRACTION OF NOISE

As we reach into the candy box we notice a piece of Turkish delight labeled "Noise"! Ever-present and constantly distracting noise! Screwtape hated silence and despised music. (Lewis wrote before the emergence of the pulsating beat of certain types of rock music of which I am sure Screwtape would approve.) What Screwtape said about music was this: "Music and silence—how I detest them both! How thankful we should be that ever since Our Father entered Hell [remember, 'Our Father' for Screwtape would be Lucifer]—though longer ago than humans, reckoning in light years, could express—no square inch of infernal space and no moment of infernal time has been surrendered to either of those abominable forces, but all has been occupied by Noise—Noise, the great dynamism, the audible expression of all that is exultant, ruthless, and virile—Noise which alone defends us from silly qualms, despairing scruples and impossible desires. We will make the whole universe a noise in the end. We have already made great strides in this direction as regards the Earth. The melodies and the silences of Heaven will be shouted down in the end."[81]

I don't know how your life is, but I find my life often filled with a great deal of Noise. This encompasses the larger dimensions Lewis speaks of in the preceding quotation, as well as the simpler variety that always seems to buzz around our ears like an annoying insect. I have nothing against modern technology. (The transistor radio was newly invented and popular when Lewis was writing, and he did not view it favorably.) I've often wondered what he would think of the myriads of personal entertainment devices we find on the market today. They're tools, of course. They're good, and in some cases even needful. But they can also surround us with a great deal of noise, probably more noise than is good for that spiritual part of us which flourishes in a more quiet and restful ambience.

In a poem, Lewis wrote:

> Clamour shall clean put out the voice of wisdom. . . .
> . . . Harpy wings,
> Filling your minds all day with foolish things,
> Will tame the eagle Thought: till she sings
> Parrot-like in her cage to please dark kings.[82]

I am not, nor do I suppose Lewis would be, deeply opposed to the technology we have today. However, we may have cause to be a little uneasy. I work with college students, and it is interesting what I see around me when I walk across campus or I ride the light-rail line to work. I would estimate that at least 60 percent of all people I see around me anymore have little wires coming down out of their ears attached to some sort of noise. Undoubtedly some is edifying in nature. That is not the issue. It may not be the quality of what we listen to that is critical, but the amount of noise drowning out the needed silence in our lives. "Their devices for saving them have banished leisure from their country," Lewis wrote.[83] He knew the need for leisure was not simply for more entertaining stimulation but for thought and reflection.

It wasn't just noise but the denying of solitude that bothered Lewis and pleased Screwtape. We understand that not all the sounds going into our ears are negative. It is just that there is so much sound. We have a need in our lives for time to meditate, to reflect, to ponder. The Spirit rarely shouts. We must invite it. It is not in the habit of intruding when we are not listening or attentive to its whisper. Sometimes sheer busyness crowds it out. I repeat, the sounds we invite into our lives are not always negative, but the accumulated amount can effectively remove solitude from our lives. We don't experience quiet enough—time to form deep friendships, family relations, relations with the Spirit, with God.

Lewis wrote, "There is a crowd of busybodies, self-appointed masters of ceremonies, whose life is devoted to destroying solitude wherever solitude still exists. . . . And even where the planners fail and someone is left physically by himself, the wireless has seen to it that he will be . . . never less alone than when alone. [How interesting that for him, the radio was 'the wireless,' while today that same word describes so much of the noise-producing technology we are discussing here.] We live, in fact, in a world starved for solitude, silence, and privacy, and therefore starved for meditation and deep true friendship. . . . When the modern world says to us aloud, 'You may be religious when you are alone,' it adds under its breath 'and I will see to it that you are never alone.' . . . That is one of the enemy's great stratagems."[84]

Screwtape, interestingly enough, was always very interested in the mind. There are a number of chapters in *The Screwtape Letters* dealing with the human mind and what he was either trying to take out of it or put into it. But there is no question as you read *The Screwtape Letters* that Screwtape was more interested in what he could keep out of the mind than what he could put into it. Screwtape makes this interesting observation: "It is funny how mortals always picture us as putting things into their minds: in reality our best work is done by keeping things out."[85] Today, he is very effective in keeping a lot out through noise, busyness, hurry, constant electronic or technological stimulation. When this happens often the most important things are sacrificed for those least essential. We really cannot "text" our way into any relationship that will have enduring meaning.

EXTREMES

Let us return to our box of Turkish delight, choose another enticement, and taste its flavor. This next piece is a small one, but it is very effective. I call it the Turkish delight of Extremes. Extremes, in whatever context, are rarely healthy. The historical backdrop of *The Screwtape Letters* is World War II, but Screwtape isn't very interested in the war. In and of itself, the war was effectively neutral as an agent in destroying the Christian soul the letters center on. So long as extreme positions were taken, the war could be useful in manipulating the "patient" Wormwood is tasked with destroying in a number of different ways. Screwtape writes to Wormwood, "Give me without fail in your next letter a full account of the patient's reactions to the war, so that we can consider whether you are likely to do more good by making him an extreme patriot or an ardent pacifist. There are all sorts of possibilities."[86] In a later letter, Screwtape writes: "I had not forgotten my promise to consider whether we should make the patient an extreme patriot or an extreme pacifist. All extremes, except extreme devotion to the Enemy, are to be encouraged."[87] (Again, by "the Enemy," Screwtape means God.)

Lucifer doesn't care if we have deep crippling guilt or easy rationalization. He's as effective with questioning cynical skepticism as he is with mind-numbing blindly obedient rigidity. He is equally pleased with a militant atheist as with an intolerant zealous fanatic. As long as the extreme is reached, the Turkish delight will do its damage.

There is a verse of scripture that others sometimes use as a challenge to Latter-day Saint claims of additional revelation or other books of scripture. It is found at the very end of the book of Revelation, where we read that we are not to add to nor diminish from the writings of the book (Revelation 22:18–19). Often these verses are used to suggest that we shouldn't have a Book of Mormon or a Doctrine and Covenants because that's adding to the scriptures. At the end of Revelation, John is himself quoting from Deuteronomy. The more accurate interpretation of this scripture, of not adding or diminishing from the scriptures, consists in not making a commandment, a principle, a policy, a standard, a position, an ordinance, or a prophecy more than it is. And, on the other hand, not to make it less than it is.

One of the reasons we call the path we are to walk the strait and narrow path follows from this admonition. We do not have much room to push things to either one side or the other on that path. Walking that path is a balancing act, much like walking a tightrope. Often people will have gospel hobbies or push overemphasized ideologies. They become extreme in advocating their position or defending it or compelling others to believe or follow it. The Lord, through his messengers, has to step in and say, "Wait a minute—you're making the commandment more than the commandment is." Or a person will diminish a commandment or doctrine and the Lord will need to say, "Wait a minute— you're making it less than it is." We need to stay on the strait and narrow and not fall off either on the broad side of the path, the "additions" side of the path, or to the other side, the "diminishing" side of the path. We should neither add to nor diminish from the proper balance. We must be careful of the Turkish delight of Extremes.

MATERIALISM

We reach back into the candy box. Here we find a glitzy Turkish delight, one that is very appealing. It is one of the first we may be tempted to pick up. It is the Turkish delight of Materialism. Lewis wrote a great deal about it. In *The Voyage of the Dawn Treader,* there is a scene when the children are exploring an island and come upon a mysterious pool of water. As they look down into the depths of the pool they see a golden statue lying at the bottom. The statue's hands are raised above its head as a diver would, and the statue appears to be made of solid gold. They discuss how to retrieve it. One character, to test how deep the water is, takes a spear and lowers it into the water. But as he lowers it, the tip of the spear turns to gold and becomes so heavy he has to drop it. As it falls into the pool it too looks like solid gold. Perhaps it has something to do with the sunlight? Then one of the children notices that the toes of his shoes have turned to gold where they came in contact with the water. The truth dawns on them that everything the water in this pool touches turns to gold, and that the man at the bottom must have been a passerby who unthinkingly dived into the pool. They back away immediately. Looking up, they see Aslan sitting on a ridge growling at them as they begin to argue about who gets to claim the water. Obviously anyone who controls the pool would be fabulously wealthy. Aslan growls his warning and they back away. They decide to name the pool "Death Water." Death Water! Materialism is a very dangerous thing. The desire to turn everything into gold must be guarded against constantly.

"Prosperity knits a man to the World," Lewis wrote. "He feels that he is 'finding his place in it', while really it is finding its place in him. His increasing reputation, his widening circle of acquaintants, his sense of importance, the growing pressure of absorbing and agreeable work, build up in him a sense of being really at home on earth."[88]

Lewis felt that we were not supposed to feel too much at home on earth. Our home, our happiness, and our joy were to be found somewhere else. But materialism dulls the longing of our hearts. Remember, we are made for another country. To be overly comfortable in this one may not be a good sign. It is not just having money or things that Lewis warned us about, but the demanding, exhilarating, serious feeling of success that was also captivating—the proud intoxication of material competence. In an essay he wrote, Lewis shared the following insight: "Otherwise we merely confirm the majority in their conviction that the world of Business, which does with such efficiency so much that never really needed doing, is the real, the adult, and the practical world; and that all this 'culture' and all this 'religion' . . . are essentially marginal, amateurish, and rather effeminate activities."[89]

I don't think Lewis was against business per se—many of us are in involved in business—but he does see that there is danger in a society that is too much involved in buying and selling. There is a very real danger when one begins to think they do not need God. The scriptures call this feeling "carnal security." It is the "all is well in Zion" problem. This focus on materialism is the real meaning of that phrase. There is money in the bank, a soaring stock market, profits are high, and all these are the expected fruits of our own wise and skillful investment-oriented drive.

"Everyone has noticed," Lewis wrote in *The Problem of Pain*, "how hard it is to turn our thoughts to God when everything is going well with us. We 'have all we want' is a terrible saying when 'all' does not include God. We find God an interruption. As St Augustine says somewhere, 'God wants to give us something, but cannot, because our hands are full—there's nowhere for Him to put it.'"[90]

The scriptures have very little good to say about wealth. I sometimes offer my students a challenge—find any verses of scripture that have good things to say about wealth. The ones that they find are not always negative about wealth, but when they are not, inevitably they contain words of warning. As you discover when you search the scriptures with the topic of wealth in mind, you will find many warnings. In a book called *God in the Dock* (the title refers to where the defendant stands in British courts), Lewis broadens our understanding of the dimensions of riches. "Christ said it was difficult for 'the rich' to enter the Kingdom of Heaven, referring, no doubt, to 'riches' in the ordinary sense. But I think it really covers riches in every sense—good fortune, health, popularity, and all the things one wants to have. All these things tend—just as money tends—to make you feel independent of God, because if you have them you are happy already and contented in this life. You don't want to turn away to anything more, and so you try to rest in a shadowy happiness as if it could last for ever."[91] Hence, in Lewis's philosophy, there is a need for trials occasionally.

Suffice it to say, we need trials to remind us of what is truly important in life lest we become like "the rich fool" who built greater barns for his increasing affluence. The more he had, the bigger he wanted, for wealth does not know the word "enough." You and I see this in the ever-increasing dimensions of houses, for instance. Lewis says, "One of the dangers of having a lot of money is that you may be quite satisfied with the kinds of happiness money can give and so fail to realise your need for God. If everything seems to come simply by signing cheques, you may forget that you are at every moment totally dependent on God."[92]

PRIDE

Materialism leads to the next Turkish delight we must learn not to acquire a taste for. This one has a foil wrapper on it, metaphorically speaking, as it is so useful in the adversary's arsenal and so deceptively appealing. For Lewis, it was "the great sin," "the essential vice"—pride.[93] As Latter-day Saints we might say the great sin is immorality. Lewis said a lot about immorality, and much has been written and said about that vice—warnings against pornography and sexual relations outside boundaries God has established—so much that I'm not going to discuss it here. Lewis did write about immorality, but he felt pride sat right in the center of the Turkish delight box, a foil-wrapped piece of candy that was tempting to all in so many ways. The problem with pride, that which creates its momentum, is the idea of competition, and we tend to be a competitive race. In *Mere Christianity,* Lewis wrote, "The point is that each person's pride is in competition with every one else's pride. It is because I wanted to be the big noise at the party that I am so annoyed at someone else being the big noise. . . . Now what you want to get clear is that Pride is *essentially* competitive—is competitive by its very nature—while the other vices are competitive only, so to speak, by accident. Pride gets no pleasure out of having something, only out of having more of it than the next man."[94]

President Ezra Taft Benson, in his landmark talk on pride, quoted from this very section of *Mere Christianity.*[95] Lewis writes, "We say that people are proud of being rich, or clever, or good-looking, but they are not. They are proud of being richer, or cleverer, or better-looking than others. If everyone else became equally rich, or clever, or good-looking there would be nothing to be proud about. It is the comparison that makes you proud: the pleasure of being above the rest. Once the element of competition has gone, pride has gone."[96]

The idea that "more makes you better" is a very difficult temptation to resist. I think pride is one of the greatest dangers for us, and I think Lewis felt it was the greatest danger for us because any difference between two people is an invitation to pride. And therefore, almost every minute of the day, as long as we can see that we are different from somebody else somehow, some way, the idea might come into the mind that what makes us different is better than what makes the other person different. In Jacob 2 the Nephites are challenged by pride. Their leader, Jacob, says something to his people that is an echo of Lewis's words: "The hand of providence hath smiled upon you most pleasingly, that you have obtained many riches; and because some of you have obtained more abundantly than that of your brethren ye are lifted up in the pride of your hearts . . . because ye suppose that ye are better than they" (Jacob 2:13). Do you see that—the more equals better idea? Any two things in competition because of an element of difference is an invitation to pride.

At Brigham Young University a number of years ago, when I was teaching about the lesson on pride found in the book of Jacob, I asked my students to do an experiment with me. We decided to each carry a little notebook in our pockets for a week. Every time the thought came into our minds *I'm better because* of some difference, we would write it down. Not that we gave into that thought, but just that the thought was there. After a week of focusing on the possibilities of pride, we would compare what we found. It was enlightening to return the next week and see what my students had experienced. Here are some from the list we compiled as a class:

- Physical appearance, everything from eye color to hairstyles.

- The apartment complex in which you lived, some apartment complexes were better than others.

- What you were majoring in. Engineering was worth more in most of their minds than Elementary Education.

- Whether you were getting a Bachelor of Arts or a Bachelor of Science degree. A BS required science, left-brain thinking. Others said, "No, the BA is more important."

- Language. Every cultured person, according to my students, can speak at least two languages.

- What state they were from originally. California ranked higher than, say, Idaho. (With all due respect to people from Idaho—I'm just reporting what was said.)

- The car they drove.

- Their girlfriend or boyfriend.

- Some other obvious inclinations to pride included the clothes they wore, their grade point average, their church calling.

- The work they had on- or off-campus. Working at the Missionary Training Center ranked higher than working as a janitor in the Wilkinson Center.

And on and on the list went. I had decided I would complete this little experiment in pride with them as well. So I had my little card and I wrote everything down during that week. As fate would have it, that week my uncle, who ran a very exclusive clothing store in Ogden, was moving to Palm Springs and liquidating his entire inventory. He had a $600 overcoat he could not sell. This was more than twenty years ago. I don't know what a $600 overcoat would cost today. It was beautiful—the most beautiful coat I had ever seen. He gave it to me because he wouldn't need it in Palm Springs. It was brand new. I remember putting that on and walking across campus, looking at everybody else in their London Fog overcoats. Mine was a light beige camelhair, with bone buttons, fully lined. I can't wear that coat. I finally had to take it off because that coat will take me right to hell, I just know it. It's hanging in the closet. I would give it to

Deseret Industries, but I don't want to tempt somebody else. What a rascal pride is . . . and so subtle.

During that experiment, I beat pride down all week long. I tried to beat down every thought that "I'm better because I have more or I'm different" from morning to night. By the end of the week I was feeling pretty good about the whole thing. But then I learned something. Pride is like a gopher in the backyard of your soul with a hundred holes. He pops his head up constantly to say, "You're better because . . ." You have to take the bat of humility and beat him down wherever he pops up. I did that all week long. At the end of the week I stood there with my bat looking at the backyard of my soul, and no gopher of pride was poking his head up. I said, "By golly, I have conquered pride. There aren't very many people who can conquer pride. I must be better than other people." And suddenly, I was proud of my humility, and the gopher had won. At that point, if you can laugh at yourself you have come a long way.

Lewis noticed this dilemma. He has Screwtape remark: "All virtues are less formidable to us once the man is aware that he has them, but this is specially true of humility. Catch him at the moment when he is really poor in spirit and smuggle into his mind the gratifying reflection, 'By jove! I'm being humble', and almost immediately pride—pride at his own humility—will appear. If he awakes to the danger and tries to smother this new form of pride, make him proud of his attempt—and so on, through as many stages as you please. But don't try this too long, for fear you awake his sense of humour and proportion, in which case he will merely laugh at you and go to bed."[97]

Lewis felt that the solution to pride was to meet God, in particular to know his greatness, from the greatness of his mind and power to the greatness of his own humility. "In God you come up against something which is in every respect immeasurably superior to yourself. Unless you know God as that—and, therefore, know yourself as nothing in comparison—you do not know God at all. As long as you are proud you cannot know God. A proud man is always looking down on things and people: and, of course, as long as you are looking down, you cannot see something that is above you."[98]

God is above us all. Meeting God and truly knowing God will cure pride as gratitude can cure pride, for pride and gratitude can't exist in the same soul at the same time. Therefore, if we have much through the mercy and graciousness of God, let us be grateful to God for those gifts. In doing so we dull the taste of the Turkish delight of Pride which is so appealing.

In a letter, Lewis wrote of pride. Once we conquer pride then "one can really for the first time say 'Thy Kingdom come': For in that Kingdom there will be no pre-eminences and a man must have reached the stage of not caring two straws about his own status before he can enter it."[99] As in almost all of Lewis's writings, the result of putting oneself in line with God and God's desires is joy. Happiness always is the result and would be the result of peeling off layers of pride. He believed there was not only joy in humility, but also tremendous relief.

We are too prone to playing what I call, "Watch me, Daddy!" My children, as they were growing up, would often say, "Watch me, Daddy! Watch me!" If you have children, your children did that too, didn't they? "Watch me, Daddy! Watch me!" Some of us never grow beyond playing "Watch me, Daddy!" We do it with the houses we build and with the cars we drive and in many other aspects of our lives. In so many ways people say, "Watch me! Watch me!" (I wish I had overcome "Watch me, Daddy." I play the game as well as the next fellow, but I try to follow Lewis's counsel here.) Lewis, in *Mere Christianity,* addressed this problem: "[God] wants you to know Him: wants to give you Himself. And He and you are two things of such a kind that if you really get into any kind of touch with Him you will, in fact, be humble—delightedly humble, feeling the infinite relief of having for once got rid of all the silly nonsense about your own dignity which has made you restless and unhappy all your life. He is trying to make you humble in order to make this moment possible: trying to take off a lot of silly, ugly, fancy-dress in which we have all got ourselves up and are strutting about like the little idiots we are. I wish I had got a bit further with humility myself: if I had, I could probably tell you more about the relief, the comfort, of taking the fancy-dress off—getting rid of the false self, with all its 'Look at me' and 'Aren't I a good boy?' and all its posing and posturing. To get even near it, even for a moment, is like a drink of cold water to a man in a desert."[100]

JELLY PEOPLE

Let us return to our box of adversarial Turkish delight and see what else may waylay our journey to joy. Turkish delight, for you who may never have tasted it (I mean the real Turkish delight, not the metaphorical), has a jelly core inside a layer of chocolate. Coincidently, jelly is the appropriate center for the next Turkish delight we will discuss. I call it the "Jelly People Instinct." We sometimes call it the "Herd Instinct." It is the desire to be like everybody else. There is a distinct paradox here, in that humans love the more equals better differences of the competitive world of pride, yet have a deep-seated desire to be like everyone else. We see this from such frivolous things as clothing styles to the latest political correctness. Youth are especially prone to this type of Turkish delight.

I obtained the phrase "Jelly People" from something Lewis wrote centering on a toast that Screwtape makes at a banquet for all the devils. It is a somewhat sarcastic and humorous bit of writing. The devils are feasting on the souls they have deceived. There is a casserole of adulterers, and a roast of embezzlers. You get the idea. While the devils are crunching on souls, Screwtape rises and toasts the desire of humanity to constantly conform. "How should a *jelly* not conform?" he gloats.[101] Unfortunately there are so many who are Jelly People, constantly wondering what the crowd will think and conforming thereto. If the world says we're supposed to think, or look, or act a certain way, people flow or pour themselves into that mold. If the style or emphasis shifts, they conform to the new standard. No real backbone, just jelly. To Screwtape's way of thinking this was a delightfully helpful instinct. Part of the reason for that delight was its ability to thwart God's purposes. God would have us like him, not painted in the latest style of the day.

Lewis felt that in Godhood, the destiny to which we travel, all the unique individualities would be brought out in greater number. Only in wickedness is everybody the same. In goodness, everyone is different, wondrously unique. Here is a section of Screwtape's toast: "[God] wanted to make Saints; gods; things like Himself. Is the dullness of your present fare not a very small price to pay for the delicious knowledge that His whole great experiment is petering out? But not only that. [Here we read some insightful words, considering Lewis wrote this before the 1960s.] As the great sinners grow fewer, and the majority lose all individuality, the great sinners become far more effective agents for us. Every dictator or demagogue—almost every film-star or crooner—[We would say rock stars today] can now draw tens of thousands of the human sheep with him. They give themselves (what there is of them) to him; in him, to us. There may come a time when we shall have no need to bother about *individual* temptation at all, except for the few. Catch the bell-wether and his whole flock comes after him."[102]

Modern mass media with their partner, advertising commercialism, has been the engine that drives this in many ways. It is one of the downsides of the global village. Continuing with Screwtape: "I am credibly informed that young humans now sometimes suppress an incipient taste for classical music or good literature because it might prevent their Being like Folks; that people who would really wish to be—and are offered the Grace which would enable them to be—honest, chaste, or temperate, refuse it. To accept might make them Different, might offend against the Way of Life, take them out of Togetherness, impair their Integration with the Group. They might (horror of horrors!) become individuals."[103]

If you are like me, you're probably nervous about your children and grandchildren. It is interesting (and sometimes devastating) that a parent can devote—invest—fourteen, sixteen, eighteen, twenty years to a child and then a few weeks with a questionable friend can begin to unravel everything instilled. They enter in their teens what I call the "friend-worship" stage of life. It becomes very important during that phase that they like what everybody likes. Screwtape knew that that was material to work with: "The deepest likings and impulses of any man are the raw material, the starting-point, with which the Enemy [again, from Screwtape's perspective, God] has furnished him. To get him away from those is therefore always a point gained; even in things indifferent it is always desirable to substitute the standards of the World, or convention, or fashion, for a human's own real likings and dislikings. I myself would carry this very far. I would make it a rule to eradicate from my patient any strong personal taste which is not actually a sin, even if it is something quite trivial. . . . You should always try to make the patient abandon the people or food or books he really likes in favour of the 'best' people, the 'right' food, the 'important' books."[104]

"One of my own patients said on his arrival down here, 'I now see that I spent most of my life in doing *neither* what I ought *nor* what I liked.'"[105]

There is a wonderful image in the book of Daniel when Shadrach, Meshach and Abed-nego valiantly and boldly stand while everybody else falls before the great idol when the music sounds (see Daniel 3). Far too often what happens today is that the music of the world plays and everyone bows. Will we bow too? It is very difficult to stand alone amidst the bowing masses. Can you see those three young men standing in the middle of the plain, the great idol in the background, with everybody else on their knees?

For adults, the bowing sometimes comes in the temptation of what we call political correctness. If possible without too great a compromise of principle, we want to conform to the things of the world. "The use of Fashions in thought," Screwtape says, "is to distract the attention of men from their real dangers. We [meaning Screwtape and his group of devils] direct the fashionable outcry of each generation against those vices of which it is least in danger and fix its approval on the virtue nearest to that vice which we are trying to make endemic. The game is to have them all running about with fire extinguishers whenever there is a flood, and all crowding to that side of the boat which is already nearly gunwale under. Thus we make it fashionable to expose the dangers of enthusiasm at the very moment when they are all really becoming worldly and lukewarm. . . . Cruel ages are put on their guard against Sentimentality, feckless and idle ones against Respectability, lecherous ones against Puritanism [I might add that in our time, it is pornographic ones against Censorship]. . . . The Enemy loves platitudes. Of a proposed course of action He wants men, so far as I can see, to ask very simple questions; is it righteous? is it prudent? is it possible? Now if we can keep men asking 'Is it in accordance with the general movement of our time? Is it progressive or reactionary? Is this the way that History is going?' they will neglect the relevant questions."[106] As Lewis wrote elsewhere, "Jesus Christ did not say 'Go into all the world and tell the world that it is quite right.'"[107]

Lewis also wrote, "All that is not eternal is eternally out of date."[108] Yet sometimes we are deeply interested in moving with the times. There was a standard Lewis felt we could use to judge all kinds of politically correct ideologies, fashions or movements; and that was the standard of pure Christianity. He wrote, "The standard of permanent Christianity [the emphasis must be on the word 'permanent,' because Lewis was often distressed about movements within Christianity that did not reflect the Savior's teachings] must be kept clear in our minds and it is against that standard that we must test all contemporary thought. In fact, we must at all costs *not* move with the times. We serve One who said 'Heaven and Earth shall move with the times, but my words shall not move with the times.'"[109]

For Satan to succeed it was essential to isolate every generation from every other generation. The scriptures originally were called a book of Remembrance. That is a very purposeful and suggestive title. It means that the Lord's book of Remembrance contains the ideas, the people, the principles, the lives, the truths, and the examples that God wants us to remember. We have over 6,000 years of human experience to draw upon. We must not cut off present generations from those of the past, yet that is exactly what the Adversary would have happen. Some of Lewis's essays have been collected in a little book titled *Fern-seed and Elephants.* One of the essays in the collection contains this passage: "A man who has lived in many places is not likely to be deceived by the local errors of his native village; the scholar [we could say the scriptural scholar] has lived in many times and is therefore in some degree immune from the great cataract of nonsense that pours from the press and the microphone of his own age."[110] We will recognize in studying the past the problems we face in the present. The past can be an excellent lens into the future. We can see how others dealt with their challenges and problems and be forewarned and forearmed. Screwtape said, "Since we cannot deceive the whole human race all the time, it is most important thus to cut every generation off from all others; for where learning makes a free commerce between the ages there is always the danger that the characteristic errors of one may be corrected by the characteristic truths of another."[111]

JUDGING OTHERS

One of the greatest dangers among all the temptations in the box of Turkish delights is the "delight" of Judging Other People. I say that because, unfortunately, I know that delight. There's a certain sticky, syrupy, and sweet taste to the natural man's palate that comes from judging others. Part of that taste comes from pride. In the Chronicles of Narnia the children are almost always interested in how Aslan dealt with somebody else. They frequently wanted him to explain what he had done with another character in the story. We, like them, are quite the bunch of busybodies. Aslan would always respond in this manner: "I am telling you your story, not hers. I tell no one any story but his own."[112] Human nature seems to be always interested in everyone else's story; since it is so easy to find fault in everyone else, why not look?

Lewis did have a lot to say about trying not to judge individuals, organizations, or other religions. One of the reasons he was a successful writer was this non-judgmental attitude. Almost all Christian groups claim Lewis—we claim him, the Baptists claim him, the Methodists claim him, the Catholics claim him! We all are spiritually fed by him. Somehow he was able to talk about Christianity in a non-judgmental way. He didn't engage in the comparisons we use to condemn and judge one another's religion.

In *The Screwtape Letters,* Screwtape suggests that church is a good place for the Christian victim they're trying to destroy because in church he'll be able to see other people's faults and can, therefore, accuse them all of hypocrisy. It is a clever temptation: "When he gets to his pew and looks round him he sees . . . his neighbours. . . . You want to lean pretty heavily on those neighbours. . . . All you then have to do is to keep out of his mind the question 'If I, being what I am, can consider that I am in some sense a Christian, why should the different vices of those people in the next pew prove that their religion is mere hypocrisy and convention?' You may ask whether it is possible to keep such an obvious thought from occurring even to a human mind. It is, Wormwood, it is! Handle him properly and it simply won't come into his head."[113]

When there are so many motes in everybody else's eyes, it is difficult to look at the beams in our own eyes. My favorite story about Joseph Smith—I really love this story—deals with the moat and beam disparity in judging others. It was written by a man named Jesse Crosby: "I went one day to the Prophet with a sister. She had a charge to make against one of the brethren for scandal. . . . [The Prophet] offered her his method of dealing with such cases for himself. When an enemy had told a scandalous story about him, which had often been done, before he rendered judgment he paused and let his mind run back to the time and place and setting of the story to see if he had not by some unguarded word or act laid the block on which the story was built. If he found that he had done so, he said that in his heart he then forgave his enemy, and felt thankful that he had received warning of a weakness that he had not known he possessed.

"Then he said to the sister that he would have her to do the same: search her memory thoroughly and see if she had not herself unconsciously laid the foundation for the scandal that annoyed her.

"The sister thought deeply for a few moments and then confessed that she believed that she had.

"Then the Prophet told her that in her heart she could forgive that brother who had risked his own good name and her friendship to give her this clearer view of herself."[114] I wish I were at that level of self-inspection.

God is the only proper judge. The Lord says to us all, "I release you from the need to judge others. You are all released. I will do all the judging." The reason that God is the judge is because he is the only one who can see all the factors. He can see the man from the inside out. You and I can only see him from the outside in. "What can you ever really know of other people's souls," Lewis wrote, "of their temptations, their opportunities, their struggles? One soul in the whole creation you do know: and it is the only one whose fate is placed in your hands. If there is a God, you are, in a sense, alone with Him. You cannot put Him off with speculations about your next door neighbours or memories of what you have read in books. What will all that chatter and hearsay count (will you even be able to remember it?) when . . . the Presence in which you have always stood becomes palpable, immediate, and unavoidable?"[115]

At the end of the Gospel of John, the resurrected Jesus tells Peter of Peter's own impending crucifixion. That revelation is shocking news to Peter, who has professed his love for the Savior three times. Peter turns and sees John the Beloved following, and does a very human thing. Peter asks, "And what shall this man do?" Jesus responds, "If I will that he tarry till I come, what is that to thee? follow thou me" (John 21:21–22). The only person we should worry about is ourself and whether we are following or not following the Master.

What we tend to do with individuals, we do with religions. We judge them, and often harshly and outside the light of Christian charity. Screwtape was, ironically, grateful for religion. "The wickedness of other religions," he says, "was the really live doctrine in the religion of each; slander was its gospel and denigration its litany. How they hated each other up there where the sun shone! . . . All said and done, my friends, it will be an ill day for us if what most humans mean by 'religion' ever vanishes from the Earth."[116]

Too much of people's faith is what we could call anti-faith. It isn't so much what one strongly believes in, but that what others believe in is wrong. Too much faith is really anti-faith. Lewis went through a great turmoil in his own life trying to find truth. In his autobiography, *Surprised by Joy,* he finally came to a remarkable conclusion: "The question was no longer to find the one simply true religion among a thousand religions simply false. It was rather, 'Where has religion reached its true maturity?' . . . Where was the thing full grown? or where was the awakening?"[117]

You and I would answer by saying we believe that The Church of Jesus Christ of Latter-day Saints is where religion has reached maturity—not full stature, but maturity. This leaves us open to explore and examine wonderful things in other faiths. In St. Patrick's Cathedral in Dublin, we find some compelling words spoken by Jonathan Swift, who served as minister there. He said, "We have enough religion to hate each other, but not enough to love each other."

Lewis compared Christianity to a house containing a long hallway with rooms leading off it. The different rooms were the different faiths. He said, "It is more like a hall out of which doors open into several rooms. If I can bring anyone into that hall I shall have done what I attempted. But it is in the rooms, not in the hall, that there are fires and chairs and meals. The hall is a place to wait in, a place from which to try the various doors, not a place to live in. . . . It is true that some people may find they have to wait in the hall for a considerable time, while others feel certain almost at once which door they must knock at. I do not know why there is this difference, but I am sure God keeps no one waiting unless He sees that it is good for him to wait. . . . You must keep on praying for light: and, of course, even in the hall, you must begin trying to obey the rules which are common to the whole house."[118]

I should say here that, having studied many different faiths, both Christian and non-Christian, there is much in common within the whole house of faith. In all religions, certainly within Christianity, there is more to unite us than divide us. Too much of zealous faith is really opposition to others' faith. It is not hard to discern in most religious conflicts throughout the world a lack of brotherly love dressed up as a defensive posture for God—hate masquerading as godly fervor. To continue Lewis's analogy: "Above all you must be asking which door is the true one; not which pleases you best by its paint and panelling. In plain language, the question should never be: 'Do I like that kind of service?' but 'Are these doctrines true: Is holiness here? Does my conscience move me towards this? Is my reluctance to knock at this door due to my pride, or my mere taste, or my personal dislike of this particular door-keeper?'" I love how Lewis ends this comparison: "When you have reached your own room [for you and I, the Latter-day Saint room], be kind to those who have chosen different doors and to those who are still in the hall. If they are wrong they need your prayers all the more; and if they are your enemies, then you are under orders to pray for them. That is one of the rules common to the whole house."[119]

The Pains and Trials of Life

This leads to the last Turkish delight we will discuss—not because it's the last Lewis wrote about, but because it's the last that space will permit, and the last of his life. That Turkish delight consists of pain and trials. Pain was a double-edged sword for Lewis. He wrote a whole book about it titled *The Problem of Pain*. He wrote a very personal account of pain and trials in *A Grief Observed*, which we will discuss here. Pain can drive you towards God or drive you away from him. In *The Silver Chair*, one of the Chronicles of Narnia, there is a "Marsh-wiggle" named Puddleglum. He was one of Lewis's favorite characters in the Chronicles. Puddleglum is half human, half frog. He had webbed feet. In the passage we're discussing, he and the children are underground in the Green Witch's domain, who is strumming on a type of mandolin. There is a fire burning, into which the Green Witch has cast enchanted dust that will lull them all into a state of not believing in Aslan or Narnia or anything else they hold true. The numbing incense fills the room. Puddleglum, sensing what is happening, sensing they are being quietly deceived into a state of non-faith, does a very courageous thing. He sticks his webbed foot onto the fire, burning himself as he extinguishes the incense. Lewis writes, "The pain itself made Puddleglum's head for a moment perfectly clear and he knew exactly what he really thought. There is nothing like a good shock of pain for dissolving certain kinds of magic."[120]

Pain sometimes can drive you to God. "My own experience," Lewis wrote, "is something like this. I am progressing along the path of life in my ordinary contentedly fallen and godless condition, absorbed in a merry meeting with my friends for the morrow or a bit of work that tickles my vanity today, a holiday or a new book, when suddenly a stab of abdominal pain that threatens serious disease, or a headline in the newspapers that threatens us all with destruction, sends this whole pack of cards tumbling down. At first I am overwhelmed, and all my little happinesses look like broken toys. Then, slowly and reluctantly, bit by bit, I try to bring myself into the frame of mind that I should be in at all times. I remind myself that all these toys were never intended to possess my heart, that my true good is in another world and my only real treasure is Christ. And perhaps, by God's grace, I succeed, and for a day or two become a creature consciously dependent on God and drawing its strength from the right sources. But the moment the threat is withdrawn, my whole nature leaps back to the toys. . . . Thus the terrible necessity of tribulation is only too clear. God has had me for but forty-eight hours and then only by dint of taking everything else away from me. Let Him but sheathe that sword for a moment and I behave like a puppy when the hated bath is over—I shake myself as dry as I can and race off to reacquire my comfortable dirtiness, if not in the nearest manure heap, at least in the nearest flower bed. And that is why tribulations cannot cease until God either sees us remade or sees that our remaking is now hopeless."[121]

Pain can drive us to God. It can also do just the opposite, but our response to it lies largely within ourselves. Toward the end of his life, Lewis faced the great crisis of personal pain. His theories came to the demanding test of reality, and not in another's pain, but in his own. Lewis was a bachelor for the majority of his life. In his later years he met a woman named Joy Gresham, a Jewish convert to Christianity, as he had been an atheist convert. They shared a wonderful relationship because they had both covered such vast spiritual distances to find unity and a faith in Christ. She had a sharp wit, a deep intellect, and Lewis came to love her. He married her first so she wouldn't have to leave England—as a nice gesture to her, as something he would do for a friend—but he came to be deeply devoted to her, especially as she was dying of cancer, and considered her then, truly and fully, his beloved wife.

Before he met Joy, he wrote about the danger of love and how love may give us some of our greatest trials, and deepest grief: "There is no safe investment. To love at all is to be vulnerable. Love anything, and your heart will certainly be wrung and possibly be broken. If you want to make sure of keeping it intact, you must give your heart to no one, not even to an animal. Wrap it carefully round with hobbies and little luxuries; avoid all entanglements; lock it up safe in the casket or coffin of your selfishness. But in that casket—safe, dark, motionless, airless—it will change. It will not be broken; it will become unbreakable, impenetrable, irredeemable. The alternative to tragedy, or at least to the risk of tragedy, is damnation. The only place outside Heaven where you can be perfectly safe from all the dangers and perturbations of love is Hell."[122]

Lewis felt the reality of his own words as Joy was diagnosed with cancer and died a slow and painful death. His faith in God was put to the test. He survived that test of his faith by writing his thoughts day by day in a notebook while he went through this great crisis. Anyone who has ever had problems, faced the pain of mortal trials such as the death of a loved one, or endured deep trials that crushed all the happiness out of you will understand some of what he wrote.

From *A Grief Observed:* "It is hard to have patience with people who say 'There is no death' or 'Death doesn't matter.' There is death. And whatever is matters. And whatever happens has consequences, and it and they are irrevocable and irreversible. You might as well say that birth doesn't matter. I look up at the night sky. Is anything more certain than that in all those vast times and spaces, if I were allowed to search them, I should nowhere find her face, her voice, her touch? She died. She is dead. Is the word so difficult to learn?"[123]

In another reflective moment, Lewis wrote, "Meanwhile, where is God? This is one of the most disquieting symptoms. When you are happy, so happy that you have no sense of needing Him, so happy that you are tempted to feel His claims upon you as an interruption, if you remember yourself and turn to Him with gratitude and praise, you will be—or so it feels—welcomed with open arms. But go to Him when your need is desperate, when all other help is vain, and what do you find? A door slammed in your face, and a sound of bolting and double bolting on the inside. After that, silence. You may as well turn away. The longer you wait, the more emphatic the silence will become. There are no lights in the windows. It might be an empty house. Was it ever inhabited? It seemed so once. And that seeming was as strong as this. What can this mean? Why is He so present a commander in our time of prosperity and so very absent a help in our time of trouble?"[124]

Lewis tries to talk himself out of his pain and back into a robust faith in God. I am, myself, a rational, reasonable, somewhat more thinking than feeling person. I understand perfectly well trying to argue yourself out of not hurting. "Do I hope that if feeling disguises itself as thought I shall feel less? Aren't all these notes the senseless writhings of a man who won't accept the fact that there is nothing we can do with suffering except to suffer it? Who still thinks there is some device (if only he could find it) which will make pain not to be pain? It doesn't really matter whether you grip the arms of the dentist's chair or let your hands lie in your lap. The drill drills on."[125]

In time Lewis began to rebuild the faith he had so ably defended for so many years. He did this by considering the alternatives. What were the choices offered us about God? Is he a bad God? An apathetic God? There is no God? Or is there a good God? If there is a good God and pain exists then all these things must be necessary. "But is it credible," he wrote, "that such extremities of torture should be necessary for us? Well, take your choice. The tortures occur. If they are unnecessary, then there is no God or a bad one. If there is a good God, then these tortures are necessary. For no even moderately good Being could possibly inflict or permit them if they weren't. . . . And so, perhaps, with God. I have gradually been coming to feel that the door is no longer shut and bolted."[126]

At times, our own cries may drown out God's comforting voice. Joseph Smith, in Liberty Jail, did not receive peace, God's consoling assurance, until he had received letters from three people—his wife Emma, his brother Don Carlos, and his friend Bishop Partridge. These letters calmed his soul and enabled him to hear God. Lewis experienced a similar realization. "I have gradually been coming to feel that the door is no longer shut and bolted. Was it my own frantic need that slammed it in my face? The time when there is nothing at all in your soul except a cry for help may be just the time when God can't give it: you are like the drowning man who can't be helped because he clutches and grabs. Perhaps your own reiterated cries deafen you to the voice you hope to hear. On the other hand, 'Knock and it shall be opened.' But does knocking mean hammering and kicking the door like a maniac?"[127]

Other factors may be part of the equation of pain. The trials may teach us things about ourselves, our testimonies, that we cannot learn any other way. Maybe the trials are not a test or a proof, but a revelation about ourselves to ourselves. Lewis felt, "God has not been trying an experiment on my faith or love in order to find out their quality. He knew it already. It was I who didn't. In this trial He makes us occupy the dock, the witness box, and the bench all at once. He always knew that my temple was a house of cards. His only way of making me realize the fact was to knock it down. . . . When I lay these questions before God I get no answer. But a rather special sort of 'No answer.' It is not the locked door. It is more like a silent, certainly not uncompassionate, gaze. As though He shook His head not in refusal but in waiving the question. Like, 'Peace, child; you don't understand.'"[128]

This lack of understanding does not mean that we do not know what to do. In typical, practical, Lewis fashion he comes right to the heart of the matter. In our grief, we may not always comprehend the Lord's designs, but we should have no question about how we are to live. In the living we find the answers. "And now that I come to think of it, there's no practical problem before me at all. I know the two great commandments, and I'd better get on with them."[129]

Lewis's faith was renewed and life continued along the narrow path. At the end, he regained the comfortable, conversational relationship with Deity he had for so long believed in, enjoyed, and recommended to all of us. Notice the trusting, childlike tone, of some of his final words: "Sometimes, Lord, one is tempted to say if you wanted us to behave like the lilies of the field you might have given us an organization more like theirs. But that, I suppose, is just your grand experiment. Or no; not an experiment, for you have no need to find things out. Rather your grand enterprise. To make an organism which is also a spirit; to make that terrible oxymoron, a 'spiritual animal.' To take a poor primate, a beast with nerve-endings all over it, a creature with a stomach that wants to be filled, a breeding animal that wants its mate, and say, 'Now get on with it. Become a god.'"[130]

He's back to the hub. He's back to the central idea, the polar star of his life and ours. We are to become gods, and that is no simple transition. We may trust, as did Lewis, that our Father knows how to do it. Our challenge is to just stay on the path.

Another of Lewis's favorite creatures in Narnia was a little mouse called Reepicheep. In *The Voyage of the Dawn Treader,* the main characters are sailing toward Aslan's home country. There comes a moment when they have to decide whether to turn back or keep going. Reepicheep, who usually has much to say, is silent. Lucy asks him what he thinks. I believe his answer portrays what Lewis would want all of us to feel as we try to walk the path to godhood.

"'Aren't you going to say anything, Reep?' whispered Lucy.

"'No. Why should your majesty expect it?' answered Reepicheep in a voice that most people heard. 'My own plans are made. While I can, I sail east in the *Dawn Treader.* When she fails me, I paddle east in my coracle. When she sinks, I shall swim east with my four paws. And when I can swim no longer, if I have not reached Aslan's country, or shot over the edge of the world in some vast cataract, I shall sink with my nose to the sunrise.'"[131]

Someone will be waiting for Lewis and Reepicheep in the sunrise. I suppose for Lewis, someone will be standing next to his beloved Aslan—his Beloved Christ, the Being who at times in his life Lewis had tried so hard not to meet. I assume Joy, the love he found in the last years of his life, will also be there.

Speaking with Joy of his own death when she was so near that transition herself, Lewis said, "Once very near the end I said, 'If you can—if it is allowed—come to me when I too am on my deathbed.' 'Allowed!' she said. 'Heaven would have a job to hold me; and as for Hell, I'd break it into bits.' She knew she was speaking a kind of mythological language, with even an element of comedy in it. There was a twinkle as well as a tear in her eye. But there was no myth and no joke about the will, deeper than any feeling, that flashed through her."[132] I'm sure when he passed away (almost unnoticed, because it was the same day President John F. Kennedy was assassinated) that Joy and Jesus were waiting for him.

And so we come to the end of our journey. I conclude with Lewis's own testimony; I think it only fitting he conclude and not myself. In an address titled "Is Theology Poetry?" he wrote, "I believe in Christianity as I believe that the sun has risen, not only because I can see it, but by it I see everything else."[133]

CHAPTER FOUR

THE FOURTH WATCH

~

When Your Prayers Seem Unanswered

LETTERS FROM FATHER

A number of years ago my eldest daughter went to Russia. This was before e-mail was the popular and convenient means of communication it has become. Russia was just opening up to the world, and she was going to teach English in Moscow. Our ability to communicate with her would be intermittent at best, and we were concerned about her welfare. In order for us to support her at such a long distance, I decided to write some letters before she went just in case we couldn't talk to her during her six-month stay. She was just out of high school, and as a parent, I was somewhat concerned. I tried to imagine every problem, dilemma, emotion, concern, feeling of loneliness, elation (from the high to the low), she might experience in that time period. I then wrote a letter of counsel, comfort, or advice that she could read there, since I couldn't otherwise readily communicate with her. I labeled each letter on the outside: "When You're Discouraged," "When You Get Homesick," "When You Are Tempted," and so forth. During our good-byes at the airport, I handed her the large packet of letters that I hoped would aid her in solving any concerns she might have.

I was not omniscient about everything she would face during those six months, but I did hit a number of them. Some of the letters she opened after her return home, just to see what I had written, even though she hadn't faced that particular concern.

I believe there is a parallel to this situation in all of our lives. In a manner of speaking, the scriptures are like a handful of letters from our Father in Heaven, who has anticipated the questions and concerns we might have from time to time during our mortal existence. Unlike me, he knows all the varied and multiple experiences his children will face, and so he has provided answers for us before we even ask the questions, face the temptations, or are challenged by life's trials.

During many years of teaching, I have been asked a number of questions, but one stands above the rest because of how often it has been asked and the number of different age groups that have shared its concern. It is sometimes phrased in different words, but the theme is essentially the same: "How do I get answers to prayer?" "Why does the Lord deal with us the way he deals with us?" "Why, sometimes, do we appear not to get answers at all?" "Why do others receive their desires and I do not?" "How can I know the answers are coming from God and not from my own mind?"

Maybe if I describe the details of an extreme case it will cover everything to a lesser degree. The scriptures do tend to deal with extremes for that very reason.

"DID HEAVEN LOOK ON?"

There are two lines from Shakespeare I often quote to myself when I face certain dilemmas in life. I repeat: These represent extreme situations, but they quite succinctly state the difficulty most of us face. The first is from *The Tragedy of King Richard III.* Elizabeth, who is the dispossessed former queen, receives word that the two princes, her two young sons, have been executed in the Tower of London by their uncle, Richard III. She raises her eyes to heaven and prays:

"Wilt thou, O God, fly from such gentle lambs, And throw them in the entrails of the wolf? When didst thou sleep when such a deed was done?"[1]

The second quote is from *The Tragedy of Macbeth.* Macduff learns that Macbeth has killed Macduff's entire family. Once again, there is a turning to heaven and a wondering and a questioning why there was not help in such a desperate situation. Macduff in his agony cries, "Did heaven look on, and would not take their part?"[2]

In lesser moments in my life—and perhaps in lesser moments in your life—I must admit I am sometimes tempted to be critical of the way that God is running the universe, at least our corner of it. I have a tendency occasionally to look heavenward and quote Shakespeare, and say as Macduff said, "Did heaven look on, and would not take their part?"

The issue at hand is not always one concerning my own desires or needs. It often occurs when I see someone I love seemingly denied righteous longings or called to endure life's trials beyond reason. On a broader scope, even a cursory perusal of the nightly news can provide sufficient fodder for a heavenward glance and a quiet quoting of Macduff.

I think about a daughter who was born wanting to be a mother but who hasn't yet been able to have children; another daughter longing to be married who just turned thirty-two and still hasn't had that joy in her life; a wife who, in spite of blessings and prayers and temple rolls, lives in pain everyday. And these are just some of the concerns in the great ocean of human experience. I'm convinced all of us have those disappointing, trying times when we wonder why "heaven [looks] on, and [will] not take [our] part."

THE FOURTH WATCH

I would like to suggest some things that go through my mind in those difficult moments of life. Hopefully they'll be of value to you as they have been to me. They are the letters I peruse from a kind Father in Heaven, who knew beforehand we would face such dilemmas and questions. One of the first of those scriptural letters contains a principle I call "The Fourth Watch."

A New Testament day was divided into twelve hours, beginning at six in the morning. The third hour would be nine o'clock, the sixth hour would be noon, and the eleventh hour, though we visualize it as being just before midnight, actually was five o'clock in the evening. The night was divided into four watches: The first watch was from six in the evening until nine at night. The second watch was nine until midnight, the third watch from midnight until three in the morning, and the fourth watch from three in the morning until six, about sunrise.

The Savior had just fed the five thousand. He instructed his disciples to get into a boat and pick him up later, after he had dismissed the multitude and spent some solitude in prayer. The disciples obeyed. It was late afternoon or early evening when they got into the ship and pushed out into the Sea of Galilee. Jesus sent the multitude home and then turned to commune with his Father. He prayed into the evening and long into the night.

In the meantime, a storm had swept down on the disciples in their voyage: "And when even was come, the ship was in the midst of the sea, and he alone on the land. And he saw them toiling in rowing; for the wind was contrary unto them" (Mark 6:47–48). In Matthew's version it says, "The ship was . . . tossed with waves" (Matthew 14:24), and in John's account we read: "And the sea arose by reason of a great wind that blew. So when they had rowed about five and twenty or thirty furlongs . . ." (John 6:18–19).

A furlong is about 220 to 225 yards. So if they have rowed twenty-five to thirty furlongs, they've rowed about sixty-five to seventy football fields, into the wind during the storm. As would be expected, they are exhausted and fearful. Mark's version adds one tiny little point that the others don't, something I think is really important. Mark relates that Jesus "saw them toiling in rowing" (Mark 6:48). They did not know that he was aware of their danger. They didn't realize he was up on the hill looking down watching them. They only knew that they had rowed a long time, the wind remained contrary, they were exhausted, and they needed help.

And then we read: "About *the fourth watch* of the night he cometh unto them, walking upon the sea, . . . [and] they . . . saw him, and were troubled. And immediately he talked with them, and saith unto them, Be of good cheer: it is I; be not afraid. And he went up unto them into the ship; and the wind ceased" (Mark 6:48–51; emphasis added).

I have a feeling that the Apostles, if they could have chosen, would have had the Lord come in an earlier watch. I put it to you, as I frequently put it to myself—when I toil in rowing against the wind, when the sea arises and I'm frightened and it's dark and the storm keeps blowing, and I want help—I want him to come in the *first* watch. I'm a first-watch type of a person. Aren't we all?

But there is also something inside of me that channels my thinking to the realization that it is good to toil in rowing against the wind—that there's something to be gained by exercising spiritual muscles that are stretched in facing trials and opposition. All right, we can accept that. But if he doesn't come in the first watch he certainly ought to come in the second watch. However, it appears that we worship a "fourth-watch" God. And it is important for us to *realize* that we worship a fourth-watch God.

Sometimes I pray: "Lord, I know you're a fourth-watch God and that I'm a first-watch person. Couldn't we compromise and have you come at the end of the second watch or at the beginning of the third watch? Wouldn't that be fair?" But the compromise rarely comes, and in my better moments I know it's good that it doesn't. He's a fourth-watch God.

There are a number of scriptures that help us understand that he truly is a fourth-watch God. Take Joseph Smith's experience, for instance. Doesn't this sound like a fourth-watch response? "At *the very moment when I was ready to sink into despair* and abandon myself to destruction—. . . *just at this moment of great alarm,* I saw a pillar of light exactly over my head" (Joseph Smith–History 1:16; emphasis added). The Lord tends to come at the moment of great alarm, when we're "ready to sink into despair."

The story of Hagar in Genesis 21 contains a wonderful "fourth-watch" phrase in describing her desperation: "The water was spent in the bottle" (Genesis 21:15). She was out wandering in the wilderness of Beer-sheba with her son, Ishmael, when "she cast the child under one of the shrubs. And she went, and sat her down over against him a good way off, as it were a bowshot: for she said, Let me not see the death of the child. And she sat over against him, and lift up her voice, and wept. And God heard the voice of the lad; and the angel of God called to Hagar out of heaven, and said unto her, What aileth thee, Hagar? fear not; for God hath heard the voice of the lad where he is. Arise, lift up the lad, and hold him in thine hand; . . . And God opened her eyes, and she saw a well of water; and she went, and filled the bottle with water, and gave the lad drink" (Genesis 21:15–19).

God often comes to us when "the water [is] spent in the bottle," then shows us the previously undiscovered, life-giving waters of the nearby well.

In 1 Kings 17, another widow, desperate in a time of famine, does not know help is just around the corner when Elijah meets her at the gate. The prophet directs her: "Bring me, I pray thee, a morsel of bread in thine hand. And she said, As the Lord thy God liveth, I have not a cake, but an handful of meal in a barrel, and a little oil in a cruse: and, behold, I am gathering two sticks, that I may go in and dress it for me and my son, that we may eat it, and die" (1 Kings 17:11–12).

Elijah appears just at the moment she is gathering those two pathetic tiny sticks for the last meal. When the water is spent in the bottle; at the moment of despair; when we're preparing the last meal, that's when the Lord tends to come.

When we advance into the second watch and he doesn't come, a certain cold fear often begins to spread through us as the wind's velocity does not diminish. As we move into the third watch we may be tempted to make some assumptions that are very dangerous and foolish to make. "God is not listening to me." "He doesn't care." Or, more dangerous yet, "He is not there." At times the universe can seem so very empty—all that dark space filled with cold stars. Or, very common to Latter-day Saints, we assume, "I'm not worthy." "He's not listening." "He doesn't care." "No one is there to respond." Because if he were there and if he were listening or if I were worthy, he would certainly come.

When you feel somewhat desperate, when it seems like your prayers aren't answered and the winds still blow, take comfort in the knowledge that he is on the hillside watching. Remember, you might not know that he's watching as you struggle in the boat, but he is on the hillside watching, and he will come. But he generally comes in the fourth watch—after we have done all we can do.

TIGHT LIKE A DISH

Occasionally I have told that story, shared that principle, and I've had people come up afterwards and say, "You know, I'm sure I'm past the fourth watch. I think I'm in the seventh, or the eighth, or the ninth watch, and he still hasn't come." We need another letter from the Father, for without doubt he foresaw just such extremities. There is another principle that applies in such cases. For those times when I've reached my fourth watch and he hasn't come, then I say these words to myself: *My ship is tight like a dish!*

In Ether we read of storms and mountainous waves that threaten to sink the Jaredite barges and immerse their inhabitants in a salty grave. I'm an English major, and I tend to subconsciously edit just about everything I read. When I read the scriptures I am often very impressed by the beauty of their language and the depth of their truths, but occasionally I come across a verse where I think, *Lord, this could be stated a little better.* I used to read Ether 2:17 and find it hard to resist the temptation to edit it. If I were an English teacher assessing the account of the Jaredite crossing, I would put a red line through Ether 2:17, accompanied by the word *redundant.*

This is the description of the barges that the brother of Jared (Mahonri Moriancumer) was instructed to build: "They were built after a manner that they were exceedingly tight, even that they would hold water *like unto a dish.*" Point made: they're waterproof. But notice how the author seems to belabor that point: "And the bottom thereof was *tight like unto a dish;* and the sides thereof were *tight like unto a dish;* and the ends thereof were peaked; and the top thereof was *tight like unto a dish;* and the length thereof was the length of a tree; and the door thereof, when it was shut, was *tight like unto a dish*" (Ether 2:17; emphasis added).

As I say, in my weaker moments of intellectual insight, I used to criticize that description. It took me a while to realize that God knows what he's doing in his scriptures, and there is one thing he wants us to understand about that ship—and he *really* wants us to understand it—and that is: "It is tight like unto a dish." It isn't going to sink! If I really grasp that truth, the application to life is powerful.

The brother of Jared discovers two problems with the boats he is constructing: 1. They lack oxygen; no one can breathe in them. 2. They are so dark inside the pilot cannot see to steer the ship. (Maybe it was Mrs. Moriancumer who pointed out those two defects: "Are you sure, dear, that you got the barge instructions right? Maybe we should check the blueprints again.") The narrative seems to suggest that God designed the ships, and I think he designed them in a way to teach Moriancumer and, through Moriancumer, all of us some great principles.

The brother of Jared climbed a mountain and asked the Lord for solutions. The Lord instructed him to cut some holes that could be blocked when the waves washed over the deck and buried the ship underwater. This would solve the problem of air. But he left the solution of light and steerage to Moriancumer to figure out. He did give him some parameters to work within: "Ye cannot have windows, for they will be dashed in pieces; neither shall ye take fire with you, for ye shall not go by the light of fire" (Ether 2:23).

The Lord has a pretty good sense of humor, I think. I can just see him saying: No light, no air? I can't imagine how I missed that in the design, but let's see, how about windows? No, no, that won't work; you know waves would break them. How about fire? No, no, that won't work; oxygen is a problem anyway, and with all the pitching and rolling of the ship, fire would be a hazard. Difficult predicament. You figure something out.

Then the Lord says something that is really amazing to me. Put yourself in Moriancumer's position—you get to solve the problem, right? Tell me what solution you would come up with when the Lord says this: "Behold, ye shall be as a whale in the midst of the sea; for the mountain waves shall dash upon you." Now, let's pause for a second. What causes mountain waves in the ocean? Wind. Wind creates waves and storms, hurricanes, and tempests. Then the Lord explains: "Nevertheless, I will bring you up again out of the depths of the sea" (Ether 2:24). The mountain waves are going to crash over the boat and submerge it for a while and then it will bob up again. They're not submarines. They'll come up to the surface again, but there will be times when the waves wash over the top and everything will be underwater.

Then the Lord makes this remarkable statement: "For the winds have gone forth out of my mouth, and also the rains and the floods have I sent forth" (Ether 2:24).

What solution would you offer to God at that point? This would be my reply: "Lord, we don't have a quandary with air or light at all in these boats. If waves are the problem and wind causes the waves and you're the cause of the wind—*then blow softly.* 'Breeze' us to the promised land. We don't need to have a mountain wave crash over us ever. We'll sit on deck, we'll get suntans, we will fish, we will play shuffleboard. We will do a cruise to the promised land. Still the storms, calm the seas, rebuke the winds." Isn't that a wonderful solution?

Are there precedents for God stilling storms? We just referred to one. The night Jesus walked on the water he calmed the wind afterward, and the scripture specifically says: "And immediately the ship was at the land whither they went" (John 6:21). Isn't that the ideal finale to the crises of our lives? "Please calm my storms, Lord, and *immediately* get me to my destination." He can do it, can't he? When the storms are blowing in my life, that is usually the solution I desire— simply still the storm, at least still it in the second watch. But if we arrive at the darkness of the fourth watch and he hasn't stilled it, we likely have learned something—something wonderful and powerful, something about ourselves.

The next verse says: "Behold, *I prepare you* against these things; for ye cannot cross this great deep save *I prepare you* against the waves of the sea, and the winds which have gone forth, and the floods which shall come. Therefore what will ye that *I should prepare for you* that ye may have light when ye are swallowed up in the depths of the sea?" (Ether 2:25; emphasis added).

Given the choice between helping us by calming the storms or preparing us before they ever come, which do you think the Lord prefers? He's a fourth-watch

God; he's also a tight-like-a-dish God. If we arrive at the fourth watch and he has not come, what do we know about our ships? *They are tight like a dish.* Our Father in Heaven already foresaw all the storms, complete with their mountain waves. He foresaw all the problems, all the disappointments and frustrations, the temptations, and the trials of life; and before the wind ever started to blow, he prepared us to withstand it. We're not going to sink. We're going to be all right. Because if our ships weren't tight like a dish, and there was fear that the mountain waves would capsize or drown us, what would he do? He would still the storm. If he doesn't still the storm, if he doesn't come by the fourth watch, we know our vessels are tight like a dish.

I think that assurance is, in part, the meaning of a promise Isaiah made. Here are the Lord's comforting words: "And it shall come to pass, that before they call, I will answer; and while they are yet speaking, I will hear" (Isaiah 65:24). Before we ever call out to him in the storms, the Lord knew they would come, and he has prepared our vessels. We need not fear. We'll feel the promised land under our feet.

WHEN HE COMES IN THE FIRST WATCH

There is one area of our lives where the Lord is willing and anxious to come to us in the first watch. In fact, if the Lord said to us, I will let you choose one part of your life where I will come to you in the first watch, or, if you would like me to, I will choose the area for you, hopefully we would have the wisdom to say to him, I'll trust your judgment. You choose the times in my life when you'll be a first-watch God for me. That area would be in forgiveness. The Savior is anxious and eager to come to us when we cry to him for forgiveness, even in the first watch. When the pain and the trial we are going through is repentance, when we struggle with the agonies of guilt, then he is a first-watch God. That truth is attested to countless times in the scriptures.

One of my all-time favorite scripture stories is that of the prodigal son. Contained in that parable is a powerful "first-watch" example that shows the eagerness the Lord feels to forgive. "And when he came to himself, he said, How many hired servants of my father's have bread enough and to spare, and I perish with hunger! I will arise and go to my father, and will say unto him, Father, I have sinned against heaven, and before thee, and am no more worthy to be called thy son: make me as one of thy hired servants" (Luke 15:17–19).

This parable was given to answer a question, which can be stated as follows: "When I 'come to myself,' when I return, when I seek forgiveness, do I return as a son or a servant?" The prodigal himself felt unworthy to return as a son; he was content to return as a servant. Should he be for the rest of his life a kind of second-class citizen of the kingdom? The parable answers: "There are no servants in the kingdom, only sons." Here is our first-watch verse: "He arose, and came to his father. But when he was yet a great way off, his father saw him, and had compassion, and ran, and fell on his neck, and kissed him" (Luke 15:20).

Sometimes it is very important to get the tone of a scripture right. Should we read the son's next comment with a tone of confession or one of amazement? I prefer that of astonishment at the greeting he has just received from his father. "And the son said unto him, Father, I have sinned against heaven, and in thy sight, and am no more worthy to be called thy son" (Luke 15:21). We might add, "Why do you treat me as one?"

"But the father said to his servants, Bring forth the best robe, and put it on him; and put a ring on his hand, and shoes on his feet: and bring hither the fatted calf, and kill it; and let us eat, and be merry: For this my son was dead, and is alive again; he was lost, and is found" (Luke 15:22–24).

As we progress through the Book of Mormon we see a theme begin to emerge as we read story after story. Everybody in the Book of Mormon who asks for forgiveness receives it. And they receive it immediately. The book of Mosiah speaks of "the immediate goodness of God" (Mosiah 25:10), and Amulek promises the humble Zoramites that "the great plan of redemption" will be brought unto them "immediately" if their hearts are soft (Alma 34:31). It's as if the Lord says: Maybe you won't receive that message if I only include it once or twice. Maybe you won't realize how important the message is, so I'm going to put it in again and again, so you'll realize when the wind that blows against you has to do with guilt and forgiveness and repentance and transgression, I will come to you in the first watch.

We read in Enos: "There came a voice unto me, saying: Enos, thy sins are forgiven thee, and thou shalt be blessed. . . . And I said: Lord, how is it done? And he said unto me: Because of thy faith in Christ, whom thou hast never before heard nor seen" (Enos 1:5, 7–8). It's as though the Lord ponders: *I wonder if they understand clearly from Enos's example? Let's state it again with Benjamin's people.* And a few pages later, we read: "They all cried aloud with one voice, saying: O have mercy, and apply the atoning blood of Christ that we may receive forgiveness of our sins, and our hearts may be purified; . . . And it came to pass that after they had spoken these words the Spirit of the Lord came upon them, and they were filled with joy, having received a remission of their sins, and having peace of conscience" (Mosiah 4:2–3).

Perhaps the Lord reflects once more: *I wonder if they got the message. We'd better remind them again.* We turn a few more pages and come to Zeezrom, to whom Alma says: "If thou believest in the redemption of Christ thou canst be healed." To which Zeezrom answers, "Yea, I believe according to thy words. And then Alma cried, . . . O Lord our God, have mercy on this man, and heal him according to his faith which is in Christ. And when Alma had said these words, Zeezrom leaped upon his feet, and began to walk" (Alma 15:8–11).

As if the conviction is not yet deep enough in our hearts the Lord imprints it deeper with the story of Alma and the sons of Mosiah. In agony of guilt, Alma cries out: "O Jesus, thou Son of God, have mercy on me, who am in the gall of bitterness, and am encircled about by the everlasting chains of death. And now, behold, when I thought this, I could remember my pains no more; yea, I was harrowed up by the memory of my sins no more. And oh, what joy, and what marvelous light I did behold" (Alma 36:18–20).

Are we convinced yet? In case we need more evidence we next turn to the Lamanites. *Include the prayers of Lamoni and his wife,* the Lord whispers to Mormon as he collects from the many records those chosen few needed for the latter-day world. Lamoni prays: "O Lord, have mercy; according to thy abundant mercy which thou hast had upon the people of Nephi, have upon me, and my people" (Alma 18:41). When Lamoni revives from his little sleep, he testifies, "As sure as thou livest, behold, I have seen my Redeemer; and he shall come forth, and be born of a woman, and he shall redeem all mankind who believe on his name" (Alma 19:13). Then Lamoni's wife, a short time later, adds her witness to the growing list: "O blessed Jesus, who has saved me from an awful hell! O blessed God, have mercy on this people!" (Alma 19:29). Lamoni's father receives forgiveness, and Lamoni's servants also understand the "immediate goodness" of our Savior.

Even the Lamanites who had come into the prison to kill Nephi and Lehi were "filled with that joy which is unspeakable and full of glory. . . . And it came to pass that there came a voice unto them, yea, a pleasant voice, as if it were a whisper, saying: Peace, peace be unto you, because of your faith in my Well Beloved, who was from the foundation of the world" (Helaman 5:44, 46–47). When we yearn for forgiveness, we worship a first-watch God.

I have emphasized the Savior's willingness to come to us in the first watch when it regards the forgiveness of our sins and transgressions. Of course this implies that we have done all we can do on our part to be worthy of that level of mercy. In Alma 24, the Anti-Nephi-Lehies refer to themselves as the "most lost of all mankind." But the Savior's mercy covered even them. It should be noted, however, that we read three times in that chapter that the Anti-Nephi-Lehies did "all [they] could do to repent sufficiently" (Alma 24:11–15). If we are willing to do as much as we can do, even though we may consider ourselves the most lost of all mankind, the Savior will come to us in the first watch, and we will know by experience the meaning of the words, "the immediate goodness of God."

Jesus instructed his disciples to forgive their brothers when they repented and asked for forgiveness. Then he added the following, "And if he trespass against thee seven times in a day, and seven times in a day turn again to thee, saying, I repent; thou shalt forgive him" (Luke 17:4). I do not believe the Lord is going to expect of us a higher standard than he himself is willing to give. If, therefore, he anticipates we will forgive one another when repentance is offered, seven times in a day, surely that means he will abide by an equal if not a greater standard. Let us do all that we can do, then with full assurance, with a confidence born of hope engendered by the Savior's many examples, we may go to him seven times in a single day and know that every time we will hear the words, "I forgive you. Go in peace."

Holding Places of the Heart — Promises Resolution in time

Occasionally, answers aren't given or the blessings we desire don't come or the trials we bear continue because there is no place in our hearts for God to put the answer we need. Life must carve or hollow out this place. The very experiences we are going through help to create these holding places. Yet he still hears our prayers and promises the resolution will come in time.

When the Missouri persecutions were raging, the Lord comforted the Saints by telling them: "Fear not, let your hearts be comforted; yea, rejoice evermore, and in everything give thanks; waiting patiently on the Lord, for your prayers have entered into the ears of the Lord of Sabaoth, and are recorded with this seal and testament—the Lord hath sworn and decreed that they shall be granted" (D&C 98:1–2). Not yet, nevertheless they will be granted. "He giveth this promise unto you, with an immutable covenant that they shall be fulfilled; and all things wherewith you have been afflicted shall work together for your good, and to my name's glory" (D&C 98:3).

Moses once asked the Lord a question after having been shown the multitude of God's creations. Why do you create all these wonders? he puzzled. The Lord answered, I have my reasons. These are his words: "For mine own purpose have I made these things. Here is wisdom and it remaineth in me" (Moses 1:31). Now that's a very polite way of saying, *I'm not going to answer your question, Moses. You want to know why I create all these things? I have a purpose and it's a wise purpose, but I'm not going to make it known to you right now.* We know that God eventually answered Moses' question. The answer is a very famous one: "This is my work and my glory—to bring to pass the immortality and eternal life of man" (Moses 1:39). I create all these worlds to make men gods, the Lord was saying. I have often asked myself why the Lord didn't answer Moses when he initially asked the question. A close reading reveals that God wanted Moses to understand a few things before the answer came—things that would make the answer even more powerful. He was creating a holding place in Moses' heart to receive it.

Let me illustrate this particular concept by a personal story. When I was just a baby, my father, because of concerns in his own life and challenges that he was having, left our family. Our mother alone, therefore, raised my sisters and me, and as I was growing up, my father had very little to do with us as children. I realize he was working with things in his own life, but his decisions created certain challenges and hardships for my mother, my sisters, and me. At age fourteen or fifteen, if you were in my situation, and you knelt down and said: "Father in Heaven, help me find peace concerning my father leaving us and really having nothing to do with us for all these years. Help me forgive my father," would you not think that was an appropriate prayer, one that deserved an answer? But no answer came at age fourteen and fifteen. Twenty, twenty-one comes, same prayers, still no answer. Twenty-five, twenty-six passes, same prayers, yet still no answer. Thirty, thirty-one, thirty-three, thirty-four all come and go. Surely I'm in the fourth watch by now, would you not agree?

Then one day I was asked to prepare a talk on families. I thought I would speak about my mother. My mother was a saint. In my eyes she could do no wrong. I would talk about my mother—her wisdom and goodness, and how she raised us. But the Spirit seemed to whisper, *Speak about your father.* And I thought, *What am I going to say about my father? I have hardly had anything to do with my father growing up.* Yet the Spirit seemed to urge that I think about him.

Just at that moment, my two sons came into the room where I was working. I was married, and I had two daughters and two sons at the time. The eldest son was about six, his younger brother was around two, and they stood in front of me, just stood there staring at me. I looked at my boys and all at once the Spirit literally flooded my mind with wonderful memories of things that I had shared with them.

We are told that a whole life can pass before us just before we die and we see everything all at once. It was that kind of experience. All the simple little memories, none of them major, came into focus—carving Halloween pumpkins; trick-or-treating with bags bulging with candy; Christmas mornings and the aroma of gingerbread; listening to their tiny-voice prayers; their first tearful, hesitant Primary talks; a squirming puppy wrapped in the tangle of their arms; walks by the pond to see the turtles; piggy-back rides; reading stories at night with mimicked voices; catching a fish out of the same hole where I caught my first fish twenty-five years earlier; the smell of saddle leather as I lifted them up for their first horseback ride. All these simple, tiny, little, everyday memories that I shared in those years with my sons washed into my soul.

And then the Spirit said: *I am now ready to answer your question. Now that you are a father, now that you know a father's love, would you be the son who lost his father, or the father who lost his son?* When I heard those words, I just began to weep. I grabbed my sons and hugged them and just sobbed and sobbed.

My wife came into the room; I was holding those two boys and crying. Not for *me!* For *my father!* Because I knew what he had missed. He doesn't know what he missed. There's a mercy in that. But I knew what he missed, and I knew it was a greater tragedy to be the father who lost his son than to be the son who lost his father.

My wife became concerned and said, "For heaven's sake, Mike, what is the matter?" I said, "I can't talk about it now." I went up and shut myself in the bathroom and cried myself dry. Have you ever done that? There are no tears coming—you're still crying, and there's nothing coming?

Why didn't my Father in Heaven give me that answer at fifteen, or twenty-one, or twenty-five, or when I was married, or when my daughters were born? He needed to wait until I was a father of sons and had enough experiences with my boys to understand what a sweet thing it is to be a father and share memories with sons. The holding place had to be carved in my heart, and as soon as I could really receive and comprehend the answer, the Lord gave it to me. Maybe we are in the fourth watch, but the Lord is saying to us: *I'll answer your prayer. I'm aware of your needs. It is recorded in heaven, and I'm going to answer it. But right now in your life there's no place for me to put the answer. Life will create a holding place, and as soon as you are able to receive it, I will give it to you.*

STONES OR BREAD

There are times in my life when I think he answers, but I misunderstand the message. I think I'm in the fourth watch, but I'm really not; it's just that I expected one answer and got another. In the Gospel of Luke the Lord urges us to come to him for answers: "Ask," he says, "and it shall be given you; seek, and ye shall find; knock, and it shall be opened unto you." (He is always telling us that. It's one of those principles he repeats many, many times because he does not want us to miss it.) "For every one that asketh receiveth; and he that seeketh findeth; and to him that knocketh it shall be opened" (Luke 11:9–10).

He then illustrates that truth: "If a son shall ask bread of any of you that is a father, will he give him a stone? or if he ask a fish, will he for a fish give him a serpent? Or if he shall ask an egg, will he offer him a scorpion? If ye then, being evil [meaning being human—imperfect], know how to give good gifts unto your children: how much more shall your heavenly Father give [good gifts through] the Holy Spirit to them that ask him?" (Luke 11:11–13).

There are times in our lives when I think the Lord says, I gave you bread, but it wasn't the kind of bread you wanted and because you keep thinking about the kind of bread you wanted you've turned my bread into a stone. I gave you a fish, but it wasn't the flavor of fish that you wanted, and you've turned the fish into a serpent. Or I gave you an egg, but I cooked it differently from how you ordered it, and you think I've given you a scorpion.

C. S. Lewis speaks of two kinds of good—the *expected* good and the *given* good. All things given from God are good. There are times in my life I have to remind myself God does not give stones, and when we need bread, a stone is something useless. God does not give stones—only bread. God does not give serpents or scorpions—they are harmful things. He only gives eggs and fish. But if I'm not careful I may hatch the scorpion out of the egg; I may interpret the given good as something bad by constantly thinking of what I wanted instead of what I received. Does that make some kind of sense?

Let me give you an illustration. When I was young I wanted to go on a mission. I dreamed of that mission. I thought I should learn a language, so I took French starting in the eighth grade. I took it in the ninth grade, the tenth grade, and the eleventh grade. I quit after the eleventh grade because I didn't like the French teacher. She was from Paris, was very proud of her language, and if you mispronounced a word (for instance the French *R,* which is rather difficult for an American to get right), she would throw chalk at you. She would literally pelt you with chalk. If you really insulted her ears by butchering her language, she would throw an eraser at you. And I got pelted quite a bit. I thought, *If this is what the French are like, the last place on earth I want to go on a mission is France.* Besides, I loved all things Danish—I'm half Danish. My mother would say the good half of me is the Danish half. My grandfather went to Denmark, my uncles went to Denmark, my cousins went to Denmark. It was tradition in the family for the boys to go to Denmark on their missions. I wanted to go to Denmark, wanted it as much as I have ever wanted anything. I wanted to do Danish research in family history. I figured the Lord would recognize my need to go to Denmark. I prayed I would go to Denmark. But I had the feeling of impending doom that I was not going to go to Denmark—I was going to go to France. So I began to plead with the Lord that he would send me to Denmark. I prayed night after night for a Danish mission.

As the bishop and I began to fill out the missionary papers, I had a feeling it probably was not appropriate to tell the Lord to which country he should send you on your mission, but I didn't think it was inappropriate to eliminate one country out of the hundreds in the world. I changed my prayers. I began to pray he would send me anywhere but France.

I remember vividly the day my call arrived. I was at work. I knew it was at home. Nobody notified me; I just knew the call was waiting for me in the mailbox. We've all seen the videos of the excited missionary who runs home and opens the letter, complete with the accompanying jubilation. I knew my call was in the mailbox, and I knew it said France. Don't ask me how I knew, I just did. I did not want to go home and open it. I lingered at work until the last moment. I was so discouraged over the fact that I was going to France that I actually—and you're going to think I am making this up, but I actually did this (I was eighteen; you'd think an eighteen-year-old would have more sense)—I pulled to the side of the road, parked the car, bowed my head, and said, "Father in Heaven, I know my call is at home; I know it says France. Thou art all-powerful! Thou canst do all things! Please change it in the envelope. I will go anywhere, I don't need to go to Denmark, I will go anywhere, just please, please don't send me to France!"

I ended my prayer, drove home with a spark of hope, and opened the envelope. What did it say? France. Actually, I sometimes think that originally it said Denmark, and the Lord looked down and said, *We really need to teach this young man something, so let's change it in the envelope. He needs to go to France.*

So I went to France. Now I could have ruined my mission. The *expected* good was Denmark. Or, after a while, any place on earth. That was the expected good. The *given* good was France. It didn't take me very long in France to love the French people. I love the French people—wonderful people. They have a beautiful language. Their culture went right to the center of my heart. I had a marvelous mission. We were successful. I found out later, when I returned home, that I had French ancestors, some of them living in the very cities and areas I had served in. I didn't know that at the time, but the Lord did.

I repeat: All things given of God are good. He doesn't give scorpions; he only gives eggs. He does not give stones; he only gives bread. Whatever he gives is good!

That is true of callings. When we moved to Utah about twenty years ago, I hoped I could be the Gospel Doctrine teacher. My favorite calling in the church is Gospel Doctrine. I love to teach the scriptures—it's rewarding, tremendous fun. We'd been in the ward only a few months and, lo and behold, they released the Gospel Doctrine teacher! That afternoon the bishop asked me to come with my wife to his office to receive a calling. Well, I *knew* it was going to be Gospel Doctrine—this is an inspired church, this bishop was called of God—obviously he would have seen that I needed to be the Gospel Doctrine teacher.

called to deacons advisor

I sat down, and he said, "Brother Wilcox, we have a call for you. We would like you to teach the deacons, to be the deacons quorum advisor." My first response was (I didn't say it, but I was thinking it), *Who called you to be a bishop? I work with college kids. What language do deacons speak? I don't speak deacon.* But as the good member, like anyone would, I said, "Thank you for the call. I would be very happy to teach the deacons." I went home and said to my wife, "Oh, I thought this was an inspired Church."

Could I have ruined that call? I could have if I kept thinking every Sunday: *I should be teaching Gospel Doctrine.* That would have made it a miserable call, but I got to really love those little guys, and the Lord helped me the first Sunday when I went into the classroom and, so to speak, met the enemy. The Spirit just whispered, *Teach them well. One day one of them might be your son-in-law.* I had daughters who were deacon age and just under deacon age. My daughters didn't marry any of those boys, but I think the Lord was saying that somewhere, someplace there is a deacon who will be your son-in-law—teach these boys as well as you hope another advisor is teaching his boys.

I had a wonderful experience with the deacons. You can call me to be the deacons quorum advisor any time and I will celebrate. God did not give me stones; he gave me bread in all of those moments.

THIS WAY

Sometimes the answer we receive is simply: *No, not this way.* When the Lord gives that kind of answer, our impatience sometimes causes us to say, *Well, then, which way do you want me to go?* I've always been intrigued with Paul's second missionary journey. If you look at it on the map, he's crossing Turkey, Asia Minor, in a very logical, methodical way—east toward west, south toward north. It's very logical. We read in Acts: "They had gone throughout Phrygia and the region of Galatia" (Acts 16:6). Now, if you look at the map the very next logical spot for Paul to preach the gospel would be Ephesus in Asia; that's logical, and that's where he was headed. But we read, "[They] were forbidden of the Holy Ghost to preach the word in Asia" (v. 6). *Okay, you don't want me to preach in Ephesus, so I'll go to the north instead of the west of Turkey, to a place called Bithynia.*

They tried to go into Bithynia, but the Spirit "suffered them not. And they passing by Mysia came down to Troas. And a vision appeared to Paul in the night; There stood a man of Macedonia, and prayed him, saying, Come over into Macedonia, and help us" (Acts 16:7–9). Responding to his vision, Paul skips Ephesus and jumps to Greece where he establishes churches in Thessalonica, Philippi, Athens, and Corinth before the Spirit allows him to go back to Turkey and preach in Ephesus. Paul does a backward circle, and the Lord never tells us in the scriptures why he didn't want Paul to preach in Ephesus at that time.

Notice, however, how the instructions came. The Lord didn't say, *Paul, would you go over to Corinth? I want you there.* It was instead, *No, not this way.* And sometimes the Lord in our lives says, *No, not this way.* Far too often our response is, *Well, then, which way?* but he doesn't always specify it. Then we try another way. *No, not this way,* comes the answer. Eventually we receive the vision and know where we're supposed to go, but there is some trial and error involved in the process. We must be patient. The Lord knows what he is doing.

THE POOREST SOIL

While we are waiting for the fourth watch there is always hope even in the most desperate situations or trials. I was at a "Time Out for Women" event a few years ago, and one of the other speakers was conducting a question-and-answer session with the women who were there. One of the sisters asked a series of questions that resonated with many of the other women gathered on that occasion. I could tell by the response of the audience. The questions were: "Why did my life not turn out like I thought it would when I was young?" "Why does it seem that everything in my life goes wrong?" "I get trial after trial after trial and, yet, when I look at other sisters, their lives seem to be going so smoothly. How come my life can't go smoothly like their lives? I recognize that I don't know all they are going through and, yet, so many of my expectations have failed to appear and some of my worst fears have come. Why?"

I listened to those questions and thought of my own life. Her life turned out, we might say, worse than expected, and I thought, *My life's turned out better than I anticipated. God has been very kind to me.* Maybe that is so because I didn't expect a great deal when I was young and received so much more. It's made me believe that when you don't expect a lot from life and you obtain so many blessings, the natural result is gratitude, and that is an emotion that is wonderful to feel. She had touched some of my deepest sympathies, and I wondered about the fairness of life with a twinge of guilt as I reflected on my own. *She was living such a difficult life while others seem to have such a good life. Why doesn't God help her in ways that he has helped others?*

I found an answer in the Book of Mormon and turned to it as I sat in the auditorium reflecting on her situation. In the allegory of the tame and the wild olive tree we find an encouraging truth. I like to read Jacob 5 not as an allegory, but as a parable—a parable that is designed to teach us some important things about life. We could call it the Parable of the Good Vineyard Owner. Notice this section of that story as it applies to that concerned woman's questions and her experiences with life.

The Lord of the vineyard, accompanied by his servant, is making the rounds of the vineyard, surveying the different branches of the original tree that he scattered. Remember, he had taken the tender branches and planted them in different spots of his vineyard. They have been growing for a while, and it's time to check their progress, to monitor their growth. This time as we read the story let us think of the trees as individual people trying to grow and progress as best they can while here on the earth.

The Lord visits the first tree and says: "Behold these; and he beheld the first that it had brought forth much fruit; and he beheld also that it was good. And he said unto the servant: Take of the fruit thereof, and lay it up against the season, that I may preserve it unto mine own self; for behold, said he, this long time have I nourished it, and it hath brought forth much fruit" (Jacob 5:20).

The servant then asks the master something that we all often ask the Lord in one way or another. When I look toward heaven and cry: "Did heaven look on, and would not take their part?" I try to remember this part of the allegory. It is comforting. The servant said: "How comest thou hither to plant this tree, or this branch of the tree? For behold, it was *the poorest spot in all the land of thy vineyard*" (Jacob 5:21; emphasis added). Now that's what that good sister was asking, isn't it? She was saying, *Why did I get planted in the poor spot of the vineyard?*

My heart echoed her question: Yes, Lord, that's a good question. Why did she get planted in the poorest spot of the vineyard, because I know a lot more poor-spot-of-the-vineyard people who are wondering the same thing. We all know poor-spot-of-the-vineyard people. Maybe we think we are a poor-spot-of-the-vineyard person; and we may be right.

The Lord of the vineyard answered his servant and said unto him; "Counsel me not" (Jacob 5:22). In other words, *I know what I'm doing in my vineyard*. It is sometimes so very difficult not to give in to the temptation to counsel the Lord on his running of the world, especially as it concerns our own lives. But we get some information in the Lord's comments that I think is comforting, certainly for those who are in the poorer spots of the vineyard or have reached the fourth watch and wonder why the wind is still blowing. The Lord replies: "I knew that it was a poor spot of ground" (Jacob 5:22). That's comforting—he knows! *I know the situation in your life isn't the best*, he whispers to us, *I know that*. We don't need to try to pretend things are really better than they are, to live an illusory, put-your-best-face-forward satisfaction or happiness. That does not mean we don't count our blessings or that we just give up and sink into despair, but it does

Jacob 5, as a parable →

mean the Lord is aware in a very honest way that our soil isn't as ideal as we both would like it to be.

Notice then the Lord's next comment: "Wherefore, I said unto thee, *I have nourished it this long time*" (Jacob 5:22; emphasis added). That's the second piece of information he deeply desires us to comprehend. *I know it's a poor spot, so I have nourished it a long time. I have not left you to fare as best you can in a difficult situation.* A lot of nourishing has been going on, much of it in ways that are challenging for a mortal to understand, but it is there nonetheless.

A third thing he wants us to understand about life in the vineyard is contained in his next words to the servant: "Thou beholdest *that it hath brought forth much fruit*" (Jacob 5:22; emphasis added). Even in the poorest spots of ground, good fruit can be produced because of the nourishment God has provided. These are the fruits of character, nobility, patience, compassion, empathy, and godliness, even genius, all of which have and will continue to rise out of some of the most debilitating of soils. Then the Lord of the vineyard calls our attention to another tree, saying, "Look hither; behold I have planted another branch of the tree also; and thou knowest that this spot of ground *was poorer than the first*" (Jacob 5:23; emphasis added). That's the fourth thing he wants us to recognize. There are others who are in even a poorer situation than the one we find ourselves in. That may be poor comfort, but it is effective nonetheless. What does he do for them? His words to his servant reveal this. "But, behold the tree. I have nourished it this long time, and *it hath brought forth much fruit*" (Jacob 5:23; emphasis added). I sense a slight tone of righteous pride in the Lord's words, "But, behold the tree." Even in the poorest of the poor spots of ground, God can bring forth good fruit.

Then, almost as if to seal the principle, he says to the servant: "Look hither, and behold the last. Behold, this have I planted in a good spot of ground" (Jacob 5:25). What kind of fruit would we foresee growing from this last spot of good ground? Since the soil is so rich, would it not be anticipated that the fruits would be comparable? The best fruit produced from the best ground? Yet we read: "I have nourished it this long time, and only a part of the tree hath brought forth tame fruit, and the other part of the tree hath brought forth wild fruit; behold, I have nourished this tree like unto the others" (Jacob 5:25).

It isn't the spot of ground we're planted in that matters; it's how we respond to the Lord's nourishing. The poorest of the poor spots of ground can bring forth some of the sweetest fruits. We must believe this or else we will allow our circumstances and environment to determine our lives and the quality of our souls.

It's how we respond to Lord's nourishing

THE GREATNESS OF GOD

We can also find comfort in the knowledge that God will turn all things in our lives to good. This is a principle that is taught often in the scriptures. No situation is ever negative in the long run and, therefore, life is always fair. Whatever happens to us, God can turn it to good if we trust him and stay on the path. He teaches that principle in every book of scripture. In the Book of Mormon, Lehi testifies to his son Jacob: "In thy childhood thou hast suffered afflictions and much sorrow, because of the rudeness of thy brethren. Nevertheless, Jacob, my firstborn in the wilderness, *thou knowest the greatness of God; and he shall consecrate thine afflictions for thy gain* (2 Nephi 2:1–2; emphasis added). Part of God's greatness consists in his ability to turn even the most negative of situations into positive truth and learning.

The Lord instructed Joseph Smith in this principle while the Prophet was suffering in Liberty Jail. We can all quote this one: "All these things shall give thee experience, and shall be for thy good" (D&C 122:7). Paul, who also suffered a great deal, bore witness: "We know that all things work together for good to them that love God" (Romans 8:28). Joseph in the Old Testament named his two sons Manasseh and Ephraim, in a manner that teaches the principle. *Manasseh* means "forgetting," and *Ephraim* means "fruitful." As he named his two boys, Joseph said: "God . . . hath made me forget all my toil, and . . . hath caused me to be fruitful in the land of my affliction" (Genesis 41:51–52). Our Father in Heaven can turn even the most negative situations to good for us, if we will trust him and stay true to his gospel.

C. S. Lewis once wrote a little piece that very poignantly taught this truth. He said: "Ye cannot in your present state understand eternity. . . . But ye can get some likeness of it if ye say that both good and evil, when they are full grown, become retrospective. . . . All their earthly past will have been Heaven to those who are saved. . . . All their life on Earth too, will then be seen by the damned to have been Hell. That is what mortals misunderstand. They say of some temporal suffering, 'No future bliss can make up for it,' not knowing that Heaven, once attained, will work backwards and turn even that agony into a glory. And of some sinful pleasure they say 'Let me have but *this* and I'll take the consequences': little dreaming how damnation will spread back and back into their past and contaminate the pleasure of the sin. Both processes begin even before death. The good man's past begins to change so that his forgiven sins and remembered sorrows take on the quality of Heaven: the bad man's past already conforms to his badness and is filled only with dreariness. And that is why, at the end of all things, when the sun rises here and the twilight turns to blackness down there, the Blessed will say, 'We have never lived anywhere except in Heaven,' and the Lost, 'We were always in Hell.' And both will speak truly."[3]

WIPE AWAY ALL TEARS

We also are promised by the Lord that all sorrows, all trials, all storms, and all fourth, ninth, or tenth watches will one day end. When I served as a bishop I soon discovered that the main purpose of a bishop was to hand out tissues. It didn't take me very long to realize that I would see a lot of tears in my five years of service. I would always carry tissues—I still do. I always have them in my pockets, because on any given Sunday I would see tears—tears of sorrow over the death of loved ones, tears of guilt in confession, tears of children over the divorce of parents, tears of parents over rebellious children, tears of wives over inactive husbands, tears of old tired bodies longing for death—so many different kinds of tears. I would hand them a tissue and watch them wipe the tears from their cheeks. I became very frustrated because I wanted to help them wipe the tears off their souls, not just off their faces. Then one day I came across a beautiful verse in the book of Revelation, a promise God makes to all of us. This is what he assures us: "God shall wipe away all tears from their eyes; and there shall be no more death, neither sorrow, nor crying, neither shall there be any more pain: for the former things are passed away" (Revelation 21:4). That is promised twice in the book of Revelation and originally in Isaiah. I realized at that moment, though I as a bishop could not wipe away the tears, there was One who could do so. One day he will do so. He will wipe away all tears.

That's an intimate image. He didn't say, *I will hand them a tissue.* He said, *I'll wipe the tears away.* When I think of my own experiences, who has ever wiped tears from my eyes? My mother, my wife, maybe a child, but only in the most intimate and deepest of relationships would one dare to reach out a gentle thumb and sweep it across the cheek to wipe away a tear. Yet the promise is that the Lord will do that for us all.

In the New Testament the Lord then reminds us of one of his titles: "I am Alpha and Omega, *the beginning and the end*" (Revelation 21:6; emphasis added). If we take that title, given in the context of wiping away all tears, and apply it to the promise, and then ask the question, *What is he the end of?* we learn a marvelous truth. He answers us: *I am the end of death, I am the end of crying, I am the end of sorrow, I am the end of pain.* Now if we ask the question, *What is he the beginning of?* he will answer: *I am the beginning of peace, I am the beginning of forgiveness, I am the beginning of life and happiness and glory. I am the beginning of all joys.*

One day, no matter what reason we may have for unhappiness—whatever trials we may face, have faced, or are then facing—one day they will all come to an end. Right at the end of his agonies on the cross, Jesus said, "It is finished" (John 19:30). He certainly meant that his Father's will had completely been accomplished, but there is something more in those simple words. His *suffering* was also over. No man suffered more than he did, and if *he* came to a point in his life where he could say of his suffering, "It is finished," all of *us* will come to the point in our existence when we, too, will say, "It is finished." And it will be finished, no matter what it was. The tears will be wiped away. That end we may hope for. That end we may be assured of. In the meantime we may know that whatever happens, he is going to turn it into good for us. So let the fourth watches come. Let the mountain waves crash. Life will be sweet eventually.

The Burning Bush

I have long loved the story of God's appearance to Moses in the burning bush. I think it is a wonderful image to hold on to when we think of our Father in Heaven: "Now Moses kept the flock of Jethro his father in law, the priest of Midian: and he led the flock to the backside of the desert, and came to the mountain of God, even to Horeb. And the angel of the Lord appeared unto him in a flame of fire out of the midst of a bush: and he looked, and, behold, *the bush burned with fire, and the bush was not consumed*. And Moses said, I will now turn aside, and see this great sight, why the bush is not burnt" (Exodus 3:1–3; emphasis added).

It is so very critical to believe, and to believe firmly, that God is a burning fire that is unique above all other fires. He will give us warmth! He will give us light! He will cleanse and purge us as does the refiner's fire! But he will not consume us. The flame of his love is meant only for good—it is not a destroying fire. Of this we may be certain. "The bush was not consumed," nor will we be in our encounters with the God of Light.

I conclude with this final thought. I believe every good thing in life that we desire is on the strait and narrow path. As long as we stay on the path, every truly enjoyable and fine thing life and eternity can offer will be ours. Sometimes while seeking for happiness or fulfillment we may stray from the path, vainly believing we will find our hearts' desires beyond the road our Savior has established, but if we'll stay on the path, everything we want in life will be ours. It's a wish-fulfilling path designed to lead us to every good, noble, and righteous thing we want if we'll just follow it. In truth it will provide greater things than we can even imagine, for did not the Lord say: "Since the beginning of the world men have not heard, nor perceived by the ear, neither hath the eye seen, O God, beside thee, what he hath prepared for him that waiteth for him" (Isaiah 64:4).

I usually want the desirable blessing to be just a few feet ahead of me on the path. However, sometimes the Lord has to give me a pair of binoculars and say, *Well, it's on the path, but it's in the distance there.* Then I must be patient, confident that if I'll just walk the path, all will, in due time, be well.

May we walk that path, trusting that every desire of our hearts that truly brings happiness will be there. May God bless us in our fourth watches. May our ships be tight like a dish. May we have the patience to wait for life, measured by the wisdom of God, to carve the holding places in our hearts. May we remember God does not give stones or serpents, he only gives bread and fish. May we understand that all things God gives are good, and even the negative ones he can make good. May we respond to his nourishing and bring forth good fruit in spite of the soil in which we may have been planted. May we trust that the Lord himself will in time wipe away all tears. May God's burning fire give us warmth, light, and cleansing. And may the Lord bless us as we walk his path of happiness.

This is my prayer for myself, my family, my friends, and for all of God's children wherever they may be.

CHAPTER FIVE

KING NOAH BLINDNESS AND THE VISION OF SEERS

~

SEE-ERS

As a high school English student, I read *Oedipus Rex* by Sophocles. Perhaps you have read this Greek tragedy before. The climax of the play comes when Oedipus discovers he has done some very evil things, albeit without knowing, and as self-punishment blinds himself. That scene was always tremendously troubling to me when I was young. The thought that somebody could reach a level of despair so deep that he would deliberately blind himself struck a sensitive place in my heart. As a result, I've never been able to reread *Oedipus Rex* since. Self-inflicted blindness was simply too disturbing. However, there is a certain kind of blindness that the Book of Mormon speaks of which is equally disquieting. The Bible also presents this type of blindness as a warning to us all. This is a self-induced blindness that, unfortunately, many people in the world, particularly young people, inflict upon themselves. That sightless condition, for lack of a better name, we can label "King Noah Blindness." If teaching from the Old Testament, we could equally call it "Jezebel Blindness," but we'll focus mostly on the Book of Mormon here.

The power of the scriptures has to do with their relevance in our lives. They speak to the human condition. We should never just merely tell scripture stories. We should always teach what the scriptures teach so that as we're looking at them, we're forever trying to draw out of them lessons that are germane, pertinent, and relevant in our own lives.

What I truly admire about the scriptures is how powerful they are in a literary sense. God never wrote a bad book. Whether we are studying Habakkuk, Mosiah, or Revelation, they're all significant, applicable, and nourishing. They are literarily powerful—full of metaphor and irony and simile and alliteration.

They also signal to the reader major themes to be discovered as one progresses through the storyline.

The major theme in the central sections of the book of Mosiah—the stories of Abinadi, Alma the Elder, King Noah, and Amulon with his coterie of wicked priests—has to do with blindness and seeing. That theme begins in Mosiah 8, when we are introduced to this section of Book of Mormon history. Notice what we are told in the thirteenth verse: "Now Ammon said unto him: I can assuredly tell thee, O king, of a man that can translate the records; for he has wherewith that he can look, and translate all records that are of ancient date; and it is a gift from God. And the things are called interpreters, and no man can look in them except he be commanded, lest he should look for that he ought not and he should perish. And whosoever is commanded to look in them, the same is called seer" (Mosiah 8:13). If we were to truly spell *seer* the way we ought to spell it in order to grasp the root idea from which the word originates, we would spell it with three *E*s. A seer is a *see-er*—one who sees.

When King Limhi learns that there is a see-er in Zarahemla, he comes to a personal, yet somewhat questioning, conclusion. He states: "A seer is greater than a prophet" (Mosiah 8:15). Ammon corrects him by including the title *seer* with its two most common companions, "A seer is a revelator and a prophet also; and a gift which is greater can no man have" (Mosiah 8:16). As Latter-day Saints, we are aware that these three words go together, prophet, see-er, and revelator— we have fifteen of them in the Church today! At every conference we raise our hands and sustain them; in every temple recommend interview we are asked if we accept these fifteen men as prophets, see-ers, and revelators.

Ammon tells Limhi what a see-er, a prophet, and a revelator can do. A revelator, by definition, is one who reveals. What does he reveal? The answer is self-evident—he reveals what he sees! Ammon's description is, "A seer can know of things which are past" (Mosiah 8:17), meaning a see-er can see into the past, take the lessons found there, and make them relevant and pertinent to our own situation. He can do this because he perceives the past and its lessons clearly without limiting biases or overly subjective thinking.

Ammon continues to describe the functions of a see-er by stating they can also see "things which are to come" (Mosiah 8:17). Seers can understand, based on the decisions we are making now or the emphasis we give to our lives or to our society, where those decisions or emphases will take us in the future. What long-term consequences will we face, given our present path? "By them shall all things be revealed," Ammon adds, "or, rather, shall secret things be made manifest, and hidden things shall come to light, and things which are not known shall be made known by them, and also things shall be made known by them which otherwise could not be known" (Mosiah 8:17). He concludes, "Thus God has provided a means that man, through faith, might work mighty miracles." The miracles Ammon is talking about, however, are the miracles of clear vision, wise understanding, and sound counsel. "Therefore he becometh a great benefit to his fellow beings" (Mosiah 8:18). I repeat: We have fifteen such benefits in the Church today.

The story in Mosiah that demonstrates these teachings is of a see-er named Abinadi. The people are going to have to make a choice. Who will they follow? Will they choose King Noah and his band of wicked priests, led by Amulon? Will they accept their vision? Or will they follow Abinadi and his counsel and vision? We are told something about the general mass of people who provide the backdrop to the main protagonists. Here, where the thesis, the theme of this part of the Book of Mormon is so profoundly introduced to us, we learn about the blindness of the people. "O how marvelous are the works of the Lord, and how long doth he suffer with his people; yea, and how *blind* and *impenetrable* [notice those two keywords; they both have to do with seeing] are the understandings of the children of men; for they will not seek wisdom, neither do they desire that she should rule over them!" (Mosiah 8:20; emphasis added).

So the stage is set in Mosiah 8, the introductory chapter, for the tragedy of King Noah Blindness that is to follow. Before we know anything about Abinadi or King Noah, a theme is introduced to us as readers. The scriptures invite us, saying: "Look for themes dealing with the eyes, with seeing, with blindness, and with seers, because in those details you'll be able to make the story deeply relevant to your own situation."

"MAY THE LORD BLESS MY PEOPLE"

With that introduction, we turn to Mosiah 11. Zeniff has died and the kingdom has been turned over to his son Noah. I have to admit I sense a little gallows humor in the last phrase that Zeniff writes, just before he turns the kingdom over to King Noah: "And now I, being old, did confer the kingdom upon one of my sons; *therefore, I say no more. And may the Lord bless my people*" (Mosiah 10:22; emphasis added). I may be putting my own inflection in those last two phrases, but I can't help but read it as Zeniff hoping for the best, but resigning himself to what he sees coming in the reign of King Noah. When we study the scriptures we usually look for lessons and principles in the lives of the major characters. That is generally where we concentrate our efforts and searches—we study the Nephis and the Lehis and the Alma the Youngers; we search the lives of Jesus and Paul and Peter, but often it is helpful to shift our focus a little and look at those who provide the backdrop for the larger characters: the nameless masses—the people. In this story, the people—those who we are told are blind and impenetrable—have a tremendous message for us.

Noah begins to change the workings of the kingdom almost immediately. "For behold, he did not keep the commandments of God, but he did walk after the desires of his own heart. And he had many wives and concubines. And he did cause his people to commit sin. . . . And he laid a tax of one fifth part of all they possessed. . . . And all this did he take to support himself, and his wives and his concubines; and also his priests, and their wives and their concubines; thus he had changed the affairs of the kingdom" (Mosiah 11:2–4). We read on: "Noah built many elegant and spacious buildings" (Mosiah 11:8). He filled them with luxurious things. He had special seats made so his priests could lounge and lean over on them while they were teaching the people (see Mosiah 11:11). He built towers. He went to war against the Lamanites for spoil. Because his armies won a few victories, he felt he was the great warrior of the Nephites. All this he supports by taxing the people.

If you ask almost any group of people anywhere in the world, "How many of you like taxes?" you're not going to get a positive response. If you then asked, "How would you feel if you knew your tax dollars were going to support the immoral lifestyle of your leaders?" you would likely get an even-stronger negative response. But these are the strangest people you have ever met. They don't seem to mind it at all. We are told, "Thus they [meaning the wicked priests and King Noah] were supported in their laziness, and in their idolatry, and in their whoredoms, by the taxes which king Noah had put upon his people; thus did the people labor exceedingly to support iniquity" (Mosiah 11:6).

They don't seem to be bothered at all by the waste and licentiousness. They love these guys. They're the best thing that has come into their lives since bread and butter. They have autographed posters of King Noah on their walls. I've often thought that a great name for a rock band would be Amulon and the Wicked Priests. Why do they feel this way about them? I suppose it is because Noah, Amulon, and the priests justify in their teachings, their conversations, and their lifestyles, those "natural man" things that are so congenial and appealing to our appetites and passions. In a sense, they are "soothe-sayers." A soothe-sayer is the opposite of a see-er. Soothe-sayers say soothing sayings. They tell you what you want to hear, and Noah and the wicked priests, with Amulon at their head, are soothe-sayers. The people think they're wonderful. When Abinadi arrives to warn the people of what he sees up ahead (he sees unhappiness, he sees misery, he sees problems), the people are not in the mood to hear it.

God is not going to deliberately put this misery and unhappiness on them; God has no pleasure in punishment. There's enough pain in the world already.

God doesn't want any more. But he knows that certain behaviors and actions lead to natural consequences. We are usually punished more *by* our sins than *for* our sins. When Abinadi arrives on the scene and can see what's coming, you would think the people would rally around him and say, "We don't like our leaders, the lazy lives that we're supporting with our hard-earned wages and labor." Yet, after Abinadi speaks, we read these words: "Now it came to pass that . . . [the people] were wroth with him, and sought to take away his life; but the Lord delivered him out of their hands. Now when king Noah had heard the words which Abinadi had spoken unto the people, he was also wroth; and he said: Who is Abinadi, that I and my people should be judged of him, or who is the Lord, that shall bring upon my people such great affliction?" (Mosiah 11:26–27). Abinadi flees at the people's rejection of his words and their hostility toward him. Mosiah 11 ends with this blunt assessment of their wisdom, "Now the eyes of the people were blinded" (Mosiah 11:29). They are King Noah–blind!

NOAHS OR ABINADIS

We can encapsulate the message of this story and what follows next with a very simple phrase: *"We simply must learn how to distinguish between the King Noahs and the Abinadis in our lives."* Often, when we are blinded by the Noahs in our lives, we cannot differentiate between the true friend and the false one. When someone else comes to our aid—the Abinadis of our lives—and tries to warn us because they see more clearly and see the unhappiness that is coming, we treat them sometimes as the enemy. We simply must learn how to distinguish between the true friend and the true enemy.

We see examples of the problem of King Noah Blindness almost everywhere. It's in the young man raised in the Church, a good boy, who begins to associate with a smaller group of friends whose standards aren't quite the same; they begin to pull him down. His grooming, his language, his activities, the movies he watches, and the music he listens to begin to change. Mom and Dad start to notice, and maybe a priesthood leader comments, or another friend senses an alienation. They say to him, "We're concerned—we're troubled a little by the things you're doing, the direction you're headed, the shift in your values." Almost inevitably that young man will say, "You're judging. So what if my friends have long hair or an earring or dress in a certain way? You're judging. You don't really know them." Remember that King Noah was enraged that he and his priests were "judged of [Abinadi]."

Two years pass and Abinadi returns with an intensified message. We find here another one of those details that causes me to laugh a little bit. There is some humor in the Book of Mormon. Abinadi comes back—in disguise, we're told—but the first words he says are these, "Thus has the Lord commanded me, saying—Abinadi, go and prophesy unto this my people" (Mosiah 12:1). I wonder if he said, "Oh, I just blew my cover."

When he comes back the second time with his second warning, which is stronger than the first one, again it is the people who are angry. It is the people who arrest him. It is the people who haul him before King Noah, because they support King Noah. Noah is wonderful! Notice what they say: "And now, O king, what great evil hast thou done, or what great sins have thy people committed, that we should be condemned of God or *judged of this man?* And now, O king, behold, we are guiltless, and thou, O king, hast not sinned; therefore, this man has lied concerning you, and he has prophesied in vain. And behold, we are strong. . . . Thou hast prospered in the land, and thou shalt also prosper" (Mosiah 12:13–15; emphasis added). One of the signs of King Noah Blindness is the justification or defense of the negative element with the counter-accusation that one is being judgmental.

My wife was serving as the Young Women's president in a former ward when she tried to help a young woman who became King Noah–blind. She was very close to this girl, who was raised in a solid Latter-day Saint family, received her Young Women's recognition award, and did everything she was supposed to do. She left home to go to college, where she met a young man whose standards weren't very high, who was less-active in the Church, and who had some substance abuse problems. She fell in love with this young man and set a goal to save him from his self-destructive patterns.

Now that's an honorable thing to desire, but before attempting to pull someone to a higher behavioral and spiritual plateau, one had better make sure to stand firmly on solid ground oneself. It is not always easy to ascertain if you're standing on solid ground. Moral gravity works against you. You don't jump into a raging river in an effort to save a drowning person or the two of you may both meet disaster. You throw them a rope and pull them to you while maintaining solid footing on the shore. But this young woman jumped into the river to try to save her boyfriend. He began to influence her, and her values and her standards and her behavior began to drop.

Who is usually the first to notice these subtle changes? Her mom and dad, her bishop, and a former Young Women's president could all see what was happening. They tried to warn her. They went to the sources we almost always utilize—the words of seers, *For the Strength of Youth,* and other counsels. In this girl's mind, who became the enemy? The young man? Never! Mom and Dad became the enemy. The bishop was the enemy. The former Young Women's president was the enemy. Who was the friend? The boyfriend! We could call him her "boy-Noah." No matter what people said to her, she always responded with the age-old defense, "You're judging. You don't really know him. You don't understand. I see clearly. You're the ones who are blind." My wife later remarked, "A temporary loss of judgment became a permanent one, when she considered every true friend her enemy."

I work with college students a great deal. I have been privileged to teach them in a number of different places and settings. Sometimes they'll become enamored with a professor, or an idea, or a popular philosophy that's sophisticated, and modern, and accepted, one that in their eyes makes the Church look rather provincial, rather puritanical, rather old-fashioned. Occasionally I get to talk to these students and try to teach them the nature of King Noah Blindness. When you attempt to point out the flaws or dangers in the person or idea or movement that has so captivated them—when you attempt to help them see they're being blinded—you become the enemy.

FRIEND OR ENEMY

Do you understand King Noah Blindness? In the Old Testament we see it with Ahab and Jezebel and Elijah. In an Old Testament context we could word our principle a little differently. We could say: "We simply must learn how to distinguish between the Jezebels and the Elijahs of our lives."

Do you remember this story? King Ahab covets Naboth's vineyard. Naboth would not sell it to him. It's his family inheritance. And so Ahab returns to his palace, turns his face to the wall, and pouts. He has a little pity party for himself, like a spoiled child. In comes Jezebel.

"What's the matter dear?" she says.

"Naboth won't give me his vineyard," he replies with the appropriate amount of self-pity.

"That's all right, dear," she says, "I'll get it for you. You're the king; you can have what you want." She exits and promptly has Naboth and his sons killed by falsely accusing them of blasphemy. They are stoned by a mob. Jezebel then returns to her pouting husband.

"You can take Naboth's vineyard now, for he is dead."

In Ahab's mind Jezebel is the best friend he has. *She* loves him! *She* gives him what he wants! *She* doesn't criticize him! *She* doesn't try and cause him to do things he doesn't want to do or live a lifestyle he doesn't want to live! *She* lets him give in to his weaknesses! *She* is his friend. So Ahab goes down from the palace to enjoy his new possession. He walks up and down the rows of grapevines. He's a proud new owner! You can just see him tasting the grapes. Then who arrives to spoil all his fun? Elijah! What unfortunate timing! How does Ahab greet Jezebel's nemesis?

"Hast thou found me, O mine enemy?"

To which Elijah answers, "I have found thee: because thou hast sold thyself" (1 Kings 21:20).

Tragically, this situation is all too familiar. We simply must learn to distinguish between the Jezebels and the Elijahs, between the Abinadis and the Noahs. Who really loves Ahab and has his eternal happiness at heart? Elijah is his best friend. Who's his worst enemy? Jezebel is his worst enemy. Who has the Nephites' best interests at heart? Who wishes to promote their eternal long-term happiness? Abinadi! Abinadi is the best friend they have. Who is their worst enemy? Noah is their worst enemy, and Amulon, and the wicked priests. The Nephites can't see this truth, but it is as sure and plain as anything the scriptures teach. The true friend, the true brother, will never try to persuade you to disobey your Father in Heaven. They will always encourage you to walk that strait and narrow path. They'll not try to broaden it, even in the name of companionship and familiarity.

I have often said that God never wrote a bad book. In all his works we should be able to find the best literary techniques. God is an excellent author. Irony is a powerful literary tool, and the Lord uses it with skill in the scriptures. Abinadi says one of the most profoundly ironic things I know of in the Book of Mormon. If we miss the irony, to a great extent we miss the message. This is what he says to the people, to his neighbors who are so smitten with their king, enchanted to the point of blindness. These are the souls who still have their posters of King Noah hanging on their walls and autographed albums by Amulon and the Wicked Priests. "And it shall come to pass that the life of king Noah shall be *valued* [that is the deeply ironic word] even as a garment in a hot furnace; for he shall know that I am the Lord" (Mosiah 12:3; emphasis added).

What is so ironic about Abinadi saying the life of King Noah will be valued as a garment in a hot furnace? There are a couple of layers of irony worthy of exploration. One layer becomes obvious fairly quickly. How does Abinadi die? He's burned alive. How does King Noah die? He's burned just like Abinadi. As the flames begin to engulf Abinadi, he makes a prophecy. What you do to me is a foreshadowing of what will happen to you. But the deeper irony, the deeper level is when we ask the question: Who burns King Noah? Who values his life as a garment in a hot furnace? The people burn him! The very people who at the moment of Abinadi's death think Noah is wonderful, defend him, see no wrong in him, make seers the enemy in his name—they burn Abinadi in his behalf. These same people in turn burn Noah. The disquieting truth about King Noah

Blindness is that you usually don't stay Noah-blind forever. Often when the scales of darkness fall, when sight returns, there are painful, painful moments to endure.

King Noah Moments—The Restoration of Sight

While serving as a bishop, I dreaded what I call "King Noah Moments." I could almost always tell one was coming by the tone of voice in the member who asked to see me. They came most often in confessions when someone's eyesight was cleared and he or she began to see what had really happened in his or her life. Let us look at the original King Noah Moment and then some contemporary examples. By the time we get to Mosiah 19, Alma the Elder has departed into the wilderness. He has baptized several at the Waters of Mormon, and then moved with his converts to the land of Helam, where his people begin to live really exemplary lives. Back in Noah's kingdom, however, there is trouble. A man named Gideon leads a revolt. He chases King Noah to the top of his watchtower. There he corners the wicked king, and he is just ready to slay him when Noah looks in the distance and he sees a Lamanite army coming. He cries out for his life to Gideon. "The Lamanites are upon us, and they will destroy us; yea, they will destroy my people" (Mosiah 19:7). In other words, spare me please, Gideon, this is a national crisis.

We learn something extremely important about the King Noahs in our lives in the very next verse. "And now the king was not so much concerned about his people as he was about his own life" (Mosiah 19:8). That's usually true of the Noahs in our lives. They're not as concerned about our welfare as something they themselves want. However, Gideon spares Noah's life and Noah leads a retreat.

It is always helpful when you read the scriptures—whenever you can—to put yourselves in them, imagine yourself in the story, visualize the events as best you can. Let's put ourselves in the story. Here I am, one of Noah's minions, one of his devoted followers. I have listened to this man and believed in him. I have defended him. I have justified him. I've accused anyone who criticized him of judging him. I have alienated people in his behalf. And now, once again, I follow him. He's my leader. I can see myself—I'm running and I have my family with me. I have my daughter and a granddaughter, about four years of age, with me. I don't think they're going to outrun a Lamanite army. My older daughter, like me, hates to run. I think she'll probably give up. I don't think she'll even try to run. She'll figure there's no way—go ahead and slay me. I have a couple of sons. They could probably make it, but I'm not sure their wives can. My own wife is only 5' 3"; I don't think she's going to outrun the army. There was a time in my life when I was younger that I would have said, "I can do it." But I have worries about myself now. Let's say I'm in the middle of the fleeing people. I'm holding my granddaughter's hand with one hand, my wife's hand with the other. I'm urging my family—maybe in your situation you have little children also, you've got a five- or six-year-old or a fourteen-year-old daughter or son—and we're running, running, trying to get away. I keep looking over my shoulder, and the Lamanites are advancing.

Then my hero, my king, my leader, my friend, gives a command. "Leave the women and children! Save yourselves!" I am so accustomed to following him, I actually do the unthinkable. I put my granddaughter down. I drop my wife's hand. Maybe with my two older sons I run. Maybe they wouldn't run. Maybe they would stay with their wives. But I run. I abandon my family. I do the unthinkable. I'm out of breath; I'm running and I keep looking back; we're winning the race! We're going to get away from the Lamanites! I run and I run! You're running with me. Then, somewhere out in the wilderness, in a clearing, we find ourselves safe. They're not after us anymore. We've won! I'm out of breath. I'm panting. Then I have a King Noah Moment. It hits me hard, with a numbing, stunning blow. I say, "Oh, no! What have I done? What have I done?" Because what do I then imagine happened to my daughters, my wife, my granddaughter back there when the Lamanites caught up with them? We know—now, as readers of their history—that the Lamanites didn't kill them. The women pleaded for their lives and the Lamanites, "charmed with the beauty of their women" (Mosiah 19:14), took them captive instead and spared the rest of the people. But I don't know that back in the clearing in the wilderness. I'm having my Noah Moment!

If you can put yourself in that meadow, in that clearing, in that jungle, or the forest, or the hilltop, or the valley—wherever it took place—all the eyes, the formerly blinded eyes swing in the direction of one man. *Now* I look at Noah; *now* I see him for what he really is! Is he any different than he was a year ago when I defended him or helped burn Abinadi at his behest? Is he any different? No! He's the same person. I'm just not blind anymore. Now I know. At this moment, how much do I value him? Am I willing to defend him now? No—now I value him "as a garment in a hot furnace." At that moment, because the people were not yet ready to take full responsibility for themselves, they blame everything on him. Seeing him for the first time as he really is, they burn him!

To add to the great ironies of the story, Amulon and his band of wicked priests get away. That's part of the beauty of the Book of Mormon—it's so true to life. Sometimes bad people just get away. As I read Mosiah I keep waiting for the wicked priests to get their just reward. They never do. They get away. Sometimes the wicked aren't punished in this life.

Let's discuss King Noah Moments in our time. I return to painful memories as a bishop. At times a young woman in my ward would set an appointment to confess. She had lost her virtue the night or the week before in a moment of weakness and under the assumption that the young man loved her. She was beginning to see the young man who compromised her in a different light. She is having her King Noah Moment. The value level of the affection or relationship decreases. I have heard young women in these situations say, "I hate him for what I've lost, for what I let him take from me." Then the young woman feels even greater guilt because now she has to deal with resentment, anger, hate, and bitterness. Before painful moments must be endured, we simply must learn how to tell the difference between the Noahs and the Abinadis in our lives, the Jezebels and the Elijahs. If not, we're going to have some very bitter King Noah Moments to face.

I recall teaching the Abinadi and Noah story once in a college class. Afterward, a young lady approached me and said, "Sometimes we have our King Noah Moments early enough to prevent great tragedies." She told me about such a moment in her life. She had a beautiful voice. Her parents had paid for voice lessons, but she used her talents by singing in a rock band. Their music, which wasn't edifying in the first place, deteriorated, and her mother and father tried to suggest that perhaps her talents should be used in other areas.

"I went through the whole King Noah Blindness thing," she said. "I told Mom and Dad, 'You're judging, you don't know. I enjoy it.' Then my clothing style began to change, but I justified everything in my mind. I was dressing immodestly because it was a costume; it wasn't really me. One night I came home from a concert where we had performed. I had in my room a poster of my favorite rock star. I turned the light on and looked at that poster. He had his shirt off, chains around his neck, black leather pants on." She described the poster in some detail—you know those kind of posters—and she said, "As I looked at it, it was almost as if the Savior came into the room and looked at it with me. I was ashamed. For the first time I saw the group I was in, and the music I sang, and my participation in it, as it really was. I knew it was vulgar and indecent. I tore the poster down, put up a picture of Christ and a MormonAd I had stuffed under the bed from my Mia Maid days. Then I went to find my parents. You can imagine how happy they were. They had their daughter back. I was surprised at how suddenly my view of my parents and of the Church began to change. I had come home."

The ultimate King Noah Moment would be when a whole life has been lived falsely and instead of seeing the particular Noah who has deceived us we see the adversary himself. That would be the ultimate painful Noah Moment. May none of us ever face *that* clearing in the wilderness.

THE BULLDOG FACTOR

Part of the danger of Noah Blindness is even when we finally see and are trying to pull away from those influences, the Noahs and Amulons in our lives are like bulldogs. They can be tenacious. They tend to hang on, or at least their consequences often do. We now enter the second phase of this marvelous, relevant, well-written story of King Noah and Amulon and the wicked priests. With Noah out of the way, the focus shifts to Amulon and his band of priests—the guys who always get away with it. The Noahs in our lives, or in this case, the Amulons, are likely to hang around in the wilderness. We may want nothing to do with them anymore, but at the most inopportune moments, they come back.

There are two main groups of Nephites at this point—Alma the Elder's company, who settle in Helam, and Limhi's faction, who return to the city after fleeing the Lamanites. Both of these parties have to put up with problems from the wicked priests, who hide in the wilderness, ashamed to come back to their wives and families. They watch the daughters of the Lamanites dance from the forest shadows. When only twenty-four girls are dancing, they run out, each grab themselves a new wife, and haul them into the wilderness like the Romans and the Sabine women.

This does not please the Lamanites. Who gets blamed for the abductions? Limhi's people are held responsible and face the full fury of the Lamanites. Do they attack Amulon and his nasty knot of co-conspirators? No, the Lamanites attack Limhi and his people. In Mosiah 21, we also read of some other problems that the wicked priests have caused. "For [Limhi's people] were desirous to take [the wicked priests] that they might punish them; for they had come into the land of Nephi by night, and carried off their grain and many of their precious things; therefore they laid wait for them" (Mosiah 21:21). The Noahs and Amulons in our lives, those whom at one time we thought were so wonderful, are prone to hide out in the brush and return to disturb our newly discovered fidelity to God. Limhi and his people want nothing to do with them, yet there they are!

However, the most forceful part of this story, a story that we might title "The Haunting of the Amulons," comes from Alma's people. They have truly and deeply repented. We read of their beautiful baptismal covenant in Mosiah 18. We quote their words as the best example of what the baptismal covenant is. They have formed a church. It's an all-week church, not just a Sunday church. They are living a dignified gospel life. The last thing in the world they want is anything to do with Amulon and the wicked priests, the old favorites they used to follow so religiously. But even for these now-intensely righteous people, the former priests are still out in the wilderness. Limhi's people do escape the bondage placed upon them by the Lamanites. They succeed in getting their Lamanite guards inebriated with wine and then sneak out the back gate, arriving eventually at Zarahemla. A Lamanite army chases Limhi's fleeing party and gets lost in the wilderness. (In the book of Mosiah, everybody gets lost in the wilderness. You're just not cool if you don't get lost in the wilderness.)

The Lamanite army is lost, wandering in the wilderness, and as fate would have it, who do they discover? Who else is hiding out in the wilderness? First, they discover Amulon, his wicked priests, and the twenty-four Lamanite daughters they had captured. At this point in the Book of Mormon you'd be tempted to say, "You're going to get it now! Justice will have its way! The Lamanite army is going to do a number on you!" But somehow the priests have convinced their new wives to like them. The wives approach the army and successfully plead for their abductors/husbands. Amulon and the wicked priests then join with the Lamanite army and they wander together, lost in the wilderness for a little longer.

But, as fate would have it—call it poetic justice—they stumble upon Alma the Elder's people who, as we remember, want nothing to do with the wicked priests anymore. Yet here they are on their doorstep, and with the Lamanite army in tow. Alma calms the fears of his people and they pray to God. They're not killed by the Lamanites; rather, the Lamanites say, "Show us the way to land of Nephi and we'll leave you alone." They are shown the way home, but the Lamanites don't keep their promise. They send an army back to put Alma's people in bondage. If they can't find Limhi and his followers, Alma's will provide a nice substitute. Next, "the king of the Lamanites . . . granted unto Amulon that he should be a king and a ruler over [the] people, who were in the land of Helam" (Mosiah 23:39). It's Amulon and the Wicked Priests all over again. Once again they rule over Alma and his people. Yet Alma wants absolutely nothing to do with them. Can you see the relevant power of this story? Our Noahs, our Amulons, are out there in the wilderness, lingering, haunting, ready to come back at the slightest opportunity.

Amulon begins to exercise authority over Alma and his followers. We read in Mosiah 24 that they "began to persecute him, and cause that his children should persecute their children. For Amulon knew Alma, that he had been one of the king's priests, and that it was he that believed the words of Abinadi and was driven out before the king, and therefore he was wroth with him; for he was subject to king Laman, yet he exercised authority over them, and put tasks upon them, and put taskmasters over them" (Mosiah 24:8–9).

"How Long?"

Let me try to illustrate this principle with a story that still haunts me. When I was in my last year of studies at Brigham Young University, I was called to serve as a counselor in a bishopric. At the beginning of the term, the bishopric interviewed all the incoming students. The ward needed organizing immediately, within the first few weeks, and as a bishopric we didn't know half of the arriving students. The three of us would interview for hours just to try to get to know our members. What were their likes and dislikes? What experience might they bring and where might they like to serve? Before we started our interviews, the bishop told me and my fellow counselor—we were both students and not very wise— "If, as you talk to someone, you feel that they need to speak to me as the bishop, bring them to me right away. Sometimes as members begin to attend a new ward with a new bishop, they will want a clean slate. They might feel uncomfortable talking to the bishop they've been raised with back home, but they will open up here and now. Be sensitive and listen for the Spirit."

I tried to follow his counsel. A young lady from California, my home state, came in. She had a certain worldly look about her. You can see things in people's countenances, and some things she said as I was talking to her—this wasn't a particularly intense interview—made me wonder if I should take her to see the bishop. Finally I said, "Cindy [not her real name], would you like to go see the bishop?" And she began to cry, and she said, "Oh, I need to do that." So I knocked on his door and he saw her immediately. Two or three hours later she came out, having confessed to the bishop some serious moral problems she had had with a "boy-Noah" back in high school in California. She wanted to change her life. I was married at the time, and the bishop asked my wife and me to help her. "Would you take this young woman under your wings?" he asked. "See that she has support. She feels a connection with you because you sensed she needed to see me. She trusts you, and I want you to work with her." We all became fast friends, my wife, this young woman, and I.

I watched that young woman go through the repentance process. It's a hard road sometimes—a beautiful one, but not always easy. She struggled, but never gave up. The bishop felt that it was in her best interest, given her situation and her willingness, to stay in the university ward and work with us. Over the months she just *changed*. I watched the power of the Atonement work its miracle in her life. Her countenance, spirit, language, clothing, everything was transformed. One of the great testaments in my life of the power of the Atonement to change people was to watch that young woman become as pure and wholesome and delightful and lovely and virtuous as any young woman you could ever meet. The Savior's mercy gave her back what she lost. It restored virtue, chastity, and purity to her.

Do you remember the old object lessons we would sometimes see in classes on sin and repentance? You pound a nail into a board and pull it out. Sin is likened to the nail. You can pull it out with repentance, but the hole is there afterwards. I never felt comfortable looking at the hole still in the wood. I reject the whole idea. I think Christ's Atonement re-weaves the fibers of that board as if no nail was ever driven. After long effort on her part, what this young woman lost with her behavior—her virtue and purity—Christ gave back in full restoration. What we lose, we can gain back through repentance and Christ's atoning sacrifice.

A young man, a returned missionary in our ward, began to date her. They fell in love, and toward the end of the spring semester they were engaged—she was as happy and wonderful a young woman as any on campus. During the holidays she would not go back to California because that's where her old life, her Amulon, was lurking. She was trying to avoid that. She was trying to stay out of the wilderness. But then Amulon—the consequences of old behaviors—suddenly came down a path through the woods. Not the boy-Noah she once dated, but Amulon arrived in the form of a troubling question.

She showed up at our house one night and said to me, "Mike, you know somewhat of my past. My fiancé doesn't. I've been struggling. Am I being honest? Should I tell him? I want to do everything right." I didn't know how to answer that question. How would you answer it? I said to her, "Well, as far as I am concerned, the Savior's forgiving mercy has cleansed you. When the Savior says, 'I will mention it no more,' that's pretty good counsel for all of us to follow. I can see some compelling reasons why there would be no need to. On the other hand, if you feel this will always be a wall, a barrier, a problem between you and your future husband, that there would always be that nagging doubt—What if he knew? Would he still have married me?—I can also see a reason that you might want to talk to him." I then added, "If you decide that's what you should do, we'll fast and pray for you that everything will be right. If you decide that's what you want to do, I would just tell him the basics—'I had some moral problems'—and hope that he doesn't ask for details because we shouldn't confess to a friend or a fiancé. I hope that he will be mature enough to handle it and can see what I see—the rebirth of a person, one of perfect purity."

She thought. She pondered. We fasted. We prayed. She came over to the apartment one night and said, "I feel I need to tell him." That night she told him. About two in the morning, a knock came at the door. I opened it. There she was. One look at her, and I knew he had not been able to handle it. He had broken the engagement, and she had given him back the ring. She was absolutely devastated. I remember her saying, "I feel unclean all over again."

We talked into the night. We tried to give her some measure of comfort, help her see hope in the future. As I reflect upon that young man's decision, I try not to judge him. I don't know how I would respond if I was his father and he brought that particular dilemma to me. My sympathies were all with Cindy, of course. My loyalty was to her experience. Maybe it is asking too much of a young man, age twenty-two, to have the spiritual maturity to understand the Savior's ability to cleanse and to purify in that situation—one that comes so close to our deepest needs, hopes, fears, and insecurities. I try not to judge him harshly or to have negative memories of him. But my sympathies were with her. I had seen the Atonement's power in her life and the restoring changes she had undergone. I knew she was worthy of a binding relationship of an eternal nature, a temple marriage.

Can you see Amulon's haunting presence in the wilderness of her life? She repented, just as Alma's people had repented. They had repented—so had she! They were living a good life—she was living a good life. But the Noahs and Amulons are tenacious, or at least their aftereffects can be. They don't want to let go. If they can't keep us in sin, they will still try to keep us in misery. Discouragement is a major weapon. They want to prevent us from moving forward into a new life. We must not let them be victorious!

Toward morning, Cindy began to feel better. Finally, she got up to leave. She went over to the door. I remember it all very distinctly. She stood at the door with her hand on the doorknob for what seemed like a very long time. It was probably no more than thirty or forty seconds, but in the atmosphere created in the room, it seemed like an eternity. I knew she was thinking deeply about something. I knew she had a question she wanted to ask. I sensed what it would be and feared to hear her ask it. She let go of the doorknob and turned around and looked at my wife and me. Then she asked the question: "How long will I have to pay for my sins?"

I didn't have a sufficiently hope-filled answer for her; I failed her because I did not know what to say. Because she *had* paid for her sins, and what is more important, the Savior had paid for her sins. It was obvious to all of us who knew her and knew a little bit of her past that the Savior had cleansed and renewed her just as Alma and his people in the land of Helam had been cleansed and accepted by their God. If he accepts us, who can say, "Nay"?

The Amulons prowl the wilderness and they may come back to haunt our small bounty of happiness. Therefore, may we never suffer the dark limiting scales of King Noah Blindness.

RETURNING TO ZARAHEMLA

Eventually those lost in the wilderness returned to the land of Zarahemla, as I trust Cindy eventually arrived in her land of Zarahemla. I wish I could say the end of the story is that she's married now with eight children and is the Relief Society president in such and such a ward. But we graduated, moved away, and lost contact. I hope she is happily married and that all is well in her life. We do get back to Zarahemla. This was an important moment in my life as I learned the lesson of how dangerous it is to flirt with King Noah Blindness or to allow Amulons into our lives.

I had an opportunity many years later to ask one of the members of the Quorum of the Twelve about this particular situation, because it's always troubled me and I wanted to let it rest. Maybe I told Cindy the wrong thing. I could have said to her: "You don't need to tell. You've been cleansed. The Savior has renewed you. You are born again." I felt comforted in the answer I received: "No one can really give that counsel. Those are important decisions, personal and private, that must be made under the inspiration and guidance of the Spirit. Each must find his own way." I hope and pray for us all that if we ever find ourselves in that situation, or counseling someone in that situation, that we will be given the guidance necessary for us to be wise and to offer the advice that the Lord would have us offer.

Be careful of being King Noah–blind, because even when you get your eyesight restored, the Amulons and Noahs and their influences may still hang around to bring sorrow. This is a gospel of hope and joy, and eventually, through the power of forgiveness and repentance and the kindness of the Savior, everyone gets back to Zarahemla. I have seen it time and time again in my life.

We learn some things about repentance in this story that will provide some final thoughts to ponder. These deal with the attitudes that bring final release. We can compare the people of Limhi and the people of Alma before their safe return to the land of Zarahemla. Let us begin with Limhi's party. What is their response to the Lamanite bondage they have brought upon themselves by their rejection of Abinadi's counsel? Remember, their bondage, their captivity, came as the natural consequence of their own blindness and behavior. When the consequences of King Noah Blindness come upon us, we sometimes try to remove them in an improper way. Notice the key words in the following verse: "And now the afflictions of the Nephites were great, and there was no way that they could deliver themselves out of their hands, for the Lamanites had surrounded them on every side. And it came to pass that *the people began to murmur* with the king because of their afflictions; and they began to be desirous to go against them to battle. And they did afflict the king *sorely with their complaints*" (Mosiah 21:5–6; emphasis added). Murmuring and complaining reveal an inner attitude not yet matured to full liberating repentance.

When I served as bishop, or when I sat on a disciplinary council, or when I dealt with my own children, or when I would listen to a confession or someone was working through the repentance process, I always watched for signs that signaled their attitude. When one faces consequences, the tendency is to murmur and complain. Murmuring and complaining are often indicators that the true spirit of repentance has not yet penetrated deeply in one's heart. I had a young man come into the office who had some moral problems. I said to him, "You won't be able to bless the sacrament for a while as we work through this." Then I waited for and watched his reaction. "You can't do that," he said. "I bless the sacrament every week. Everyone knows that. My parents know that. You might as well broadcast to the whole ward that I've done something wrong." I have total sympathy for this dilemma. Nevertheless, his response, although understandable, consisted mainly of murmuring and complaining. We had to work through that.

Young engaged couples have similar problems occasionally. Unfortunately, many times they make an appointment because they have a problem that needs resolving just three weeks before the wedding with the invitations all mailed. I would say, "We'll need to postpone the wedding, because you'll want to go to the temple and feel the full power and spirit of that holy house. So let's wait for a while. There will be a little embarrassment, but the way you'll feel when you go to the temple and are married without guilt, without fear, without doubts in your heart, will be worth whatever embarrassment." Once again I would watch for their reaction. Many times the couple would say, "We want to do everything right and whatever counsel you say we'll follow." When a couple brought that attitude, I would often say, "Well, it will probably be quicker than later. We can work this out." It's obvious from that response that they have the true spirit of repentance in them. One couple responded, "All the invitations are out. We might as well mail an invitation to everybody telling them we've sinned." Then they went to their student ward, got a recommend from that ward's bishop and stake president, and went to the temple anyway—all of which I discovered later.

A child may murmur and complain when a parent corrects them. As a parent, I always watch for that attitude. The people of Limhi try three times to free themselves from the consequences of their actions, and then we notice an attitude change. Listen for the key words that represent their mind-set: "They did humble themselves even to the dust, subjecting themselves . . . submitting themselves . . . And they did humble themselves even in the depths of humility; and they did cry mightily to God; yea, even all the day long. . . . And now the

Lord was slow to hear their cry because of their iniquities; nevertheless the Lord did hear their cries, and began to soften the hearts of the Lamanites that they began to ease their burdens; . . . and it came to pass that they began to prosper by degrees" (Mosiah 21:13–16). The full load of what they're bearing is not lifted, but God helps them because their attitude is right.

We turn now to Mosiah 21:31. Again, look for the words that indicate an attitude of true repentance. "Now they would have gladly joined with them [meaning Alma the Elder's people out in the wilderness]." *Gladly* is an important word. The truly repentant individual always wants to come back into full fellowship with the Saints. The fact that they want righteous companionship is a positive sign. "They themselves had entered into a covenant with God to serve him and keep his commandments" (Mosiah 21:31). Truly repentant people want to make covenants. It's the most natural thing in the world for those who are repentant to long to have the sacrament, to be baptized, to go to the temple. Their sincere desire is further stated in the very next verse: "King Limhi had also entered into a covenant with God, and also many of his people, to serve him and keep his commandments. And it came to pass that king Limhi and many of his people were desirous to be baptized" (Mosiah 21:32–33).

See that hunger for the covenants! This is why baptism naturally follows repentance. The desire to make covenants is a natural fruit of truly repentant people, but it isn't yet time for that step. Let us look at the people of Limhi's attitude at this juncture: "They did not at that time form themselves into a church, waiting upon the Spirit of the Lord. Now they were desirous to become even as Alma and his brethren, who had fled into the wilderness. [There is that hunger to be with the Saints again.] They were desirous to be baptized as a witness and a testimony that they were willing to serve God with all their hearts; nevertheless they did prolong the time" (Mosiah 21:34–35). Notice the two phrases: *waiting upon the Spirit* and *prolong the time*. Occasionally someone will want to take the sacrament again, or a child wants certain privileges that he's lost, or someone wants to be rebaptized or go back to the temple. Maybe their bishop, stake president, or parent doesn't feel that it's the right time yet. The Spirit hasn't moved them to restore privileges or blessings. They may say, "I feel we need to wait a bit more," then they give further counsel. What will the reaction be? If the person murmurs and complains, the leader or parent knows something. If the person's attitude is "whenever and whatever I need to do, I'll do," the leader or parent also knows something.

With a "whenever and whatever" attitude, do you think they'll be freed pretty quickly? As soon as they hit that point—no murmuring, no complaining, humility, desirous of making covenants, wanting to be with God's people, willing to wait upon the Spirit of the Lord, and prolonging the time—God says, "Okay, let's get you out of there." Before they know it, they arrive in Zarahemla.

CHEERFULLY AND PATIENTLY

Let us shift now from the people of Limhi to those of Alma. They have already made their covenants. They are already humble and submissive. Notice the sweetness of their attitude as stated in Mosiah 24, starting with verse 12: "And Alma and his people did not raise their voices to their Lord their God [they were forbidden by Amulon and the wicked priests], but did pour out their hearts to him; and he did know the thoughts of their hearts. And it came to pass that the voice of the Lord came to them in their afflictions, saying: Lift up your heads and be of good comfort, for I know of the covenant which ye have made unto me [there is that emphasis on covenants again]; and I will covenant with my people and deliver them out of bondage. And I will also ease the burdens which are put upon your shoulders, that even you cannot feel them upon your backs" (Mosiah 24:12–14). The Lord did this for Limhi's people, too. He gave them the strength and the ability to bear the consequences, even though it wasn't quite yet time.

"And now it came to pass that the burdens which were laid upon Alma and his brethren were made light; yea, the Lord did strengthen them that they could bear up their burdens with ease." We then read the following marvelous statement of deep repentance; it is just the opposite of the murmuring, complaining stance first taken by Limhi's people: "And they did submit cheerfully and with patience to all the will of the Lord. And it came to pass that so great was their faith and their patience that the voice of the Lord came unto them again, saying: Be of good comfort, for on the morrow I will deliver you out of bondage" (Mosiah 24:15–16). That last verse seems to suggest that it was their cheerful submitting to God's will with patience that brought the quicker deliverance.

My oldest son is a meek, mellow child. He's married now, but he rarely did anything that displeased us. Once, as a teenager, he came home far too late. He didn't tell us where he'd be, and his mother was worried—my wife won't sleep until everybody is in the house safe and accounted for. This night she was really worried—there was no phone call, and it was hours after he said he would be home. Finally, he arrived home. We talked together about what discipline would be appropriate under the circumstances. God blessed us with good children, so we had rarely ever grounded one of them, but we decided that parental discipline would warrant it this time. So we grounded him for two weeks. I recall saying to him: "Ben, you need to stay here at the house for two weeks. Sorry, you can't go out with your friends. It was so late last night and we were worried!" He said, "Mom and Dad, I'm sorry I did this. I'm at fault, I know. I should have called you. I just got caught up with my friends and I understand why you need to ground me, and I'll be okay. You don't need to feel guilty about it."

Then humbly, quietly, he walked down the stairs, opened the door to his room, went in, and shut the door. I looked at my wife, and she looked at me. "Maybe two hours will be sufficient," I said. Two hours later I went downstairs to talk with our son. "Ben, I'm sure you won't let it happen again. You go ahead and go out with your friends." Cheerful submitting and patient replies invite quick release. If this is true for Mom and Dad, who are not as merciful as Jesus and our Father in Heaven, certainly it will be true for them.

The scriptures always end in hope—always! Esau is not left crying, "Bless me, even me also, O my father" (see Genesis 27:34, 38). Esau is last seen weeping in reconciliation in his brother's arms. Even though he feels that is all he deserves, the prodigal son is not left standing outside the door in the role of servant. His father runs out to embrace him and helps him complete his journey home, putting a ring on his finger, shoes on his feet, the best robe over his shoulders, and killing the fatted calf.

I suppose we will all be King Noah–blind a few times in our lives. I suppose we all will make incorrect decisions and choices regarding the friends and influences we allow into our lives. Maybe they'll stay out in the wilderness and haunt us for a while, but the Book of Mormon's testimony is that if we can learn to submit cheerfully and patiently to all the will of the Lord, if we'll do our very best to change our lives, we will all go home. Everyone returns to Zarahemla. Even the burdensome captivity of Amulon and the wicked priests is removed in time.

May your burdens always be light because you listen to the see-ers, who, if we'll listen to them, will prevent King Noah Moments and very painful experiences in our lives. The see-ers will also always be there to help us complete our journey home, for they see the needs of the soul and the invitation to return home will ever be there. May we never leave Zarahemla—but if we find ourselves lost and momentarily blinded by the seductions of a King Noah, yet in time longing to return, may the Lord help us in our journey. I'm sure he will as he has helped me and all of those I have seen who are cheerfully willing to repent.

CHAPTER SIX

SEEING AS GOD SEES

~

Discovering the Wonder of Ourselves and Others

"WHAT IS MAN?"

Two men in very different circumstances both asked the same question. One was David and the other was Job. The answer to the question was central to the experiences of their lives. It is a question we all ask at some time or another, depending on our needs and circumstances. What was the question?

"What is man?"

David asked it in the awe of reverent wonder while contemplating the heavens. Job asked it in the anguish of suffering, sitting on an ash heap, bereft of family, abandoned by friends, and, temporarily, even by God.

These were David's words: "When I consider thy heavens, the work of thy fingers, the moon and the stars, which thou hast ordained; what is man, that thou art mindful of him? and the son of man, that thou visitest him? For thou hast made him a little lower than the angels, and hast crowned him with glory and honour" (Psalm 8:3–5).

In anguish Job cried out, "Am I a sea, or a whale, that thou settest a watch over me? . . . What is man, that thou shouldest magnify him? and that thou shouldest set thine heart upon him? And that thou shouldest visit him every morning, and try him every moment?" (Job 7:12, 17–18). Here are two men in very different circumstances, both asking the same question.

Both men centered their inquiry in trying to discover what God saw in the most noble of his creations. Both wanted to see with God's eyes and understand with God's mind. This is a desire common to most men and women. However, all of us will ultimately fail in our attempts to see with God's eyes. We see so differently—as we read in Isaiah, "For my thoughts are not your thoughts. . . . For as the heavens are higher than the earth, so are . . . my thoughts than your thoughts" (Isaiah 55:8–9). But if we can grasp even in the smallest way a vision of how our Father in Heaven views us and our mortal experiences—how he answers that most significant question—we will transform our perception of ourselves and our perception of other people. I believe that God is desirous of sharing that vision and will facilitate it for us if we will try to enter into his mind and become more keenly aware of his purposes.

How we answer the question is critical and vitally important. Paul once said, "Now we see through a glass, darkly; but then face to face: now I know in part; but then shall I know even as also I am known" (1 Corinthians 13:12). In the ancient world, bronze discs were finely polished; these were what they used as mirrors. Obviously the reflection was not as clear as a modern mirror. When you saw your face in the polished bronze, the surface was dark. This is what Paul is referring to with the phrase "through a glass, darkly." I think that's a wonderful image for how we all see ourselves and how we see one another, but the day will come when we are promised that we will see as God sees. How does he see? Though we can only see "through a glass, darkly" in our present state, perhaps through the help of some stories, through the clarification of some human experiences, and by the light of some scriptural insight, we can make an attempt at seeing as God sees.

THE BEAUTY UNDERNEATH THE SURFACE

First and foremost, God always sees the beauty under the surface. A few years ago I had an opportunity to take a tour group to the Middle East. We stopped at the Red Sea on the Egyptian-Israeli border. It is a desolate, dry, barren place. I could not see anything green for miles. When we drove across the border, I remember looking around and seeing nothing but rock and sky—nothing seemed to live there. I thought, as I surveyed the dry, desolate scenery, "Whomever God assigned to create this part of his world needs to go back and take Creation 101 again, because he didn't do a very good job here."

Later that day, I put on a snorkel mask and swam just a few feet off the coast to look at the coral reefs. In some places the reef lies just a few inches under the surface of the water. What a different world that was! Beautiful corals of every color, fish of all varieties displaying the most wonderful patterns. Here was life at its fullest! There are few places I have been where one can see more beautiful life than snorkeling in the Red Sea. As I was looking at all that magnificent splendor, I remembered my first judgment of the area. I had condemned this part of the earth's surface as a godforsaken place. As I swam along the surface of the water with my eyes peering into the depths, I could feel God's smile and his laugh—I'm sure he has a delightful laugh. I was enjoying the wonder of his creation which had been hidden from my view by just a few inches of water. When the impression was sufficiently deep the Lord whispered to me, "Michael, you must learn to see all things, and all places, and all people, as you have learned to see today." God always sees the beauty underneath the surface!

When the Lord sent Samuel to anoint a king from among Jesse's sons, and Jesse lined his strong, noble sons up for the prophet to see, Samuel was sure the man he was searching for would be among them. They were all there but the youngest—David. Jesse, himself, failed to even consider David as a possibility. As the older boys passed by, Samuel kept thinking *surely this must be the right one,* but each was rejected. Finally the Lord counseled Samuel, "Look not on his countenance, or on the height of his stature; . . . for the Lord seeth not as man seeth; for man looketh on the outward appearance, but the Lord looketh on the heart" (see 1 Samuel 16:6–7). I repeat: God always sees the beauty under the surface.

THE GALACTIC SETTING

God sees that people matter more than things. On that same trip to the deserts of Egypt, we arose in the middle of the night and drove to the foot of Mount Sinai. There we mounted camels and rode in the darkness to the top of Mount Sinai. I'll never forget watching that long solitary line of camels on the horizon, silhouetted against the night sky, lit by the softness of the moon. There is no light pollution, no dust pollution, and the stars are absolutely magnificent. You can see the band of the Milky Way. As you climb up Sinai you look right into the center of the galaxy. I had a pair of binoculars, and I could focus on different sections of the sky and see the star clusters and the double stars. The Milky Way appears as a waterfall falling from the sky down to the horizon. I remembered as I gazed into the night sky, into that vast, wonderful expanse of creation—perhaps the greatest thing I have ever set my eyes on—that it was in this very setting that God said to Moses, "Look, and I will show [you] the workmanship of mine hands; but not all, for my works are without end. . . . Worlds without number have I created; . . . innumerable are they unto man; but all things are numbered unto me, for they are mine and I know them" (Moses 1:4, 33, 35).

Against the backdrop of that tremendous setting, that cosmic vision of majestic galactic creation spread before the eyes of Moses, God said, "This is my work and my glory—to bring to pass the immortality and eternal life of man" (Moses 1:39). We are more important than galaxies. The first great choice a man ever made on earth reflected that truth—that people matter more than things or places. Given the choice between Eve or Eden, Adam chose Eve. Given the choice between the paradise or the person, the perfect environment or the relationship, he rightly chose the person, the relationship.

In another time and place, Isaiah was looking at the stars and he wrote, "Lift up your eyes on high, and behold who hath created these things, that bringeth out their host by number: he calleth them all by names by the greatness of his might, for that he is strong in power; not one faileth" (Isaiah 40:26). Isaiah describes God as sitting on the horizon of the earth with the heavens spread out before him like a tent in which he dwells (see Isaiah 40:22). Yet, against this immense backdrop again, surrounded by the grandest scenery and the greatest vista one can direct one's eyes toward, the Lord said, "Fear not: for I have redeemed thee, I have called thee by thy name; thou art mine. When thou passest through the waters, I will be with thee; and through the rivers, they shall not overflow thee: when thou walkest through the fire, thou shalt not be burned; neither shall the flame kindle upon thee. . . . Since thou wast precious in my sight . . . I have loved thee" (Isaiah 43:1–2, 4). God sees that people matter more than things, more than galaxies, more than worlds without number. If we matter more than galaxies, we certainly matter more than we often evaluate ourselves and others.

LEAD WITH THE QUEEN

God sees the power within us to do good, and he moves us into positions where we can accomplish it. When I was young I wanted very much to play chess, but there was no one to teach me. So I went down to the public swimming pool and watched the older boys playing chess on the tables surrounding the pool. Every day I picked a new piece on the board and I watched how the older boys used it. I studied the use of the bishops, the rooks, the knights, the pawns, the king, the queen. When I was finished I had at least an elementary education in the tactics of chess.

Because I loved the ranch where I spent my summers as a boy, in my mind, horses were God's noblest creature. In the order of creation, the priority of nobility, I believe, goes from woman, who is the greatest thing God created, to man, to the horse. (There are times where I think it goes woman, horse, man.) At any rate, I loved the knights because of my summer days spent on horseback. I loved the way the knights moved. They could jump over things, and they moved in an L-shaped fashion—two squares over and one up, or one over and two up. Because I was so fascinated with the knights when I played chess, I would always lead with my knights. They were the first two pieces I moved at the beginning of each game. I would jump them over the line of the pawns and maneuver them into attacking position. I always attacked with the knights. Everything I did was focused on the knights. The other pieces were for support. Now, anyone who has played chess knows that the knights are not the most powerful piece on the board. The queen is the most powerful piece on a chessboard. She has the most unfettered movement and the greatest reach. But I didn't lead with my queen. I led with my knights—I would leave the queen standing by the king to protect him against any attack by my opponent. As you can imagine, I did not win very many games. In time, I learned to lead with the queen because she was the most powerful piece on the board. In a manner of speaking, God always leads with the queen. He always sees the power within us and he will move us into positions where we can do good.

I believe there is a very specific application to that memory of playing chess. With all the respect in the world for the men of the Church, I would not hesitate to affirm that God is leading with the queen today. Women in particular are very powerful pieces on the board of life, but they often fail to see themselves as such. They often fail to realize that God today still leads with the queen—with them! I'm grateful that in my life God led with a queen, in particular, my mother. Let me give you an example.

The Lens of a Mother's Soul

When Mary met Elisabeth, as related in the gospel of Luke, she said something that I think is a reflection of the soul of all righteous mothers. She said, "My soul doth magnify the Lord" (Luke 1:46). When we magnify something, we bring it up close and fill our vision with it. I believe that a mother's soul, a woman's soul—also a man's soul to a certain degree—is the lens through which her children first see God. I first saw God through the lens of my mother's soul and she filled my vision with him; he was magnificent. She did it in very simple ways. I loved living things. I loved lizards and snakes . . . and horned toads, frogs, salamanders, rabbits, and turtles. There was a field near our house where I would go out day after day and hunt for these little animals. After having captured them, I would bring them home in triumph to my mother. As I dangled a garter snake in her presence or presented before her eyes a horned toad, she would not say, "Take that filthy thing out of the house!" She would stoop down to my level, eye to eye, look at what I had (she didn't always touch it), and say, "Which of Heavenly Father's little creatures did you bring home today, son?"

I grew up believing God made horned toads for little boys to catch. I still believe it. What other possible purpose could they have? Our family would go to the beach along the Southern California coast and, as the waves receded, the sand crabs would burrow under the sand. I would run forward and scoop my hands underneath them. My mother taught me how to catch these little bullet crabs. They would continue to dig through the sand until they hit my palm and, persisting in their digging, they would tickle my palm. I grew up believing that God made sand crabs to tickle my palm—and a God who made a horned toad for a little boy to catch and a sand crab to tickle his palm is a wonderful God. I am grateful that in my life God led with the queen. God sees the power within us to do good, and he will move us into positions where we can. He will lead with us all!

EMERGING FROM THE COCOON

God sees our potential—the final destination, the polished, liberated character we will one day achieve. Another of the things my mother did to show me the majesty of God was to have me raise caterpillars. We had an elm tree in our backyard and it housed a lot of caterpillars in the spring. I liked to climb the tree, and the caterpillars were sticky and messy so I considered them real pests. Mother said, "Why don't you bring some down?"

So I brought down seven or eight of them and she said, "Go get a jar"—that most useful of objects for little boys. I brought her a great big mason jar and she said, "Now, you feed these caterpillars." We put a stick into the jar for the caterpillars to crawl on. She said, "Every day, bring fresh elm leaves for them and we'll see what happens." So I fed the caterpillars and watched them grow. Eventually they spun their cocoons. Pretty soon I had seven or eight little cocoons dangling from the stick in the jar. We watched and waited for weeks and weeks and finally one day I saw them beginning to split. I'll never forget what a wonderful feeling it was, what a delight it was to see those caterpillars, that once I considered pests, turn into Mourning Cloak butterflies. I remember pulling the stick out of the jar and holding it up to the sun so their wings could dry. Seven or eight butterflies clung to the edges of their broken cocoons. Then, one by one, as their wings dried, they flew off. Wonderful! Simple but wonderful! I have a good friend who once shared with me this thought, "In their caterpillar brains, did they know they would one day fly?" Did they know that, pests though they were, they would one day delight?

MEANIE!

On the ranch where I spent most of my summers as a boy, we had a very mean cow. We called her Meanie. She was a milk cow and believe me, she was a nasty, mean cow. I hated that cow! She would hide in the willows along the river. It was usually my job to bring the cows home at milking time. She'd hide in the willows waiting for me to pass. As I would go by, she would charge and try to pin me right to the ground. She was just mean. She had a dislike for people. When we milked her we had to rope her around the neck and almost choke her into submission. We tied her to the fence. This involved tying her head to the fence poles, tying her back end to the fence, tying her legs to the fence, and tying her outside leg up and to the fence. Then you could milk her . . . cautiously. Every now and then she'd get that back leg free and then—look out! She would kick the milk bucket with all her soul. There are still milk buckets in orbit from Meanie kicking them. She could really kick a bucket!

One day, after she had kicked the milk bucket and my uncle was politely talking to her, I asked him, "Uncle Verland, how come Meanie is so mean?"

And he said, "She thinks she's a range cow and ought to be running wild."

So I said, "Why don't we let her be a range cow and let her run wild?"

He replied, "She's not a range cow. She's a milk cow and a darn good one. She just doesn't know it yet. We're trying to teach her."

There are times when I have worked with people or students when I have thought of that little story. There are times when we may want to give up on somebody. I have experienced that heaviness, that sense of failure or frustration. Each time I can hear my uncle's voice returning from the past. When all I can see is the caterpillar form, the pest stage of some individuals, I can hear him say, "They're sons and daughters of God. They just don't know it yet. We're trying to teach them."

CHOSEN VESSELS

This message is taught time and time again in the scriptures. Let me share just a few of the myriad examples we could call upon as evidence. Joseph Smith described himself as "an obscure boy . . . a boy of no consequence in the world" (Joseph Smith–History 1:22). God saw an inquirer after truth, one who would do "more, save Jesus only, for the salvation of men in this world, than any other man that ever lived in it" (D&C 135:3).

When God told Ananias to give Paul back his sight after Paul's experience on the road to Damascus, Ananias responded with, "I have heard by many of this man, how much evil he hath done to thy saints at Jerusalem" (Acts 9:13). But the Lord told him, "He is a chosen vessel unto me, to bear my name before the Gentiles, and kings, and the children of Israel" (Acts 9:15). Ananias saw a persecutor and an obstacle, a problem. God saw an Apostle, a witness, a key individual in the history of Christianity who would cause it to grow and survive in the world.

When Jesus called Peter to follow him, he multiplied a great catch of fish. As Peter pulled all the fish from the nets into his boat and into James and John's boat, they began to sink. At that moment, Peter sank to his knees at the feet of Jesus saying, "Depart from me; for I am a sinful man, O Lord" (Luke 5:8). But Jesus said unto him, "Fear not; from henceforth thou shalt catch men" (Luke 5:10). Peter felt unworthy of Jesus' presence. However, Christ saw a friend of intimacy worthy to be included in that sacred, most privileged circle of three.

When God called Enoch to teach the people, Enoch said, "Why is it that I have found favor in thy sight, and am but a lad, and all the people hate me; for I am slow of speech; wherefore am I thy servant?" (Moses 6:31). The Lord responded, "Go forth. . . . I will give thee utterance" (Moses 6:32). Enoch believed he was a graceless, inarticulate boy. God saw the builder of Zion, a man who would sanctify his people and lead them to translation.

When the Lord called Gideon, he said to him, "Go in this thy might, and thou shalt save Israel from the hand of the Midianites: have not I sent thee?" (Judges 6:14). But Gideon replied, "Oh my Lord, wherewith shall I save Israel? behold, my family is poor in Manasseh, and I am the least in my father's house" (Judges 6:15). Gideon saw himself as a poor, timid boy. God saw an inspirer of men and the liberator of Israel.

When we see ourselves as God sees us, when we see others as God sees them, we may rise to meet those expectations, and we may inspire others to rise to meet their expectations. May I give you a personal example from a time in my life when a lot of people saw me in the caterpillar stage? I'm not sure I'm a butterfly yet, but I'm absolutely certain that when I was in elementary school I was a caterpillar and a mean cow.

"SATISFACTORY GROWTH"

A few years ago while rummaging in some old boxes, I came across my elementary school report cards. That's an interesting thing to discover in a box— your old report cards. I was nicknamed the "Holy Terror of the Primary," so you can imagine what I was like in school. I was even worse there. When I was barely five years old, my very first teacher wrote on my kindergarten report card: "Michael makes contributions to our group discussions, expressing his opinions. He must be reminded of our rules quite often, thereby taking up more than his share of individual-teacher time. His attention span is short. He will listen to stories." By the second semester I had not improved much. Here is what she wrote. "Michael has become very interested in reading. He still must be reminded of the rules quite often."

I advanced from grade to grade. Here is another sample from Mrs. Lungren; bless her heart, I remember Mrs. Lungren. She was a sweet lady. I took advantage. She wrote: "Michael is very impatient with his written work. If he would relax and work a little slower his papers would be much neater. He must learn to be more considerate of others when they desire to share."

Here is one from Mrs. Rich: "Mike needs to strive for accuracy and neatness in every area of his work. Encourage him to work accurately and to develop handwriting skills." I never did do that. Here is one from another grade: "Mike's major problem is one of adjustment, to think before speaking. Trying to be a good sport is our main objective." Perhaps I should burn these—then I could pretend I had been a model child.

Mrs. Walter writes: "Help Mike to do better in writing. Encourage all of his work habits." Mrs. Miller's contribution includes these words: "Mike's written expression is difficult to understand. He has very poor spelling and illegible writing. He needs to concentrate!"

We used to receive little blue report cards that contained our progress in various areas of school academics and citizenship. They were divided in half. On the left-hand side was growth in character and citizenship. A student could get one of two grades—"Satisfactory Growth" or "Greater Growth Needed." On the right-hand side was growth in skills and knowledge, and you could receive one of the same two grades. There were no letter grades in my elementary school, just these two categories. I usually did fairly well in growth in skills and knowledge, but every report card I got in elementary school on the growth in character and citizenship side read like this: "Works well with others—greater growth needed. Plays well with others—greater growth needed. Shows self control—greater growth needed. Is thrifty with time and materials—greater growth needed. Completes work—greater growth needed. Assumes responsibility towards school and safety rules—greater growth needed." (At least I was consistent.) I used to hate taking my report cards home to my mother. I might point out that she was an elementary school teacher as well. On my third grade report card, in the space left for additional comments, my teacher curtly wrote, "Michael has been promoted to the fourth grade." Can you hear her sigh of relief? She continues: "His writing is quite a problem. He still interrupts continually in class. I hope he will control this next year." I can almost hear her say, "I'm glad I won't have him!"

Which brings me to my fifth grade report card. Mr. Burns was my teacher. He used to give some of his students nicknames. How many of us had a nickname (a good one)? When I was a boy, baseball was the big thing, and in Southern California you were either a Los Angeles Dodgers fan or you were a San Francisco Giants fan. I lived in Southern California which should have made me a Dodger fan, but I idolized Willie Mays. He was my boyhood hero. He could catch a baseball in a very unique manner. He played center field and so I played center field. I was a San Francisco Giants fan in a Dodgers world. That's a bit like being a University of Utah fan in Provo. Willie Mays would catch a baseball by flipping his hand over at the last second and letting the ball drop into his mitt. I tried to catch a baseball that way, but it wasn't natural to me. One day Mr. Burns saw me doing that and he came up to me and said, "Mike, I'll bet I know who your favorite baseball team is."

I said, "Who?"

And he said, "The San Francisco Giants."

I said, "Yes, how did you know?"

And he said, "I'll bet I know who your favorite player is."

I said, "Who?"

And he said, "Willie Mays."

I said, "Yes, how did you know?"

He replied, "Because you catch a baseball like Willie Mays. I'm not going to call you Mike anymore. I'm going to call you Willie because you remind me of Willie Mays."

I would have done anything for Mr. Burns. Mr. Burns saw the potential, saw something good in this "greater growth needed" boy. This is what my fifth grade report card says: "Works well with others—satisfactory growth. Plays well with others—satisfactory growth. Shows self control—satisfactory growth. Is thrifty with time and materials—satisfactory growth. Completes work—satisfactory growth. Assumes responsibility towards school and safety rules—satisfactory growth." Then he wrote this: "Mike is a good boy in every respect. He studies hard. He plays hard. All in all, I am very proud of him. His improvement is in all areas and I know he is aware of this and is trying hard. True, his writing isn't what it could be, but with constant effort and time Mike will find growth and satisfaction here in this area. Keep going, Mike."

God also sees our potential, the final destination, the polished, liberated character. Because he sees it, we will live up to it.

The Jonathan Factor

God does not measure or equate approval or progress by the positions we hold. I wish we could get rid of that whole idea in our thinking. We tend to gauge and measure our approval and our progress in God's sight far too much by position, by callings. We also, perhaps unintentionally, create that misconception by what we say in lessons or talks, and we do it at every level. I'm not being critical or judgmental of any individual in the Church, but at every level we induce this type of assessment. When we are talking to the youth, for example, we say things like, "You will be the future *leaders* of the Church! Somebody, perhaps, in this congregation or this group will be a future Apostle, stake president, bishop, Relief Society president!" As we do this over time, we are in danger of creating in people the feeling that callings in the Church, or positions, are equal to approval and progress.

May I be absolutely honest with you, totally honest, even at the risk of misunderstanding? When I was called to be a bishop, do you know what my very first emotion was? Relief! Please understand that I didn't want to be the bishop. I don't like administration. I'd much rather teach. The classroom is my natural habitat. But I felt relief because being called took the pressure off me of needing to be in a leadership position so I could feel good about myself. Relief!

After ten years of serving in a stake presidency, I realized the emotions and doubts I experienced when I was called as a bishop were not unique. A number of times when we reorganized bishoprics—not every time, but often—someone would say something; ask a tentative question; or, you could see the question in their eyes: "Why was I not called?" These were good men. They were not aspiring. They just wanted to know they were okay, they were qualified. Whenever those times came and I had the opportunity, I would sit down with them and say, "Let me teach you about the Jonathan factor."

In the book of 1 Samuel, the tragedy of Saul is told. Saul was going to be replaced as king. There were two wonderful candidates to succeed him as king of Israel—David, who would be the man anointed by Samuel to be the new king, and Jonathan. Of the two, who was in the most logical position to succeed Saul? Was it not Jonathan? He was Saul's son, and Jonathan, without question, is one of the most remarkable people in scripture. I could make a very good case that Jonathan would have been a better king than David. He was as courageous. He faced a whole garrison of Philistines on his own. David faced one Philistine in Goliath. Jonathan and his armorbearer faced an entire garrison. It is a remarkable but little-known story. Jonathan said to his armorbearer, "Come, and let us go over unto the garrison of these uncircumcised: it may be that the Lord will work for us: for there is no restraint to the Lord to save by many or by few" (1 Samuel 14:6). The two of them then climbed up a very steep cliff on their hands and knees, attacked the whole garrison, defeated them, and sent the entire Philistine army into a panicked retreat. In terms of courage and faith in God, Jonathan was every bit the equal of David.

When David was anointed, Saul felt threatened. He wanted Jonathan to use his friendship with David to have him killed. This was suggested again and again and again. Yet in spite of the pressure, Jonathan supported David. He supported him even though David was taking his place. He is the best male example that I know of in scripture, other than the Savior, who demonstrates by his life Paul's definition of charity, especially that part of the definition that says charity "seeketh not her own" (1 Corinthians 13:5). Jonathan's last encounter with

David is indicative of the majesty of Jonathan's character and fitness for leadership, "Fear not: for the hand of Saul my father shall not find thee; and thou shalt be king over Israel, and I shall be next unto thee" (1 Samuel 23:17). The man's humility and selflessness are unprecedented.

I relate this story because I know there are many Jonathans among us who, figuratively speaking, will never be king, but who display some of the deepest qualities of a godly character. I do not know why God chose David instead of Jonathan, but I am certain it was not because David was a better man, or because God approved of David above Jonathan, or because David had progressed to a higher level than had Jonathan. God does not measure or equate approval or progress by position. Nor must we!

MITE MOMENTS

God sees the importance of the smallest acts; he does not underestimate their value. There are what I call "mite moments" in all of our lives. We are on both the receiving and the giving end of these moments. There are many of these moments in our lives. I get the phrase "mite moments" from the account of Jesus standing in the temple when a certain widow entered. He looked up and saw the rich men casting their gifts into the treasury. "And he saw also a certain poor widow casting in thither two mites. And he said, Of a truth I say unto you, that this poor widow hath cast in more than they all: For all these have of their abundance cast in unto the offerings of God: but she of her penury hath cast in all the living that she had" (Luke 21:2–4).

President Gordon B. Hinckley talked about the widow's mite that he had on his credenza to remind him to be careful with the tithing funds. I don't think that "certain poor widow" even had an idea that Jesus was watching her or that he had made a remark about her. I think she walked to the treasury, put her two mites in, and walked out, unaware that two thousand years of history would watch her—that she would be an inspiration to future prophets and others. We never know the effect of tiny, "mite moments" in our lives, but God sees those effects.

I will give you an example or two by way of illustration of this principle. I remember one day sitting in Primary and the Primary chorister saying, "Children, I'm going to teach you a new song today." It was the one thing I liked in Primary—singing. She said, "I will sing it for you and then you sing it with me." And she sang these words:

The golden plates lay hidden
Deep in the mountainside,

Until God found one faithful,
In whom he could confide.[1]

Her voice was clear and high and beautiful and she took me to Cumorah. I could see Joseph walking up the hill and rolling the stone off and I knew it happened and I wanted to be a good boy so God could confide in me too. I don't remember the name of that Primary chorister. I cannot even bring her face back from my memory. She has no idea that the foundation of my love for Joseph Smith and the Book of Mormon lay in the sound of her voice. It was a mite moment.

When I was about eight years of age we participated in the construction of a new stake center. In those long-ago days the members had to help build their own buildings. The church must be true because none of those buildings fell down.

Our bishop came up to me—I was there because my mother was there working. He saw me standing there by my mother, watching. He said, "Mike, come here." Then he gave me a can of wood putty and a little putty knife. He took me into the chapel. There was beautiful wood paneling all the way around the chapel. He said, "Mike, there are nail holes in all of this paneling. I need you to fill them in with the putty so that Heavenly Father's house will look beautiful and perfect. Could you do that?" He showed me how to apply the putty and then scrape it off smooth. I felt so powerful. I filled all the nail holes in all the paneling of the chapel.

I don't think that bishop had any understanding of what that would mean to me. Every time I went into that chapel, I looked at the oak paneling and thought, *I put the putty in the nail holes in that paneling.* I don't think he realized that he taught me how wonderful it is to do things for God and to feel God's approval and to serve in his church.

When I was twelve years old the stake president called me into his office. I was a brand-new deacon. He said, "Michael, I want you to give the opening prayer in stake conference."

I was terrified, but I said, "Okay." I was a tiny little short kid. I looked about eight. I didn't grow until I started eating pastries during my mission in France. I looked like I was just a little kid, even though I was twelve. They had to lower the pulpit all the way down (and when you're a deacon, you don't want to have to use the little stepstool). I remember standing there, giving the prayer, and being barely able to look over the top of the pulpit. I'm sure I gave just an ordinary, normal prayer. Ten years later—ten years!—I had recently returned from my mission and a sister came up to me and said, "Mike, I need to thank you. You changed my life and I've never told you."

I said, "I can't remember having ever done anything for you."

"Well, you probably won't remember this," she said, "but when you were a little boy you gave an opening prayer in a stake conference."

I said, "I remember that."

She said, "I was struggling with my testimony at the time. I did not think God listened to my prayers, but I came to stake conference and saw a boy pray. It wasn't anything you said, it was just the image of a boy praying and the sense I had inside that the boy believed someone was listening to him. It reawakened all my belief in God, the belief that I had as a little girl. The crisis was over and I never thanked you. You changed my life."

Now, did *I* change that woman's life? No! I said a prayer in stake conference, but it was a "mite moment" for her, and in God's hands these simple things can have profound results. God sees the importance of the smallest acts.

Jacob taught that "the righteous shall have a perfect knowledge of their enjoyment, and their righteousness" (2 Nephi 9:14). I think that might mean that in the hereafter we will know how all of our actions righteously affected everyone else, which thing we don't know now.

IN THE IMAGE OF GOD

God sees his own image in the mirrors of his children's souls. The Lord said, "Let us make man in our image, after our likeness" (Genesis 1:26). We tend to read that verse with the physical body in mind, the outer image: eyes, ears, hands, and legs, but it also means internally. God is compassion. That wonderful trait is also in us. God is patient, longsuffering, kind, and gentle. All these things are in us too, though not yet to the degree and perfection they are in him.

I love the Greek and Russian Orthodox view of the moment in Christ's life we call the Transfiguration. We read in Matthew, "[Jesus] was transfigured before them: and his face did shine as the sun, and his raiment was white as the light. And . . . there appeared unto them Moses and Elias talking with him" (Matthew 17:2–3). In the Orthodox view of that moment, it wasn't only important that Jesus was seen in a glorified state—God appearing as God—but also to show man what he could become. Since man is in the image of God, Jesus was showing all of us our divine potential. We would one day be equally worthy of the company of Moses and Elijah. When you walk into a Greek Orthodox church or a Russian Orthodox church, there are icons all around. It is a little different for us. We don't have icons, but for the Orthodox, the icons are windows to the other world, a sort of portal. The person who is portrayed in the icon, Mary or Peter or James or Andrew or Christ, is there looking through the window and you can communicate in some measure through that window to the person behind. I remember being in a Greek Orthodox church with an Orthodox man who said, looking at the icons with great reverence, "They are all here with us. We are welcome in their company!" I think that is a good way to view the Transfiguration.

I believe God sees his image in our souls and feels we're worthy of the company of Moses and Elijah. He will send people and experiences into our lives to awaken the godliness that is within us. We awaken it in one another. I recall taking my son, McKay, to Guatemala when he was twelve years old. This was his first experience with poverty and I didn't know at the time that it rocked him to the core, but it penetrated deep. Years later, when he had an assignment to write an autobiography for a class, he wrote about those moments in Guatemala: the poverty he saw and how good the people were and how much he had learned to love them. He said, "When people ever say anything negative about Latin American people I hurt inside. I wish I could take them down there and let them see the people. They would never say anything like that again." God saw compassion in the heart of my son, and he awoke it. In those emotions and sentiments, McKay was in the image of God.

I had a teacher when I was a junior in high school named Miss Woodward. I idolized her. She was an English teacher—very tough, very strict. We were studying Dante and she said, "All churches—all Christian churches—believe in a simple concept of heaven and hell."

For some insane reason I raised my hand and said, "Not all Christians believe that."

I should have realized she'd pounce on me and so she said, "Oh, Mr. Wilcox? What do you believe?"

I began to try and explain the Latter-day Saint belief of the three degrees of glory. I made a feeble attempt, hoping she would let it go, but she turned to the class and said, "Students, do any of you have any questions to ask of Mr. Wilcox?"

For a whole hour my fellow classmates grilled me on my beliefs. It was somewhat terrifying for me. During it all, she sat on the stool at the front of the classroom without saying a word. When it was all done, she stopped and said, "Class, we have had a bit of fun at the expense of Mr. Wilcox, but I want you to know that you have seen a rare form of courage today. How many of you could have defended your beliefs in this setting as he has today?"

Coming from her, it was the greatest compliment of my life. I saw myself as timid. I would never have used the word *courage* to describe me, but God has courage and I am made in his image and he sent someone to awaken it in me.

"To Every Man Is Given a Gift"

God sees we are worthy of his most precious gifts. We are told by Joseph Smith that all people have been given a spiritual gift. "All have not every gift given unto them; for there are many gifts," he wrote, "and to every man is given a gift by the Spirit of God. To some is given one, and to some is given another, that all may be profited thereby" (D&C 46:11–12). We all have spiritual gifts. It is God's way of saying, "I need you all." No one need feel about their church attendance, *They won't miss me; I have nothing to contribute,* because we all have something to contribute.

I had an interesting dream once that I will share with you. I was wondering, as Joseph Smith had been just before Moroni appeared, what God thought of me. I wanted to know my station before him, and in response to my ponderings, I had a dream. In the dream I saw myself (interesting the images God chooses as he teaches us) as a ragged child begging in the streets of a medieval village. The roads of the village were covered in cobblestones and the houses were tightly packed along the narrow lanes. If you've been to England or other European countries and you've visited some of those little communities, that's what it was like. My hair was uncombed; I was dressed in rags; I was dirty and begging in the streets. Upon a hill above the village was a beautiful palace where the king lived. The gates swung open, the drawbridge lowered, and the king, a crown on his head filled with bright and precious gems, rode out on a beautiful white horse across the drawbridge and down into the village. He was surrounded by his lords and ladies. I stood at the side of the street with everyone else. As he approached I held up my hand begging—hoping—for something. The king, who I knew represented the Savior, reined his horse to a stop, looked down at me in contemplation and compassion, then took his crown off and turned it in his hand to look at the different gems that were there. After a few moments he pulled out a large green one and laid it in my hands. Then he said, "Lift it up high and let the light catch it. Let it shine out for all the people to see its beauty." He then rode on. I looked at my gift, my jewel. I lifted it up as he told me and it caught the rays of the sun and sent beautiful green light into every corner of the village. The people came running to see the beautiful light and in its radiance I, too, looked like a king. But I knew I was just a beggar boy in rags with uncombed hair.

All of us have been given a gem from the crown of Christ whose light will make us look like kings, whose light will draw others and bless them. God says to all of us, as he said to Solomon, "Ask what I shall give thee" (1 Kings 3:5). Solomon replied, "I am but a little child: I know not how to go out or come in. . . . Give therefore thy servant an understanding heart to judge thy people, that I may discern between good and bad" (1 Kings 3:7, 9).

Paul affirmed that everyone receives a gift from the Lord. He compared them to the various parts and functions of the human body. The eye doesn't say to the ear, "I don't need you" and the hand doesn't say to the foot, "I don't need you." Nor does the ear say, "Because I'm not the eye and I can't see, I'm not important, I'm not part of the body" (see 1 Corinthians 12:11–21). We all have been given gifts. We all have wonderful things to offer. We all have our gems to hold up so that their light can bring beauty into the lives of one another. God sees us as worthy of his most precious gifts.

RACING CHINESE CHARIOTS

God does not see with comparing eyes. Unfortunately, most of us *do* see with comparing eyes. I love a story that I found a number of years ago. It comes from the wisdom of a Chinese philosopher named Han Fei. He relates a story about a chariot driver and a king. I believe it is based on a real historical encounter. The story goes something like this: There was a great king who wanted to learn to race chariots. So he brought the greatest chariot driver in China to his kingdom to teach him. But no matter how hard the chariot driver tried, the king just couldn't do it right. Finally his teacher said, "When you fell behind, you became so anxious you whipped your horses madly. When you overtook me, you were so worried that I might catch up that you rushed forward without any concern for your horse. You were so focused on my chariot you did not mind your own. And, being so tense and anxious, how can you ever possibly drive well?"

That is, sadly, far too often the way we drive the chariots of our lives. If someone is ahead of us we may perceive they are better and we despair. If we're ahead of somebody else we might feel pride. Paul wrote to the saints in Galatia, "Let every man prove his own work, and then shall he have rejoicing in himself alone, and not in another" (Galatians 6:4).

I think it is interesting that when Jesus asked his disciples both in the Old and in the New World, "What can I do for you? What do you desire of me when I go to my father?" Peter wanted to be with Christ immediately after he had finished his work on the earth. John, however, wanted to stay and work with people. Peter, it appears, then felt maybe he hadn't chosen correctly. He did what we all do. He compared his request of Christ with John's request and wondered where he stood in God's eyes based on it. Jesus said, "I say unto thee, Peter, this was a good desire; but my beloved has desired that he might do more . . . yet among men. . . . Verily I say unto you, ye shall both have according to your desires, for ye both joy in that which ye have desired" (D&C 7:5, 8). There was no ranking, one was not better than the other, and both choices would bestow joy.

Interestingly, just the opposite thing happened with the three Nephites. When the nine Nephite Apostles said in answer to the same question, "We desire that after we have lived unto the age of man, that our ministry . . . may have an end, that we may speedily come unto thee in thy kingdom" (3 Nephi 28:2). Jesus said, "Blessed are ye because ye desired this thing. . . . After that ye are seventy and two years old ye shall come unto me in my kingdom; and . . . find rest" (3 Nephi 28:3). Then he turned to the three who were silent: "What will ye that I should do unto you? . . . They sorrowed in their hearts, for they durst not speak unto him the thing which they desired" (3 Nephi 28:4–5). They felt, perhaps, their desire, compared to the other nine's desires, would not be appropriate. But Jesus said, "Blessed are ye, for ye shall never taste of death" (3 Nephi 28:7).

We compare too much. God told Joseph Smith, "In temporal labors thou shalt not have strength, for this is not thy calling" (D&C 24:9). Are we not grateful that Joseph Smith did not compare himself in temporal labors to other people? In spiritual labors he was among the greatest, but in temporal affairs he was lacking. God does not see with comparing eyes.

"WICKED MAN" TO WITNESS

God ceases to see the negatives of the past. Whenever I go to the Peter Whitmer farm, where the Church was organized, I usually don't think about the events of April 6, 1830. I like to get away from the farm and out into the woods where the Three Witnesses saw the golden plates, because those woods are to me one of the most merciful places on earth. Martin Harris always comes to my mind when I roam those woods. Martin lost 116 pages of the Book of Mormon manuscript, and that is not a small thing to do. That is a sin none of us can commit. He lost 116 pages of sacred writing. In Doctrine and Covenants 3, the Lord does not mince any words when talking to Joseph Smith about the actions of his friend. Martin had pushed Joseph to give them to him. The Lord was not pleased. Notice particularly what God calls Martin Harris as a result of that precious loss of scripture: "When thou deliveredst up that which God had given thee sight and power to translate, thou deliveredst up that which was sacred into the hands of a wicked man, who has set at naught the counsels of God, and has broken the most sacred promises which were made before God" (D&C 3:12–13). When I read those words I say, "Ouch! Martin Harris was a wicked man . . . a *wicked* man?"

I say, "No, Lord, you mean *weak* man, not *wicked* man. He was a weak man." However, if we turn to Doctrine and Covenants 10:1, the Lord calls him a wicked man again.

On the morning the Three Witnesses were to see the golden plates, Joseph Smith came into the Peter Whitmer house and said, "'Martin Harris,' . . . '*you* have got to humble yourself before your God this day. . . . If you will do this, it is God's will that you and Oliver Cowdery and David Whitmer should look upon the plates.'"[2]

"It is the will of God . . ." Thrilling words! Martin Harris went from "wicked man" to witness, and that's a remarkable thing.

After he had seen the plates, he came into the house and said, "I bless God in the sincerity of my soul that he has condescended to make me, even me, a witness of the greatness of his work."[3]

Ezekiel testifies, "All his transgressions that he hath committed, they shall not be mentioned unto him: in his righteousness that he hath done he shall live" (Ezekiel 18:22). And Paul, viewing his own rather troubled past, wrote to the Philippian Saints, "Brethren, I count not myself to have apprehended [I've not achieved perfection; I've not achieved the celestial kingdom]: but this one thing I do, forgetting those things which are behind, and reaching forth unto those things which are before, I press toward the mark for the prize of the high calling of God in Christ Jesus" (Philippians 3:13–14). God ceases to see the negatives of the past.

How Come You're So Old?

One final thought on seeing as God sees—we certainly haven't exhausted our search, but hopefully this is a good beginning. God does not see with impatient or discouraged or anxious eyes. I remember once asking my grandfather, who died when he was ninety-three, "Grandpa, how come you're so old?" I was a little kid and he looked pretty old to me. He was probably in his late seventies then. For me, eighty is not looking quite so unattainable anymore. He smiled, thought for a minute, and then he answered, "Well, Mike, the Lord can make a good man out of some people in forty or fifty years, but your grandpa was a hard nut to crack. It will take God eighty or ninety years to make a good man out of me—but he's patient."

I remember trying to teach my oldest son how to swim. For some reason, he was terrified of the water. Teaching that boy how to swim was an agony. I was raised in Southern California, where you learn to swim when you learn to walk. I felt it was important for him to swim and yet sometimes I got discouraged. I'm sure that as my son looked into my eyes he saw that discouragement. We were working on merit badges for Scouts, and swimming was a critical talent. There were times when he looked into my eyes and could see the impatience, the discouragement, the frustration of an imperfect dad and the anxiety that he would never achieve success. Sometimes, I have to admit, I thought, *I guess it doesn't matter if my son learns how to swim or not. He'll still probably survive.* When he noticed I was wavering, bordering on giving up the lessons, he would look at me and his eyes would say, "Dad, don't give up on me. I'm trying. I want to swim. I'm afraid. Don't give up on me." I could never turn away from those eyes, and in time he learned how to swim.

Sometimes I say to God—as I strive for perfection—as my son's eyes said to me, "Father, don't give up on me. I'm trying. Don't let me fail. Please don't get discouraged." I'm always directed by the Spirit to the words of Isaiah when he wrote, "[God] shall not fail nor be discouraged, till he have set judgment in the earth" (Isaiah 42:4). Then I hear the Lord say, "Michael, if I'm not going to be discouraged until the whole world is a place of righteousness and judgment, do you think I'm going to be discouraged with you, when you want so badly to please me and to conquer yourself? I don't get discouraged. Discouragement is not part of my character. I am not impatient. I am never anxious. I do not give up. Keep trying."

There is another wonderful story from China. (I'm becoming quite fond of Chinese literature.) A Chinese philosopher named Mencius told this story. It's called "Helping the Seedlings to Grow":

"You must not be like the man from Sung. There was a man from Sung who pulled at his seedlings because he was worried about their failure to grow. Having done so, he went on his way home, not realizing what he had done. 'I'm worn out today,' he said to his family. 'I have been helping the seedlings to grow.' His son rushed out to take a look and there the seedlings were, all shriveled up."

He had pulled each of them up, just enough out of the ground to kill them all. Then Mencius says, "There are very few in the world who can resist the urge to help their seedlings to grow."[4] We must be patient with ourselves and with others. We may do damage to ourselves if we try to pull ourselves into perfection too quickly.

One of my favorite verses of the Doctrine and Covenants are these tender words Jesus offers us imperfect beings: "Verily, verily, I say unto you, ye are little children, and ye have not as yet understood how great blessings the Father hath in his own hands and prepared for you; and ye cannot bear all things now; nevertheless, be of good cheer, for I will lead you along. The kingdom is yours and the blessings thereof are yours, and the riches of eternity are yours" (D&C 78:17–18). In other words, "You're going to make it. You're going to be all right. I'm going to get you there and I'm not going to be discouraged and I'm not impatient and I'm not anxious about you." God does not see with impatient, discouraged, or anxious eyes.

DARKNESS TO A WORLD OF COLOR

One of the great stories in the New Testament is about seeing. It is the healing of the man born blind. The Savior takes some clay and he puts the clay on the young man's eyes and then he says, "Go, wash in the pool of Siloam" (John 9:7). The young man follows the Savior's instructions. He washes in the pool of Siloam and he leaves the place seeing. I often try to visualize in my mind the stories of the scriptures. I try to put myself in the position of that young man. What must it have felt like to see for the very first time? You and I can't remember that experience, can we? We can't remember it; we were babies. We were born seeing. But what must it be like to be born in absolute darkness and suddenly one day, as the clay is washed away, to look up and see the trees, and the blue sky, and people's faces; to see colors and light and shadows for the first time ever? What a dramatic and powerful moment that must have been for him.

I have a feeling that one day in the future we will all have a similar experience when the dust of the earth, when the clay of this mortal life, is washed away and for the first time we see ourselves as God sees us and we see others as God sees them. Surely that will be just as remarkable an experience. It will be like going from darkness into the brightest light of day and we will see all the radiance and all the colors and all the beauty that we could not see here because the dust of mortality is in our eyes.

May you and I not see in a "glass, darkly" as Paul indicated in his hymn to charity. May we learn to see as God sees and help each other to see as God sees, that we may live up to and become all that he sees in his children.

WHEN ALL ETERNITY SHOOK

~

Finding Hope and Healing in the Savior's Sacrifice

THE FEARS OF OUR LIVES

When I was little, I had a fear and a terror of roller coasters. Every time we would go to an amusement park, all my friends would want to ride the roller coaster. Even with all that peer pressure, I just could not get myself on the roller coaster. I had the very real sense that once the cars reached the top and began their rapid plunge toward the bottom that they would just keep going—right through the tracks and into the bowels of the earth. Now, I knew intellectually that my fear was not realistic, but emotionally, I could not get over it. What was fun and thrilling for others was pure agony for me. Consequently, I have never ridden a roller coaster.

I have noticed, as I am sure you have, that most people have fears and that most of those fears are not very rational. A large percentage of our anxieties have nothing to do with logical analysis of the potential harm or danger. My wife and I travel a lot, directing tours to foreign countries. I've observed many people who are nervous, either about traveling on airplanes or to the Middle East when we're visiting Israel and Jerusalem. I have gathered a few statistics about various risks, both to assuage their fears and mine. Statistically, one's chances of dying of heart disease are one in 300, and those chances increase to a great extent if one does not take a vacation for five years or more. My chances of dying in a car accident are one in 18,800; of falling in my house, one in 20,700; of dying in a car/pedestrian accident while crossing the street, one in 45,200; a boating accident, one in 402,000; skiing or snowboarding, one in 6,330,000; dying in an airline accident, one in 8,450,000. I would have to fly every single day for 8,200 years to be in an accident with multiple fatalities. The odds of dying of a terrorist attack are one in 9,270,000; and my original fear, dying at an amusement park on a roller coaster: one in 70,000,000.[1] But I have still not yet ridden a roller coaster. Rational thought and fear do not seem to be consistent companions.

Most of us deal with our fears to a lesser or greater extent, and fear of roller coasters is not my major fear. The major fear that I have—and I have observed this fear in many members of the Church—is the fear of failure. This is an anxiety I'm not sure we need to experience as much as we do, but I think many of us will understand the nervousness I will try to describe. I fear, and I think many of us do, failing the great test of life, and just missing the celestial kingdom. Most Latter-day Saints don't fear that they're going to miss celestial glory by miles; we fear we're going to miss it by inches, or fractions of inches. We have what I describe as a "B+ personality."

THE B+ PERSONALITY

When I was a boy I tried very hard to get As. I would work diligently on an assigned paper, or I would study for a big exam, hoping, anticipating, that this time I would get an A. When the teacher would hand back my paper or my test, on the front page I would see, in red, the grade: B+. Because my teachers knew that I was trying so very hard, they would try to assuage my disappointment by writing "Great Effort!" on the paper. This was supposed to make me feel good, which, of course, it never did because I wanted the A. This illustrates what I fear. One day I'm going to stand before the Lord, the Teacher of all teachers, at the judgment bar, the Test of all tests, and he's going to say, "Mike—Great Effort! B+."

Then I'll say, "But I wanted the A, Lord."

He'll respond, "I know, and you tried very hard, and I have a lovely kingdom for B+ people." This is my fear and my anxiety. And again, I think many Latter-day Saints share this apprehension.

I love a quote I've heard by Michelangelo Buonarroti, who once said, "Despite thy promises, O Lord, 't would seem / Too much to hope that even love like thine / Can overlook my countless wanderings."[2] There is a Book of Mormon equivalent to Michelangelo's words. It is a verse that we all love as Latter-day Saints, contained in what has been called "Nephi's hymn," in 2 Nephi 4. We resonate with Nephi's emotions because he so profoundly states how we often feel ourselves. Nephi loves and wants to delight in the things of the Lord. He writes, "My soul delighteth in the scriptures, and my heart pondereth them. . . . My heart pondereth continually upon the things which I have seen and heard" (2 Nephi 4:15–16).

We understand that feeling. We all have it. God has been good to us. We want to rejoice in his goodness. But then Nephi voices that nagging, tugging anxiety we all sometimes feel as we view our failures. "Nevertheless, notwithstanding the great goodness of the Lord, in showing me his great and marvelous works, my heart exclaimeth: O wretched man that I am!" (2 Nephi 4:17). Nephi here echoes Paul's words, who said the same thing when he expressed a similar dilemma. (See Romans 7:24.)

"O wretched man that I am!" Nephi cries. "Yea, my heart sorroweth because of my flesh; my soul grieveth because of mine iniquities. I am encompassed about, because of the temptations and the sins which do so easily beset me. And when I desire to rejoice, my heart groaneth because of my sins" (2 Nephi 4:17–19). Then Nephi offers a wonderful and profound truth. He says, "Nevertheless, I know in whom I have trusted" (2 Nephi 4:19). Sometimes we miss that last aspect. What does Nephi trust in? He trusts in the very thing he had mentioned earlier—The Great Goodness of Christ.

THE GREAT GOODNESS OF CHRIST

Occasionally I have an urge to edit—to re-write—some verses of scripture. Fortunately the Lord has never given me the opportunity, but every now and then I feel the desire. I tend to edit everything I read anyway. Let us suppose the Lord gave me the chance. If he said, "Mike, you can edit one scripture," I would pick the fourth article of faith. This is how I would change it: "We believe that the first principles and ordinances of the Gospel are: first, faith in *the great goodness, mercy, longsuffering, patience, willingness to forgive, and compassion of* the Lord Jesus Christ. . . ." This is what Nephi trusted in and what Michelangelo alluded to. We trust in the personality and perfect character of our Savior that overflows with mercy. We hear of the "tender mercies" of the Lord quite frequently. It is a wonderful descriptive phrase, but I submit that "great goodness" is equally powerful.

Later in the Book of Mormon we read of King Benjamin's emphasis on this quality of Christ. He says, "If the knowledge of the *goodness of God* at this time has awakened you, . . . if you have come to a knowledge of the *goodness of God,* and his matchless power, and his wisdom, and his patience, and his longsuffering towards the children of men; and also, the atonement which has been prepared from the foundation of the world, that thereby salvation might come to him who should put his trust in the Lord, . . . I say unto you as I have said before, that as ye have come to the knowledge of the glory of God, or if ye have known of *his goodness* and tasted of his love . . . [this causes] exceedingly great joy in your souls" (Mosiah 4:5, 6, 11; emphasis added).

Others in the scriptures speak of the goodness of Christ. David wrote in Psalms, "The goodness of God endureth continually" (Psalm 52:1). The Lord described himself to Moses as "merciful and gracious, longsuffering, and abundant in goodness and truth" (Exodus 34:6). Jeremiah told us that the people would "flow together to the goodness of the Lord" (Jeremiah 31:12). In the Doctrine and Covenants the Lord himself tells us, "Blessed are ye if ye continue in my goodness" (D&C 86:11).

"I UNDERSTAND!"

When others are going through trials or facing difficult problems, there are two ways that we express that we understand each other. The most natural thing in the world for us to say in such situations is "I understand." Sometimes when we say "I understand," our understanding is viewed through the lens of empathy. We have not been through others' specific problems, but we think we know what it would feel like. We project our own souls onto the life experience of another. We try to put ourselves in our friend's shoes and say to him or her, "I understand!" The Spirit helps us immeasurably in this endeavor. In a certain sense, the Holy Ghost is the great empathizer and he can share his perspective with us. Occasionally those we are trying to empathize with might look at us and say, "Do you really? Do you really understand? How can you? You have not been through what I'm going through." That is the first type of understanding, one created by our empathy and enhanced by the Holy Spirit.

The other type of "I understand" comes directly from our own personal experiences. They too may be enhanced by the Spirit, but there is a depth of reality to our feelings. When we say "I understand" to someone, we are saying, "I understand your situation, challenges, grief, or trial because I have been through the same kind of experience myself."

Of the two varieties of "I understand," which does Jesus want to say to us? In which does his goodness consist? His goodness came from his premortal character, certainly, but that was refined and a dimension added to it when he took upon him flesh and shared mortality (and all that that word implies) with us. During his mortal life his goodness was deeply personalized because he wanted to say to us all, no matter our sorrows, "I understand," in the second way. Alma testified to this truth when he wrote of Christ's mortal experiences. Notice in the following verses the specific kinds of occurrences the Savior wanted to know by enduring them in his own life. "He shall go forth, suffering *pains* and *afflictions* and *temptations of every kind;* and this that the word might be fulfilled which saith he will take upon him the pains and the *sicknesses* of his people. And he will take upon him *death,* . . . and he will take upon him their *infirmities*" (Alma 7:11–12; emphasis added). Notice the critical key words in this passage: *pains, afflictions, temptations, sicknesses, death, infirmities.*

Without doubt, the Savior also knew joy and happiness and peace and love and laughter. He had to be the happiest man who was ever born because, according to Lehi, righteousness is happiness (see 2 Nephi 2:13), and no one was more righteous than our Savior. But he wanted to understand the more negative painful moments of life, and Alma tells us why. He did this all "that his bowels may be filled with mercy, according to the flesh, that he may know according to the flesh how to succor his people according to their infirmities. Now the Spirit knoweth all things; nevertheless the Son of God suffereth according to the flesh" (Alma 7:12–13). Alma explains that Jesus could have comprehended, through the Spirit, all of life's experiences—he had a depth of spiritual empathy we cannot fathom—but there was an added dimension to his goodness which came because he himself had been through mortality at its most demanding levels.

Paul also spoke of the Savior's ability to comprehend our lives in the second type of "I understand." He said, "For verily he took not on him the nature of angels; but he took on him the seed of Abraham. Wherefore in all things it behoved him to be made like unto his brethren, that he might be a merciful and faithful high priest in things pertaining to God, to make reconciliation for the sins of the people. For in that he himself hath suffered being tempted, he is able to succour them that are tempted" (Hebrews 2:16–18).

Succor is a Latin word whose roots suggest the idea of running to help or to aid. Paul later says, "Seeing then that we have a great high priest, that is passed into the heavens, Jesus the Son of God, let us hold fast our profession. For we have not an high priest which cannot be touched with the feeling of our infirmities [same word Alma used]; but was in all points tempted like as we are, yet without sin. Let us therefore come boldly unto the throne of grace that we may obtain mercy, and find grace to help in time of need" (Hebrews 4:14–16).

APPROACHING THE THRONE OF GRACE

How can we come boldly to the throne? To illustrate: I am a great fan of C. S. Lewis, and C. S. Lewis was a great fan of a man named George MacDonald. George MacDonald possessed a sweet spirituality rare in most men. I have not found anyone who describes our Father in Heaven in as wonderful a way as MacDonald. I've often said, "I want to be judged by George MacDonald's God." MacDonald preached lovingly and in the spirit of invitation. He was a minister in the Protestant faith, and some of his fellow clergymen felt that he was making God too good and teaching doctrines that, in their minds, bordered on heresy. So they effectively fired him, obtained his resignation, and he no longer preached—his ideas were too controversial. He wrote a book called *Unspoken*

Sermons. In that lively and profoundly beautiful book he teaches something about how we can boldly come to the throne of Christ:

"How the earthly father would love a child who would creep into his room with an angry, troubled face, and sit down at his feet, saying when asked what he wanted: 'I feel so naughty, papa, and I want to get good!' Would he say to his child: 'How dare you! Go away, and be good, and then come to me'? And shall we dare to think God would send us away if we came thus, and would not be pleased that we came, even if we were angry as Jonah? Would we not let all the tenderness of our nature flow forth upon such a child?"[3]

When I was working on my Ph.D., my committee chairman taught me a lesson about how we can come boldly to the throne of God. Earlier in his life he had been through the doctoral process, and he knew the anxiety that the final defense of a dissertation can create. He understood the process by experience. He sensed I had certain anxieties as I began that process. So he said to me, "Now, Mike, I don't want you to have any unease about your Ph.D. You will obtain your Ph.D. I will not let you into the examination room with the other professors on your committee to defend your dissertation until I know without question you will pass. I've been through a lot of dissertations, so you can trust my judgment. When you walk in the room, you will know that you have your Ph.D., and I will not stop helping you until I get you to that position."

And thus, when I defended my Ph.D., I went into that room with absolute confidence. I think the Savior says a similar thing to us. I think he says to us, effectively, "I understand what you are going through. I will not stop working with you until I know that when I present you before my Father that he will be as pleased with you as he was with me. You may grow and live and learn and fail and correct your mistakes and do it all without fear or anxiety." The judgment we will all face one day will be, in the words of Jacob and Moroni, "the pleasing bar of God" (see Jacob 6:13; Moroni 10:34), not a fearful or an anxious place.

THE BITTER CUP

I've often been interested in introductions. I like short introductions. We hear too many long introductions. I always thought it was wonderful that the Savior himself was introduced to Joseph Smith in less than ten words. Introductions tell you what the person doing the introducing feels is important about the individual who is going to speak. This is also true of self-introductions. They indicate those things about yourself you want people to know about you. I've been fascinated with the way that the Father introduces the Son and the way that the Son introduces himself. To the Nephites, Jesus introduced himself this way: "I am the light and the life of the world" (3 Nephi 11:11). We must understand that introduction in the context of the three days of darkness which they were experiencing when Jesus told them he was the light. In the same verse we read these introductory words: "I have drunk out of that bitter cup which the Father hath given me, and have glorified the Father in taking upon me the sins of the world, in the which I have suffered the will of the Father in all things from the beginning" (3 Nephi 11:11).

One thing the Savior wants us to know about him is that he drank the bitter cup. His goodness, the focal point of his goodness, of his mortal experience, was during that atoning period, particularly in Gethsemane. Here his understanding of life by experience came to its highest fruition. The metaphorical image that he uses is the bitter cup. The figurative symbol of the bitter cup comes from Isaiah originally, where it is called the "cup of fury," and the "cup of trembling" (Isaiah 51:17), and it needs to be visualized. Notice how the Savior speaks of this cup in another place when he talks about his own sacrifice: "For behold, I, God, have suffered these things for all, that they might not suffer. . . . Which suffering caused myself, even God, the greatest of all, to tremble because of pain, and bleed at every pore, and to suffer both body and spirit—and would that I might not drink the bitter cup and shrink—" (D&C 19:16,18).

If we visualize the image of the bitter cup we come to understand its symbolic power. When we drink something very bitter the body naturally shakes or trembles. If you were to drink a glass of strong vinegar or something equally bitter, your body would react instantly. I once taught this concept in a family home evening with my children. I wanted them to understand the metaphor of drinking the bitter cup, so I gave them a little cup of vinegar to drink and they trembled—they actually shook. It is a natural response. That is the image of the Savior which he used himself during his atoning hour. He spoke of that cup in his prayer from Gethsemane. He used the image of the cup in his deepest, most earnest moment (see Luke 22:44), when he pleaded in Gethsemane with his Father.

THE THREE PRAYERS OF GETHSEMANE

There are three recorded prayers from Gethsemane, or at least three versions of the same prayer. I don't think we have to choose which of the gospel writers is most correct, for they are all poignant and beautiful, yet they teach different truths all of which we can relate to. I favor Mark's version, but all of them tell us something about that moment in the Savior's life. We too pray in each of these ways in our own lives. Matthew records the prayer thus: "And he went a little further, and fell on his face, and prayed, saying, O my Father, if it be possible, let this cup [this bitter cup of trembling] pass from me: nevertheless not as I will, but as thou wilt" (Matthew 26:39). Do we not often pray in a similar vein? "Father if it be possible . . ." When we pray this way, the answer we desire is a matter of possibilities. It may not be possible. If it isn't possible, we will understand, but if it's possible that God can take away this trial or bring the hoped-for blessing, we would want God to do so.

Mark's prayer is more deep and poignant. The idea of possibility is removed. Mark's account is thus: Jesus pleaded, "Abba, Father, all things are possible unto thee; take away this cup from me: nevertheless not what I will, but what thou wilt" (Mark 14:36). *Abba* is a word used especially by a child, a little trusting child, to his father. It means *daddy* or *papa*. Have we not prayed this way also? "Father, thou canst do all things! Give me this blessing. Take away this trial." The question of possibility is removed in the prayer in Mark. All that is left is a cry from the innermost realms of the soul. Can a loving Father refuse such a prayer from his beloved trusting child?

The prayer in Luke doesn't present it as a matter of possibility at all. It's a matter of what God wills: "And he was withdrawn from them about a stone's cast, and kneeled down, and prayed, Saying, Father, if thou be willing, remove this cup from me: nevertheless not my will, but thine, be done" (Luke 22:41–42). This is what we might call, in a certain sense, a hinting prayer or request. We hope that God wants what we want, as a child might come to his parent and say, "If it's all right with you, this is what I desire." Regardless of which version you favor, Christ took the cup of trembling because the answer to his prayer, whichever account you prefer, was, "It is not possible. Too much is necessary for my other children that depends on these intensely painful moments."

So Jesus began to drain the bitter cup. He drinks it all through Gethsemane. It is easy to visualize the shaking that accompanied drinking that extremely bitter cup. He drank it through his trial before the Sanhedrin as well as the trials before Herod and Pilate. He drank it through Calvary and the crucifixion and finally arrived at that moment on the cross near the end when he made one request for himself. Two simple words! They are the simplest request a man in pain can make: "I thirst" (John 19:28). What did they give him? Luke writes, "The soldiers also mocked him, coming to him, and offering him vinegar" (Luke 23:36)—vinegar is bitter. David, in the Psalms, looking forward with prophetic vision to that same moment, voiced the Savior's own feelings at the moment when the vinegar was given. In Psalm 69, David wrote, "I looked for some to take pity, but there was none; and for comforters, but I found none. . . . and in my thirst they gave me vinegar to drink" (Psalm 69:20–21). When Jesus tastes the proffered vinegar, he knows that he has drunk the bitter cup to the very last drop. He then says, "Father, into thy hands I commend my spirit" (Luke 23:46). It is finished, and he dies.

THE BREAD AND THE WATER

Because he drank the bitter cup for us, there is something appropriate that you and I do every week. We also drink a cup. We drink a cup as part of the sacrament to remind us that our Savior drank the cup of trembling in our behalf. There are two symbols of the sacrament: bread and water. There were two major consequences of the fall of Adam: physical death and spiritual death. The two symbols of the sacrament correlate to those two consequences. The bread is to remind us that Jesus conquered physical death through the power of the Resurrection. When the Savior showed the Nephites his body and gave them the sacrament bread, he told them to remember this body "which I have shown unto you" (3 Nephi 18:7)—the resurrected body. The bread reminds us of the Resurrection. In like manner, the cup of water that we drink reminds us that Christ conquered spiritual death. He overcame our sins through his mercy—mercy that was again intensified in those moments in Gethsemane. In the sacrament we have one symbol for physical death and one symbol for spiritual death.

One Sunday when I was feeling "wretched," as Nephi mentioned, feeling concerned about "the sins which do so easily beset me" (2 Nephi 4:18), I had an epiphany while I partook of the sacrament. As I was pondering during those memorial minutes the Spirit said, "Always remember him!" I thought that the Spirit meant I was to think of him with greater gratitude, because when we take the sacrament we do it in gratitude and thanksgiving as we are the recipients of his mercy. I tried to feel more intensely grateful, and the Spirit whispered a second time, "Always remember him!" Once again I tried to reach a deeper level of gratitude. I said, "I do. I am. I'm thankful. I honor him." But I was not receiving the message. A third time the Spirit said, "Always remember him . . . in hope." The sacrament is a time of hope, a time to remember the great goodness of Christ, to remember that he understands our challenges and will forgive. From that time on the sacrament has been a memorial of hope as well as one of gratitude and praise.

BEARING TESTIMONY EVERY SUNDAY

Paul taught something significant about the sacrament. He said, "For as often as ye eat this bread, and drink this cup, ye do shew [or proclaim or announce] the Lord's death till he come" (1 Corinthians 11:26). The sacrament is certainly a memorial, but it is also a testimonial. I have sometimes heard criticism leveled at the members of the Church for offering in fast and testimony meeting what are termed "thank-u-monys" or travelogues instead of heartfelt testimony of the gospel. I suppose there may be some justification for those criticisms, especially when we get only one testimony meeting a month. But Paul indicated that the sacrament itself is an open proclamation of our faith in Christ. The very fact that we drink the cup and partake of the bread announces to everyone in the congregation: "I bear witness that Jesus is the atoning Christ who conquered death, both physically and spiritually." Each Sunday, therefore, is testimony Sunday, and every Sunday that we partake of those emblems, we bear our testimonies. Is not the most important testimony one can bear a declaration that Jesus truly is our Redeemer? The next time you take the sacrament, consciously think in your mind, "Today I bear my witness to everybody who sees me by this outward act that I have faith in the atoning sacrifice of Jesus."

When All Eternity Shook

Let us try and understand as best we can—we certainly won't be able to understand completely—those critical atoning hours that are so sacred in Christ's life and so essential in our own. It is interesting to me that of the four Gospel writers, the one who was nearest to Christ during those prayer-filled hours in Gethsemane chose not to document it. John (with Peter and James) was invited by Christ to accompany him deeper into the Garden of Gethsemane and there to watch and pray. Yet his account of Gethsemane moves directly from the Last Supper to the arrest and betrayal by Judas. Matthew, Mark, and Luke record the prayer of Christ in Gethsemane, but John does not. I have pondered that omission over the years.

Frederic Farrar wrote a wonderful book titled *The Life of Christ.* I think it is the finest book on the life of Christ ever written. It was composed in the nineteenth century in England by Farrar, who was a Protestant minister. When he spoke of Christ's atoning moments he said: "We may not intrude too closely into this scene. It is shrouded in a halo and a mystery into which no footstep may penetrate. We, as we contemplate it, are like those disciples—our senses are confused, our perceptions are not clear. We can but enter into their amazement and sore distress. Half waking, half oppressed with an irresistible weight of troubled slumber, they only felt that they were dim witnesses of an unutterable agony, far deeper than anything which they could fathom, as it far transcended all that, even in our purest moments, we can pretend to understand."[4] At the risk of doing what Frederick Farrar felt was essentially impossible, let us try and understand as best we can the bitter cup Jesus drank for us all.

I think Enoch helps us understand the most as we read Moses 7 in the Pearl of Great Price. Let me set the stage for Enoch's insight with another vision from the Pearl of Great Price that was given to Moses in Moses 1. Moses, as was Enoch, was shown all the inhabitants of earth and "many worlds" (Moses 1:35). We read in Moses 1 that "Moses cast his eyes and beheld the earth, yea, even all of it; and there was not a particle of it which he did not behold, discerning it by the spirit of God. And he beheld also the inhabitants thereof, and there was not a soul which he beheld not; and he discerned them by the Spirit of God; and their numbers were great, even numberless as the sand upon the sea shore" (Moses 1:27–28).

It is difficult for us to understand that kind of discernment, but somehow the Spirit had the power and the ability to allow Moses and other prophets to comprehend, in a moment of time, all the inhabitants of the earth, even those as numberless as the sands of the seashore. Let us keep that in our minds while we turn to Moses 7. In this profoundly beautiful chapter, Enoch sees God weeping over the sins of the earth. As the conversation between God and Enoch progresses, Enoch tries to understand God's heart and mind so that he can be "of one heart and one mind" (Moses 7:18) with God as well as with the people in Zion. That is what makes a Zion people, that unity. Enoch asks God why he is weeping. In the context of eternal time and the infinite multitude of creations, all which exist from everlasting to everlasting, why does God weep over the suffering and misery of a few people on a tiny dust speck called Earth, among all the worlds in the vast universe? The Lord answers him, "They are the workmanship of mine own hands" (Moses 7:32). They are his children. He has asked them simply to choose him as their Father and to love each other, but they cannot do even those two basic things. As a result they will suffer. He weeps for their suffering.

The specific suffering spoken of is the guilt we feel when we finally realize our lives are not in line with the wisdom of God. Yet it is also the suffering of those who are the victims of others' sins. They too suffer, and their misery is not self-inflicted. But there is more than just weeping—the Lord's tears will lead to redemptive action. The Lord tells Enoch, "That which I have chosen hath pled before my face" (Moses 7:39). Christ's pleading accompanies God's weeping, and then with atoning love makes our suffering his own. "Wherefore, he suffereth for their sins; inasmuch as they will repent in the day that my Chosen shall return unto me, and until that day they shall be in torment; Wherefore, for this shall the heavens weep, yea, and all the workmanship of my hands" (Moses 7:39–40).

There follows one of the most profoundly beautiful scriptures in the canon. It is my favorite scripture. If I were to be shipwrecked on an island and God only gave me one verse to take with me, I would take Moses 7:41. I will quote it as it is, then I will change it just a little to reflect those moments in Gethsemane and Calvary when Jesus drank the bitter cup.

"And it came to pass that the Lord spake unto Enoch, and told Enoch all the doings of the children of men; wherefore Enoch knew, and looked upon their wickedness, and their misery, and wept and stretched forth his arms, and his heart swelled wide as eternity; and his bowels yearned; and all eternity shook" (Moses 7:41). In this context *shook* means *overflowed*. We might ask, "What did all eternity overflow with? What was *eternity* not large enough to encompass?" The answer is compelling. Eternity overflowed with love, with compassion, with mercy, with forgiveness, with longsuffering. If we take that particular verse and put it into Gethsemane's context, the insight is profound. We picture the Savior in Gethsemane, who in a single moment of time can comprehend, as Moses did in Moses 1, or Enoch in Moses 7, all the wickedness and all the misery of all the souls who ever did or ever will exist on the earth. Let us read this wonderful verse with Christ in mind:

"And it came to pass that the [Father] spake unto [the Son], and told [the Son] all the doings of the children of men; wherefore [Jesus] knew, and looked upon their wickedness, and their misery, and wept and stretched forth his arms, and his heart swelled wide as eternity; and his bowels yearned; and all eternity shook" (Moses 7:41). It overflowed! All eternity is not big enough to hold the compassion and the mercy of the Savior. It flows over the edges of the infinite.

THE BURDENS WE CARRY

At a women's conference that I was a part of, the organizers introduced a new aspect to our presentations—a question and answer period. During the first of these sessions, I was overwhelmed by the questions that the women asked. For privacy and for candor, they wrote their questions down and during the lunch break we responded to them. It was a crushing experience for me to realize that in this assembly of about 1,200 to 1,500 women there was such a large amount of pain. Let me share a few:

- "My husband was given a blessing by priesthood holders that he would overcome his illness, but he died. Was my faith lacking?"

- "What can you do to build trust in a relationship where trust has been broken so many times before?"

- "They say the most valiant came and were chosen to live with good Mormon families. Does that mean I wasn't as good because I grew up in an alcoholic family and was abused as a child?"

- "Should there ever be secrets that I keep from my husband? Things which I have repented for and which I want to forget that he doesn't know about?"

- "How do you stand alone every Sunday with a baby and a husband who doesn't want to go to church? Every Sunday is a fight. It is so hard."

- "I have a teenage son who, after my divorce, has hardly spoken to me and wants very little to do with me. Help me know what to do."

- "My husband was excommunicated. What do I tell my kids when he can't take the sacrament on Sunday?"

- "My husband and I are in a cycle that happens every year. I'm tired of the cycle, the addictions, the pain, the blame. How do I know when he truly wants to end the cycle and isn't just saying whatever he can to make it better at the time? I'm ready to leave."

- "If your husband has left the Church and tries to persuade his kids to accept his beliefs, is it more harmful to divorce him or to keep a two-parent home?"

- "How do we as women help our husbands who are struggling with pornography without being nags, spies, or ignoring the problem?"

- "How do you give joy to a child with her own trials when the stress of your life is bringing you to the depths of despair?"

- "I married young in the temple and have had a family, been active, and tried to follow the Lord. I struggle with feeling that I made a mistake in whom I married. How do I fix this? Will the Lord forgive me? Can he make it right?"

- "After forty-five years of marriage, which I thought was a very loving relationship, I found out my husband has had several affairs. I wanted to keep my family eternal. I'm having a hard time forgiving my husband. How do I truly forgive? Is it possible under these circumstances?"

These are just a few of the questions from one small group of Latter-day Saint women, and I have to believe that the Latter-day Saint people are as good as any people on earth. Not problem-free, as we all know, but where could you find a nobler people? Trying to answer those questions was such a crushing experience and yet, those experiences are just an infinitesimally small amount of agony and distress when placed against the backdrop of the population of the world measured against the lifetime of the planet. Can we begin to understand our Savior if we magnify that pain by what Christ knew and experienced in the Garden of Gethsemane in those atoning moments of his life when all eternity shook? My heart filled with compassion that afternoon reading question after question. If I could have, I would have solved every one of those problems, but I didn't know how to solve them. I didn't know how to remove the pain.

"As Broad as Eternity"

Later in Moses 7, the Savior said, "I am Messiah, the King of Zion, the Rock of Heaven" (Moses 7:53). It is always desirable to visualize what you read in the scriptures. When you imagine Christ as a rock, what do you see? How large is that rock? If you close your eyes, what image appears when you imagine the Rock of Heaven? We get an answer from the Savior himself. Notice the words "broad as eternity"—that is a very large rock. Christ follows those words with a promise: "Whoso cometh in it at the gate and climbeth up by me shall never fall" (Moses 7:53). Why can't you fall off a rock that is broad as eternity? There are no places to fall! Isn't it wonderful to realize there is no place in the broad reaches of space where the love of God does not penetrate? His heart swelled wide as eternity and he is a rock as broad as eternity—the rock we can build our lives on is the rock of his compassion and mercy and forgiving nature. That is solid!

If It Were Allowed

There are times in our lives—there have been times in mine—when we see someone we love suffering, that if it were allowed, if God permitted it, we would take the suffering for them. I think most parents understand that. Most husbands and wives understand that. Sometimes children, in their love for each other and for parents, understand that. At times close friends understand that. However, it's not allowed us. I cannot take my wife or child's pain upon me. Through empathy I can try to share it, but I cannot transfer it and release them. But it was allowed once—during those moments when the Savior drank the bitter cup in Gethsemane, when he understood our suffering, our afflictions, our pains, the whole of human misery. I can almost hear a deeper prayer echoing beneath the vocalized one in Gethsemane, a transformation from "remove this cup," to "let me drink it for them."

Whenever I have visited Gethsemane in the Holy Land, the great emotion I feel there is one of gratitude—my gratitude for him certainly, but also a more profound gratitude, the gratitude of the Savior to his Father in Heaven for allowing him to take our pains that we would not, as he says in Doctrine and Covenants 19, need to suffer them (see D&C 19:16). So to me, amidst the groundswell of mercy which permeates Gethsemane, it is also the place of deepest gratitude on earth. The experiences the Savior had there intensified his forgiving nature, refining the already eternal refinement he brought with him to that stable of Bethlehem. Throughout his life and ministry he demonstrated that forgiveness, as if he knew we'd need constant encouragement in our need for constant mercy.

TEN-THOUSAND-TALENT, SEVEN-TIMES-A-DAY FORGIVENESS

There are verses that I often turn to when I feel, as Nephi, that "I am encompassed about, because of the temptations and the sins which do so easily beset me" (2 Nephi 4:18). In these scriptures we come to understand Christ's great goodness. In Matthew 18, Jesus relates a parable about our need to forgive each other, but there is also in his teachings a hint about the largess of his forgiving nature.

"Therefore is the kingdom of heaven likened unto a certain king, which would take account of his servants. And when he had begun to reckon, one was brought unto him, which owed him ten thousand talents. But forasmuch as he had not to pay, his lord commanded him to be sold. . . . The servant therefore fell down, and worshipped him, saying, Lord, have patience with me, and I will pay thee all. Then the lord of that servant was moved with compassion, and loosed him, and forgave him the debt" (Matthew 18:23–27).

We worship a God who can forgive ten-thousand-talent sins. That is an enormous sum. We find another parable of a similar vein in Luke 7. "There was a certain creditor which had two debtors: the one owed five hundred pence, and the other fifty. And when they had nothing to pay, he frankly forgave them both" (Luke 7:41–42). We worship a God who forgives five-hundred-pence sins as easily as fifty-pence sins. This he does easily, as the word *frankly* suggests.

In Luke 17, when the disciples asked the Savior about forgiveness, he answered them, "If thy brother trespass against thee, . . . and if he repent, forgive him. And if he trespass against thee seven times in a day, and seven times in a day turn again to thee, saying, I repent; thou shalt forgive him" (Luke 17:3–4). The Savior is certainly not going to require of us something he himself would not give. If he expects us to forgive the repentant soul seven times in a single day, we can be assured that we too can go to him seven times in a single day and every time he will forgive us. We worship a ten-thousand-talent, five-hundred-pence, seven-times-a-day God!

In Alma 24, the Anti-Nephi-Lehies used a very evocative expression to

WHEN ALL ETERNITY SHOOK

describe themselves. It intensifies the forgiveness God gave to them and instills hope in all our hearts. Their king says: "I also thank my God, yea, my great God, that he hath . . . taken away the guilt from our hearts, through the merits of his Son. And now behold, my brethren, . . . we were the most lost of all mankind" (Alma 24:10–11). We worship a God who forgives ten-thousand-talent, five-hundred-pence, seven-times-a-day, most-lost-of-all-mankind sins.

Alluring, Wooing, Kingly Forgiveness

The Old Testament book of Hosea is such a beautiful book. Hosea was married to an unfaithful and promiscuous woman, and God used Hosea's experiences to compare his own feeling for us as his people. Remember that Christ is the bridegroom and we are the bride. Hosea continued to love his wife even in the midst of his own personal grief at her unfaithfulness. There is a poignant moment in the book when the wife is described as making herself beautiful, but not for her husband: "She decked herself with her earrings and her jewels, and she went after her lovers, and forgat me" (Hosea 2:13). This is compared to Israel's following after strange gods. How would it feel for a husband to see his bride, his wife, putting on makeup, fixing her hair, adjusting her earrings and necklaces, yet not for him, but for her lovers? What does the Lord say he will do? What would most men do under those circumstances? Yet the Lord says, "Therefore, behold, I will allure her, . . . and speak comfortably unto her. . . . and she shall sing there, as in the days of her youth. . . . And it shall be at that day [here he changes from talking about her in the third person to directly addressing her], saith the Lord, that thou shalt call me Ishi [my husband]; . . . and I will betroth thee unto me for ever; yea, I will betroth thee unto me in righteousness, and in judgment, and in lovingkindness, and in mercies. I will even betroth thee unto me in faithfulness: and thou shalt know the Lord" (Hosea 2:14–15, 19–20). We worship an alluring, wooing, betrothing God.

Later in Hosea, the compelling image is changed from husband and wife relationships to that of a parent and child. "When Israel was a child," the Lord says, "then I loved him. . . . I taught Ephraim also to [walk], taking them by their arms" (Hosea 11:1, 3). We can see that tender image, one of a father holding the arms of his child, teaching him to walk, "but they knew not that I healed them. I drew them with cords of a man, with bands of love: . . . And my people are bent to backsliding from me: . . . How shall I give thee up, Ephraim? How shall I deliver thee, Israel? . . . Mine heart is turned within me. . . . I will not execute the fierceness of my anger, I will not turn to destroy Ephraim: *for I am God, and not man*" (Hosea 11:3–4, 7, 8, 9; emphasis added). In other words, the Lord is saying, "If I were a man, I could not respond that way, but I am a God."

There is a wonderful moment in the movie *Camelot* when Arthur knows that Lancelot and Guinevere have committed adultery and that they are in love with each other. Naturally, he feels deeply betrayed. He has just knighted Lancelot as one of his Knights of the Round Table. Finishing the ceremony, Arthur leaves the hall and goes out on the parapets of the castle where he draws his sword, Excalibur, and says, "Proposition: If I could choose from every woman who breathes on this earth, the face I would most love, the smile, the touch, the voice, the heart, the laugh, the soul itself, every detail and feature to the smallest strand of hair, they would all be Jenny's.

"Proposition: If I could choose from every man who breathes on this earth a man for my brother and a man for my son, a man for my friend, they would all be Lance. . . .

"Yes, I love them. I love them, and they answer me with pain and torment. Be it sin, or not sin, they betray me in their hearts, and that's far sin enough. I see it in their eyes and feel it when they speak, and they must pay for it and be punished. I shan't be wounded and not return it in kind. I'm done with feeble hoping. I demand a man's vengeance!" He raises his sword on that last agonizing cry for retaliation. Then his face softens and he lowers the sword and continues, "Proposition: I'm a king, not a man. And a civilized king. Could it possibly be civilized to destroy what I love? Could it possibly be civilized to love myself above all?"[5]

And he forgives them. And he goes right on forgiving them until the very end, until everything is destroyed. Then, in contrition, they come to him as the Round Table is broken in pieces, the Knights are scattered in rebellion, and the old brutal days of war return. Even in the midst of the shattered pieces of his life's dream which remind him of all he longed for and all he has lost, he still forgives both Lancelot and Guinevere. Arthur has a final moment alone with his once deeply beloved Jenny. She is going into a convent and they will now be separated forever. She says, "So often in the past, Arthur, I would look in your eyes and I would find there forgiveness. Perhaps one day in the future it shall be there again. But now I won't be with you. I won't see it." Arthur opens his arms wide, enfolds her, and says, "My love, my dearest love," and forgives her once again. She knows he will always forgive her! There is something profoundly beautiful in forgiveness, especially this Hosea-like always-loving-in-the-midst-of-pain forgiveness.

SCARLET-TO-WHITE, RING-ON-THE-FINGER, EAST-TO-WEST FORGIVENESS

Let us turn to Isaiah. In the first chapter we read the Lord's invitation, "Come now, and let us reason together, saith the Lord: though your sins be as scarlet, they shall be as white as snow; though they be red like crimson, they shall be as wool" (Isaiah 1:18). There are, in the Church, too many of what I call "pink people." Pink people are people who don't really believe that verse, who say, in a sense, "The Lord can make my sins, though they're scarlet, a light shade of pink. I can never be totally white, completely stain-free, just pink." They have trouble forgiving themselves. We worship a from-scarlet-to-white-as-snow God. The parable of the prodigal son tells us that in a very wonderful and profound way. We worship a God who enjoys forgiving, because as God says (in so many words) in Hosea: "I do not think like man. I like to forgive. I delight in forgiveness. Forgiveness for me is not difficult. I do not need to strain and force my heart in order to accomplish it." As the publicans and the sinners draw near in Luke 15, Jesus relates three parables. First, he relates two mini-parables to set up the parable of the prodigal son—the lost sheep and the lost coin—the first perhaps directed to men and the second perhaps directed to women.

The shepherd loses one of his sheep, and after searching finds it. The Savior then says, "He layeth it on his shoulders, rejoicing" (Luke 15:5). But the joy is so great that he has to share it with somebody. "And when he cometh home, he calleth together his friends and neighbours, saying unto them, Rejoice with me; for I have found my sheep which was lost. I say unto you, that likewise joy shall be in heaven over one sinner that repenteth, more than over ninety and nine just persons, which need no repentance" (Luke 15:6–7). God, like the shepherd, still joys in the ninety and nine, but there is an intensity of joy for the one. There's a constant joy in the ninety and nine. God feels both types of joy, both the constant and the intense.

Next Jesus speaks of a woman who has lost a coin. She sweeps the house, searching diligently. "And when she hath found it, she calleth her friends and her neighbours together, saying, Rejoice with me; for I have found the piece which I had lost" (Luke 15:9). Once again the joy needs to be shared.

With these two introductory parables the Savior now has his audience prepared for the finding of a lost man—the prodigal son. A young man goes on a long journey with his newly acquired fortune to a "far country"—Babylon, we might say—where he wastes his substance in "riotous living" (Luke 15:13). In a Babylonian world one wastes their "substance." That may consist of integrity, health, resources, testimony, love. How much does Babylon want from us? The parable gives an answer. "And when he had spent all, there arose a mighty famine in that land; and he began to be in want. And he went and joined himself to a citizen of that country; and he sent him into his fields to feed swine. . . . And no man gave unto him" (Luke 15:14–16). Babylon will take all you have and give nothing in return. "And when he came to himself, he said, How many hired servants of my father's have bread enough and to spare, and I perish with hunger!" (Luke 15:17). The phrase "came to himself" is a beautiful phrase; we might say "his real self," because the real you is you at your best. He was not really a prodigal. He was his father's son.

The son wants to go home, yet he doesn't feel he can go home as a son. He can only go home as a servant, but he's now content to go home as a servant. In his mind he is no longer worthy to be a son. The relationship has changed because of his wasteful expenditure of his father's generous inheritance. There are people in our Church who have not had the best past, who feel they'll never be equal to those who seem to have never sinned, or not committed serious sin. They just want to come home. They just want to be servants and be near the Father. The prodigal makes a decision. "I will arise and go to my father, and will say unto him, Father, I have sinned against heaven, and before thee, And am no more worthy to be called thy son: make me as one of thy hired servants" (Luke 15:18–19).

When we return from inactivity, or from wasting ourselves in Babylon, do we return as a son or as a servant? That is the question this parable addresses. Remember, many of those listening to the parable were sinners. "And he arose, and came to his father [who doesn't even know at this juncture why he's returning]. But when he was yet a great way off, his father saw him, and had compassion, and ran, and fell on his neck, and kissed him" (Luke 15:20). The father receives him as a son, not a servant. "And the son said unto him [I think in a tone of amazement], Father, I have sinned against heaven, and in thy sight, and am no more worthy to be called thy son. But the father said to his servants, Bring forth the best robe, and put it on him; and put a ring on his hand, and shoes on his feet: And bring hither the fatted calf, and kill it; and let us eat, and be merry: For this my son was dead, and is alive again; he was lost, and is found" (Luke 15:21–24). That may be the most elevated moment in all Christian literature, perhaps in all religious literature. We worship a ring-on-the-finger God. The prodigal's father received him as a son. There are no servants in this church— only sons, only daughters. There are no "pink people," because we worship a ring-on-the-finger, crimson-to-white God.

Let me share one more beautiful, hope-filled passage from Psalms. David— who should certainly have known something about forgiveness—says, "The Lord is merciful and gracious, slow to anger, and plenteous in mercy. He will not always chide. . . . He hath not dealt with us after our sins; nor rewarded us according to our iniquities. For as the heaven is high above the earth, so great is his mercy toward them that fear him. As far as the east is from the west, so far hath he removed our transgressions from us. Like as a father pitieth his children, so the Lord pitieth him that fear him. For he knoweth our frame [he understands]; he remembereth that we are dust. . . . the mercy of the Lord is from everlasting to everlasting" (Psalm 103:8–14, 17).

"I Don't Remember That"

May I add a personal experience? We could have added many more assurances from the scriptures—the Lord really wants us to realize that we worship a ten-thousand-talent, five-hundred-pence, seven-times-a-day, most-lost-of-all-mankind, alluring, wooing, betrothing, scarlet-to-white, ring-on-the-finger, east-to-west, high-as-heaven forgiving God. If all those assurances were not enough, sometimes the Lord will give us personal, private experiences to help us understand his mercy. I have the opportunity of traveling by air often. When I get on an airplane I always feel the pressing duty that I ought to share the gospel, so I try to engage my fellow passengers in some kind of conversation. It is always somewhat awkward. I don't know how to do it well, apparently. We all have our own tactics for that. If somebody would just sit down next to me and say, "You look like a Mormon. I'd love to hear about your church," it would be positively enjoyable. But it never happens that way, so I'm always a little uncomfortable as I'm getting on an airplane. When I sit down and no one is sitting next to me, or if I'm with my wife, then I feel relieved. I think, *At least on this flight I'll be spared the awkwardness.* The problem is that as soon as I think that, I immediately feel guilty about feeling relieved. So I'm never comfortable when I'm flying on an airplane. I'm either feeling guilty for being relieved, or I'm trying to engage in an awkward conversation.

I have discovered that the Lord can, through our imaginations (which is a great revelatory tool), teach us. I call these moments in my own life "ponderings." When we ponder it is an invitation for the Lord to teach us. One day I was sitting on an airplane, and no one was sitting next to me. I was relieved and then instantly felt guilty for being relieved. At that moment the Lord took over my imagination and showed me an interesting scene. It was a judgment scene. I was the man who would "stand in the dock," so to speak. It was a very comfortable scene, however. There were two Queen Anne chairs placed in a conversational position. I have always loved Queen Anne–style furniture. The Savior entered the room and sat down in one of the chairs, graciously inviting me to sit in the other.

I knew I was going to be judged. I knew that was what it was all about, but there was something very comfortable and disarming in the setting.

He asked me his first question. He said, "Mike, did you proclaim the gospel?" There I was, sitting on an airplane feeling relieved that no one is sitting next to me. I thought, *Oh, he would start with that!* I answered his inquiry probably the way anyone would answer it.

I said, "Lord, I tried."

And he said, "Let us see."

Then, as I watched in my mind's eye, it was as if there was a little stage between us. Images appeared between the two chairs as he showed me all the efforts I had ever made to proclaim the gospel. He showed me invitations to my friends as a boy to attend my MIA activities, a three-week mission I went on as a teenager, my full-time mission, stake missions, invitations to neighbors to spend time together, preparing my children for their missions and supporting them while they were away, and every conversation on every airplane I had ever had.

When he was done showing me these things, he turned to me again and he said, "So, Mike, did you proclaim the gospel?"

I still wasn't quite sure how I was supposed to answer and so hesitantly and timidly I said, "Yes?" When that "yes" was out of my mouth, suddenly all my failures flooded into my mind and I said, "But Lord, what about my failures? You didn't show me my failures."

He said, "Tell me your failures."

So I told him. It was such a relief to unload all my guilt and my sense of falling short. "What about all the times I *didn't* talk on the airplane? I should have been a better full-time missionary. I should have set a better example for my friends and acquaintances who were not members of the Church. I should have prepared my own children better for their missions. I should have spent more time and effort on my stake mission." I could remember those failures so well, and he listened patiently.

When I was finished, he replied, simply, "I don't remember that."

I looked at him in amazement, and he smiled, and asked the second question. "Did you redeem the dead?"

I said, "Lord, I tried."

And he said, "Let us see."

Once again the scenes opened between us. Once again he showed me every effort I had ever made in temple work. Every temple session I had ever been to—baptisms for the dead as a boy, endowments, sealings, initiatories, searching for my ancestors, filling out my first pedigree chart in Cub Scouts, babysitting so that other people could go to the temple. Then he turned to me and said, "So, did you redeem the dead?"

I said, still timidly, "Yes, Lord, but what about my failures? You didn't show me my failures."

Again I heard the gentle invitation, "Tell me your failures."

I recounted them to him with relief mingled with my own guilt and fears. "I should have researched better. I should have gone to the temple more often. I should have been more alert when I was in the temple." He listened again very patiently and then said, simply, "I don't remember that."

Then he smiled and asked his third question. "Did you perfect the Saints?"

I said, "Lord, I tried."

And he said, "Let us see."

Again the scenes appeared; every effort I made for the kingdom was displayed, every calling I've ever had in the Church, every home teaching visit I had ever made (even on the last day of the month), every talk or lesson or fireside, every seminary and institute class I had taught, he had recorded and they paraded before my eyes.

Then he turned to me again. "So did you perfect the Saints?"

I said, "Yes, Lord, but what about my failures?"

"Tell me your failures," he responded again. It was such a relief to lay them before him. "I should have tried harder with my home teaching families. I should have served in my callings more diligently. I should have been more dedicated. I should have loved more purely."

Once again I heard those words that filled me with loving awe: "I don't remember that."

On and on the questions continued. "Did you follow the Brethren? Were you a good husband? Were you a good father?"

"I tried."

"Let us see."

Then all the positive things I had done were shown me.

"But what about my failures?"

"Tell me your failures."

There was always that great relief in unburdening them. Each time those final wonderful words that filled me with such hope were shared: "I don't remember that." In those moments while sitting on that airplane, I tasted, I think, something of the "great goodness" of Christ, and my soul overflowed with hope. Perhaps this is what is meant in the Book of Mormon by the phrase "the pleasing bar of God" (see Jacob 6:13; Moroni 10:34).

What Do We Need to Do to Be Forgiven of Our Sins?

Paul was so concerned that we would abuse the great goodness of the Lord that he reminded us that "the riches of his goodness and forbearance and long-suffering" (Romans 2:4) is to lead us to repentance, not to sin. We may take advantage of God's gracious mercy because it is so freely given. We debate sometimes the statement, "I can always repent." I would say, "Yes, we can always repent and our repentance will be accepted if it is sincere." What do we have to do to receive such graciousness? I think we must do two things.

If we were to ask the Savior what we need to do to be forgiven of our sins, I think he would answer differently than an average assembly of Latter-day Saints. When I ask a group of Latter-day Saints, "What do you have to do to be forgiven of your sins?" I usually hear, "You have to repent." I'm not convinced the Savior would answer it in that manner, at least according to what he stresses in the Gospels. I think he would answer it this way: "To be forgiven of your sins, you need simply to ask and to be willing to forgive others." He indicated as much in the parable of the ten-thousand-talent sinner. The servant's lord said, "I forgave thee all that debt, because thou desiredst me." The servant asked and forgiveness was offered, even at that level of sin. Then his lord followed with: "Shouldest not thou also have had compassion on thy fellowservant, even as I had pity on thee?" (Matthew 18:32–33). We ask and we forgive others. It seems an elementary focus.

"It Was a Long Time Ago"

I remember witnessing a touching scene as a bishop. It was a wonderfully tender moment between a husband and a wife. The wife had, years previous, committed adultery and she felt she was, as I've termed it, a "pink person," not able to believe that her sins could ever be completely white. In counseling with her, she never could get over that. I suppose she feels pink to this day. The husband was forgiving; the marriage was saved. Years later, she and her husband had another occasion to counsel with me as their bishop, about an incident involving one of their children. In tears, she made an allusion to her previous adultery and said, "Had I only been a better mother. Had I not sinned, this would not have happened." Her husband threw his arm around her and kissed her temples, her cheek, and her forehead. Stroking her hair, he said again and again to her, "It was a long time ago. It doesn't matter. I never think of it. It was a long time ago." As I witnessed that, I thought, *There is something deeply beautiful and divine in forgiveness.* Surely God will forgive that man, who was himself not a perfect man—I knew him well. Surely God will forgive that man of his sins because that man is willing to forgive.

Snatching Forgiveness

The account of Alma the Younger teaches us that all we need to do is ask. Alma shows us a process that we might term "snatching forgiveness." There was a moment in his two-day experience when he was, as he says, "harrowed up" and "racked" (Alma 36:12) by the memory of his sins. The thought of being in the presence of God wasn't just, as it is for many of us, an anxiety and a fear but "an inexpressible horror" (Alma 36:14). "Oh, thought I, that I could be banished and become extinct both soul and body, that I might not be brought to stand in the presence of my God, to be judged of my deeds. . . . While I was harrowed up by the memory of my many sins, behold, I remembered also to have heard my father prophesy unto the people concerning the coming of one Jesus Christ, a Son of God, to atone for the sins of the world" (Alma 36:15, 17). Think of those words. Alma is like a drowning man. Have you ever almost drowned? I nearly drowned once. I remember being under the water and reaching for anything that might pull me out. I was desperate, fearful, despairing. What would it have felt like at that moment to feel a hand reach down and grab my hand and pull me up into the life-giving air? Alma continues: "As my mind caught hold upon this thought, I cried within my heart: O Jesus, thou Son of God, have mercy on me, who am in the gall of bitterness, and am encircled about by the everlasting chains of death. And now, behold, when I thought this, I could remember my pains no more" (Alma 36:18).

When Alma recounts that experience in Mosiah, he says, "The Lord in mercy hath seen fit to snatch me. . . . I am born of God. My soul hath been redeemed from the gall of bitterness and bonds of iniquity. I was in the darkest abyss; . . . my soul was racked . . . but I am snatched, and my soul is pained no more" (Mosiah 27:28–29). Think of the unity of those two phrases used by Alma— *caught hold* and *snatched*. We can almost see the hand of Alma reaching up and God's reaching down. When Alma reaches up, the Savior responds immediately to that cry of anguish and grabs him, snatches him. We worship a God whose forgiveness is rapid and immediate—when we catch hold, he snatches us.

Ammon, who shared Alma's born-again experience, used the same word: "Who can say too much of his great power, and of his mercy, and of his long-suffering. . . . I cannot say the smallest part which I feel. Who could have supposed that our God would have been so merciful as to have *snatched* us from our awful, sinful, and polluted state? Behold, we went forth even in wrath, with mighty threatenings to destroy his church. Oh then, why did he not consign us to an awful destruction, yea, why did he not let the sword of his justice fall upon us? . . . Oh, my soul, almost as it were, fleeth at the thought. Behold, he did not exercise his justice upon us, but in his great mercy hath brought us over that everlasting gulf of death and misery" (Alma 26:16–20; emphasis added). If you ask, as Alma and Ammon asked, God snatches you. In that immediate release from the bonds of sin, your desire to forgive others is born, steadied, and intensified, but forgiveness is there for the asking.

"CHECKMATE!"

When we receive our own forgiveness, as Alma and Ammon received their great forgiveness, a desire to reciprocate that gift to the Savior is born in our hearts. May I illustrate what that desire is with a little story from my youth: When I was a boy, I wanted to play chess. Every day I went down to the public swimming pool and I watched the older boys playing chess. There were tables around the pool with chessboards on them. For the first few weeks, every day I would pick a new piece and study it—the rook, the knight, the bishop, the king, the queen, the pawn. Every day I would focus on one until I learned all the pieces, their powers, and how various players used them. Then I challenged my uncle to a game of chess. He beat me in three moves. It was devastating to hear that concluding word, "checkmate," the first time I played. A desire was born in me that day—I was going to beat my uncle in chess. So I practiced and watched the older boys play chess. I played chess with my friends, and when I thought I'd learned enough, I would challenge my uncle—and he would beat me. I bought books on chess; I studied; I practiced and practiced. I would challenge my uncle—and he would beat me. Again and again he would say, "Checkmate!" "Checkmate!" "Checkmate!"

In my mind I imagined a large chessboard, and every time my uncle said "Checkmate," I put a black piece that represented my failure, my defeat, on that chessboard. Soon, after a few years of playing chess against my uncle (I think when I started I was nine or ten), the chessboard in my mind was littered with black pieces. I wanted a white piece to represent a victory, but again and again I would hear that word: "Checkmate."

Finally, I can see the morning—I remember I was about twelve or thirteen—sitting at the kitchen table, listening to the sparrows in the elm tree outside the door, the sun filtering through the yellow plaid curtains, when I looked at the board and made my last move and said to my uncle, "Checkmate!" I had beaten him. What a wonderful feeling that was! Of all the words I've ever said in my life, only one has had more power than "checkmate" in my memory. That is when I knelt at an altar in the temple and said "Yes" to be sealed to my wife. But that "checkmate" comes close to that "yes." I wanted to put many white pieces on the board in my mind, many more victories, but for whatever reason, my uncle never played chess with me again. However, that particular day I could, in my mind, put one white piece in the middle of the chessboard. It represented my victory.

In a sense, when we sin the Savior comes to us and says, "You've been checkmated by the adversary and by your own weaknesses." In the moment of a personal prayer for forgiveness such as Alma offered, the Savior clears all the black pieces off our chessboard with one sweep of his hand and says: "You have no defeats. Your defeats will not hold you back, but there is one thing I cannot do for you. I cannot put white pieces on the board for you. Go now and win the victories and put the white pieces on your chessboard." That is what we desire to do, deep in our hearts—to win more and more victories until the board has as many white pieces as there once may have been black.

INTIMACY—WONDER—ADORATION

I conclude with one of the most tender moments in Christ's life, when he appears in the Americas, as recorded in 3 Nephi. We could discuss the cosmic aspect of the Atonement when all eternity shook, but there is something that makes this wonderful moment with Christ and the Nephites and Lamanites very personal. When Jesus descended from heaven, the people fell at his feet in worship. He then asked them to do something. He said: "Arise and come forth unto me, that ye may thrust your hands into my side, and also that ye may feel the prints of the nails in my hands and in my feet, that ye may know that I am the God of Israel, and the God of the whole earth. . . . And it came to pass that the multitude went forth, and thrust their hands into his side, and did feel the prints of the nails in his hands and in his feet; and this they did do, going forth *one by one* until they had all gone forth, and did see with their eyes and did feel with their hands, and did know of a surety and did bear record" (3 Nephi 11:14–15; emphasis added).

There are many paintings of the resurrected Christ appearing before his people. We've all seen artists' renditions of the Apostles or others standing before the resurrected Savior, with him showing them the marks of his atoning sacrifice. There are three sets of marks—in his side, in his hands, in his feet. I've pondered considerably those three marks, or signs, or symbols, or scars, or wounds, or tokens—whichever word you want to use. I've pondered those scars and what they suggest to us. In almost every artistic account, it is the wound in the hands that is most often depicted. In the past, every time I visualized myself standing before the Savior one day, I imagined it was the marks in his hands that I would look at. But if we read carefully, it is not the mark in the hand that Jesus first invites the people to touch. Remember, they approached the Savior "one by one."

The first mark they reach out to touch is the wound in his side. I try to visualize what that may have been like. One day it will be my opportunity and yours. I think the Savior will say, "Mike, it's your turn. Come forth and touch the symbols of my Atonement." I draw near. I reach my hand forward and lay it on his side. I can feel the warmth of his body as my hand rests right next to his heart. I call that mark, that symbol, the mark or wound of intimacy. There is something very private and beautiful about that interaction. The first token the surviving Nephites and Lamanites touch is the one in his side. I've never seen an artistic rendition of that. I had never visualized it myself until very late in my life, but that spot near his heart is the first mark they touch. We sing a hymn that contains the essence and the power of that particular first symbol of his atoning love. "Oh, love effulgent, love divine! / What debt of gratitude is mine, / That in his off'ring I have part / And hold a place within his heart."[6] There is our hand over his heart—the sign of intimacy.

Then we would move our hands from his side to the marks in his hands and wrists. Again, I have pondered that moment a great deal. I call these the wounds or signs of wonder—wonder at his submission. His hands, that could have refused the nails, instead submitted to them in atoning obedience, in atoning humility. We sing another hymn that gives us a sense of that: "I think of his hands pierced and bleeding to pay the debt! / Such mercy, such love, and devotion can I forget? . . . Oh, it is wonderful that he should care for me / Enough to die for me! / Oh, it is wonderful, wonderful to me!"[7] This is the mark of wonder, the wonder that he would submit, that he would obey his Father's will to that extent for the sake of his Father's other sons and daughters.

I don't think we could stand after that. We would fall at his feet and there would be presented to our eyes the third mark or symbol of his atoning sacrifice—the wounds in his feet. Again, I have pondered much about this. I call this the token of adoration, as we fall at his feet. There is a difference between gratitude and adoration, between praise and thanksgiving. Gratitude and thanksgiving say, "Thank you, Lord, for creating this beautiful world." Praise and adoration ask, "What must the God be like who can create such beauty?" Thanksgiving and gratitude say, "Father in Heaven, thank you for sending thy Son into the world." But adoration and praise ask, "What quality of being, what mercy and love would sacrifice to this extent?" What I am trying to say may be best expressed in yet another hymn: "And when I think that God, his Son not sparing, / Sent him to die, I scarce can take it in, / . . . Then sings my soul, my Savior God, to thee, / How great thou art!"[8]

Intimacy! Wonder! Adoration! For me, those words and all they represent seem to encompass much of what I feel when I think of Him in whose name we do all things, in whose name we seek forgiveness. No wonder all eternity overflowed with his compassion.

May we believe and understand as we face those moments in our lives when we feel, as Nephi, "encompassed [by] the sins which so easily beset [us]" (2 Nephi 4:18), that we have an understanding God. We worship a God of great goodness. We can trust in that great goodness. We worship a God who is a ten-thousand-talent, scarlet-to-white, ring-on-the-finger, seven-times-a-day God. May we rejoice in anticipation of that day when we will be invited to comprehend in an individual way our intimacy with him, the wonder of his sacrifice, and be given the opportunity, as have all who have gone before us, to bow in adoration, to fall at his feet. May the hope of his sacrifice and compassion rest always in our hearts. May we ever feel all eternity shaking—for when it overflowed, it overflowed into our lives also.

CHAPTER EIGHT

YOUR FAITH BECOMETH UNSHAKEN

~

Building Your Testimony Pyramid

CLOUDY DAYS

A number of years ago I came across an article called "Cloudy Days in Tomorrowland." It was published in *Newsweek*. It consisted of a number of predictions of future events, none of which were right. Looking back with the perspective of hindsight they sound silly, or foolish, or in some cases downright stupid. Some very dangerous things were allowed to develop. Some opportunities were lost. In all cases, those who made the predictions regretted their shortsightedness. Here are a few of them:

"'I must confess that my imagination . . . refuses to see any sort of submarine doing anything but suffocating its crew and floundering at sea.'—H. G. Wells, British novelist, 1901.

"'Airplanes are interesting toys but of no military value.'—Marshal Ferdinand Foch, French military strategist and future World War I commander, 1911.

"'The horse is here to stay, but the automobile is only a novelty—a fad.'— A president of the Michigan Savings Bank advising Horace Rackham (Henry Ford's lawyer) not to invest in the Ford Motor Company. Rackham ignored the advice, bought $5,000 worth of stock and sold it several years later for $12.5 million.

"'Believe me, Germany is unable to wage war.'—Former British prime minister David Lloyd George, Aug. 1, 1934. . . .

"'Who . . . wants to hear actors talk?'—Harry M. Warner, Warner Brothers, 1927.

"'There is no reason for any individual to have a computer in their home.' —Kenneth Olsen, president and founder of Digital Equipment Corporation, 1977. . . .

"'Computers in the future may . . . perhaps only weigh 1.5 tons.'—*Popular Mechanics,* forecasting the development of computer technology, 1949.

"'We don't like their sound. Groups of guitars are on the way out.'—Decca Records rejecting the Beatles, 1962. . . .

"'Stocks have reached what looks like a permanently high plateau.'—Irving Fisher, professor of economics, Yale University, Oct. 17, 1929."

And a final one: "'[Television] won't be able to hold on to any market it captures after the first six months. People will soon get tired of staring at a plywood box every night.'—Darryl F. Zanuck, head of 20th Century-Fox, 1946."[1]

Those *were* "cloudy days in Tomorrowland" for many of those people. Personally, I want to avoid cloudy days in my future. I don't wish to make decisions or mistakes based on things that aren't true, or on a false assessment of the value of things, or on a misperceived understanding of danger. We may, as I've seen many people do, throw away truth, thus assuring ourselves of cloudy days in the future, either here on earth or in an eternal sense. We need to hang on tightly to truths that are firm and stable, particularly truths that relate to the gospel. Mormon indicated this when he urged his people to "cleave unto every good thing" (Moroni 7:28).

Every day they have been alive, I have prayed for my children—and now for my grandchildren as well—that they will not make decisions similar to those just mentioned. I pray, as I'm sure you do, that those you love will stay true to the faith. I also pray for my students. I often ask, "Father in Heaven, help my children, my grandchildren, and my students hold true, to stay firm when the faith-shakers come in their lives."

THE FAITH-SHAKERS

I like the word "faith-shakers" a little better than another word that is sometimes used to describe those experiences or people who may enter our lives and trouble our faith. In the Book of Mormon they are termed anti-Christ, but anti-Christ is a name that almost doesn't mean anything anymore because so often it's been misapplied. It has taken on an aura of deepest evil that few of us have ever encountered or will ever encounter. There are four individuals called anti-Christ in the Book of Mormon. I call them faith-shakers. If I ask a class of my students, "How many of you have ever met an anti-Christ?" I rarely see a single hand go up. But if I ask my students, "Have you ever met someone who tried to shake your faith, or have you ever had an experience in life that was faith-shaking?" every hand is going to go up. We all have met faith-shakers. They come in different forms.

In the Book of Mormon the four men who fit the criteria as anti-Christ are

Sherem, Nehor, Korihor, and Zoram. They are all different. They all approach the doctrine of salvation in a different manner. Sherem teaches that something else saves you. In his particular case the law of Moses is implied. Nehor says everyone is going to be saved. Isn't that comforting news? This doctrine made Nehor very popular. Korihor asks, "Saved from what? There is no Satan. There is no sin and therefore no need of salvation of any kind." Zoram insists that his followers are saved, and everyone else is not. Salvation is selective. We can see in just these four different approaches that there are various faith-shaking people and faith-shaking experiences, and we can find all four approaches still today. I suppose if we put these four men in a room together they would quarrel and contend like cats.

I take that expression—faith-shakers—from Jacob's experience with Sherem, as recorded in Jacob 7: "And he had hope to shake me from the faith, notwithstanding the many revelations and the many things which I had seen concerning these things; for I truly had seen angels, and they had ministered unto me. And also, I had heard the voice of the Lord speaking unto me in very word, from time to time; wherefore, I could not be shaken" (Jacob 7:5). For myself and my children, my grandchildren, my students, and all of us, I hope that Jacob's last words could describe us. I hope we can all confidently say, "I could not be shaken."

We all have experiences in life that may challenge our beliefs or our testimonies. What we have always accepted as truth may be troubled. The dark clouds of doubt may arise and obscure our eternal views. Let me share some examples that I have seen with students, myself, my family, and other Church members over the years.

Even our own behaviors may cause our faith to be shaken. All faith-shakers are not enacted from without. There may come times in our lives when it would be very convenient if the gospel were not true. At times, when we are chastened for something—possibly by a parent, a bishop, a priesthood leader—that experience can shake our faith. We probably all know someone like that. I know at least a dozen people who are not active in the Church and believe it is not true because their own behaviors caused challenges in their lives or certain consequences to come from the Church. Jacob said, "O my beloved brethren, give ear to my words. Remember the greatness of the Holy One of Israel. Do not say that I have spoken hard things against you; for if ye do, ye will revile against the truth; for I have spoken the words of your Maker. I know that the words of truth are hard against all uncleanness; but the righteous fear them not, for they love the truth and are not shaken" (2 Nephi 9:40). Occasionally our own behaviors may shake our faith a little bit.

There are moments when the trials of life can shake our faith. C. S. Lewis, a great defender of Christian truth, had just such a faith-shaking trial in his own life when his wife died of cancer. This is what he wrote about that soul-searching event: "Meanwhile, where is God? This is one of the most disquieting symptoms. When you are happy, so happy that you have no sense of needing Him, so happy that you are tempted to feel His claims upon you as an interruption, if you remember yourself and turn to Him with gratitude and praise, you will be—or so it feels—welcomed with open arms. But go to Him when your need is desperate, when all other help is vain, and what do you find? A door slammed in your face, and a sound of bolting and double bolting on the inside. After that, silence. You may as well turn away. The longer you wait, the more emphatic the silence will become. There are no lights in the windows. It might be an empty house. Was it ever inhabited? It seemed so once. And that seeming was as strong as this. What can this mean? Why is He so present a commander in our time of prosperity and so very absent a help in time of trouble? . . .

"Not that I am (I think) in much danger of ceasing to believe in God. The real danger is of coming to believe such dreadful things about Him. The conclusion I dread is not, 'So there's no God after all,' but 'So this is what God's really like. Deceive yourself no longer.'"[2] Lewis continued his painful reflections by saying, "After the death of a friend, years ago, I had for some time a most vivid feeling of certainty about his continued life; even his enhanced life. I have begged to be given even one hundredth part of the same assurance about [my wife]. There is no answer. Only the locked door, the iron curtain, the vacuum, absolute zero. 'Them as asks don't get.' I was a fool to ask. For now, even if that assurance came I should distrust it. I should think it a self-hypnosis induced by my own prayers."[3]

Sometimes trials can be very faith-shaking events in our lives. From time to time overanxiety, worry, fear, focusing on a single thing—a single doctrine or event—may create a faith-shaking experience. Jacob himself also wrote, "Behold, my beloved brethren, I will unfold this mystery unto you; if I do not, by any means, get shaken from my firmness in the Spirit, and stumble because of my over anxiety for you" (Jacob 4:18). We have all experienced those moments of overanxiety.

We may encounter a teacher, a professor, an intellectual whose ideas cause our faith to tremble. We may read something that has the same effect. Often these criticisms are given in tones of mockery. We can hear the mocking tone of Korihor as he challenges the faith of the Nephites, telling them that their belief in God is "the effect of a frenzied mind." This "derangement of your minds," he indicates, comes of listening to old prophets, old men, old authorities, old traditions of the fathers, and so forth (Alma 30:16). I have had conversations with many students who have come under that style of attack, given in the same tone of sarcastic mockery.

Apathy, fatigue, being life-weary, often shakes our faith. A recently returned missionary said to me, "I don't know why I don't feel it so strongly anymore. Maybe I never did. It just becomes more and more difficult to continue." Our faith must endure through spiritual attrition, hence we must rely on the Lord's promise that "they that wait upon the Lord shall renew their strength; they shall mount up with wings as eagles" (Isaiah 40:31).

Anti-Mormon literature may be the Achilles heel for some members. Almost always this type of argument against our testimonies takes the form of what I call "a one-spoke wheel." One-spoke wheels won't hold any weight. If we visualize a wagon wheel with numerous spokes radiating out from the hub, we get an idea of how weak and ineffective a wheel would be if it contained only a single spoke. This is true of doctrinal things also. A critic, however, may pull out a statement from Brigham Young, or some scientific study, or a verse in the Book of Mormon about horses or silk. They will, then, base their whole doubt, their whole faith-challenging attack against the Church, on that one single spoke, as if the doctrines of the Church were founded on obscure statements or single verses. If we really want to know what Brigham Young thought about something, we need to get all the statements he made about it. We put all the spokes in the wheel. Clarification is uncovered in this manner. A one-spoke wheel won't hold any weight. I often say to my students, "Be careful you don't let a one-spoke wheel shake your faith." Questions about historical people or facts, polygamy, priesthood to every worthy male, and so on, may shake faith. Scientific theories or assertions, evolution, DNA studies among the American Indians, Egyptology and the book of Abraham may all cause members to pause with a troubled mind or heart.

Sometimes we have questions about perceived doctrinal stands when the Church has never taken that stand. These may rest in either cultural or traditional areas. When I was young I believed that the Native American people from Alaska to Tierra del Fuego were all the descendents of Lehi. That's a difficult position to defend, and it's never been the doctrine of the Church—it may be a traditional or cultural belief, but never the official doctrine. Lehi himself said, "The Lord hath covenanted this land unto me, and to my children forever, *and also all those who should be led out of other countries* by the hand of the Lord" (2 Nephi 1:5; emphasis added). The Book of Mormon itself allows for many more groups to have come here. If we're not careful, we may assume we have to defend ideas or positions that we never had to defend in the first place.

Often leaders' weaknesses shake faith. These may include past leaders, present leaders, Joseph Smith, the bishop, the stake president, or one of the Brethren. There is an undefined assumption that they all should be close to perfection, at least in their callings, if not in their personal lives. Can we allow men to be human in behavior, in thoughts, in opinions, in application of principles, in policies? We are too weak and frail ourselves to demand perfection of any human being regardless of their position or stature. If I desire allowances to be made for my own inadequacies, why should I not grant that same tolerance for others? We hope others will be gracious and forgiving of our weaknesses. Can we not extend that equally for our leaders?

What we call "political correctness" often shakes faith. One may question or oppose the viewpoint of the Church on gay marriage, abortion, women's issues, environmental concerns, or even a perceived leaning toward one or another of the political parties. I know a student who feels she cannot be a good Latter-day Saint because she is of a political party that she suspects other members look at questioningly. They wonder at her allegiance to it. These pressures we put on each other must be trimmed.

Friends often shake our faith. Now and then our beliefs may sound so silly, so incredible in an atmosphere of those who do not share them with us. That malaise can be difficult to overcome and may, with time, trouble even the deepest held beliefs.

Falling in love may shake faith. We must be cautious of seeing things through the sometimes distorted lens of our romantic emotions and longings. Emotion is one of the most unstable of foundations. It may distress what our reason has long ago sorted out, pondered carefully, and accepted.

Life's unfairness, its injustices, its inconsistencies can shake faith, especially for those who have been righteous and often face Job-like experiences. It may appear there is no God, or at least not the one we believed in as a child. He can seem very far away during certain moments of our lives.

There is a final faith-shaking experience I would add to our growing list. It is what I call a "black hole" moment. There are instances in life when it seems like all the light is being sucked right out of me, all the faith, all the past sweet assurances; when it all looks so unbelievably incredible. I remember being in Bryce Canyon, Utah, once, looking up at the stars through a telescope and feeling infinitesimally small, knowing that in the solar system alone, 99.9 percent of all matter is in the sun. We are one tiny little dust speck. How could I really believe that what happened on this little dust speck mattered to the Creator of all that immensity, or that he would send his Son to this particular dust speck to initiate his infinite Atonement? How could I continue to feel, with my accustomed warm intensity, that there was a Being who heard my whispered prayer or received my offered thoughts? These are times—those black hole moments—when it seems like all my faith is being pulled forcefully out of my very core and I must hold on tight lest I lose the center of my soul.

These moments come to us, and they will, in all probability, continue to come to a greater or lesser degree depending on our circumstances and personality. We are not alone, however, when we feel the spiritual earth under our faith begin to tremble. Maybe one of these isn't your particular concern. Perhaps you've never been troubled by a leader, but you might have been troubled by a historical fact. Maybe you've never had a problem with a friend, but did experience one with a professor or college class. Regardless of our own unique situations, what we want to try to create, what we need to establish, is a faith like that of Jacob, a faith that cannot be shaken.

PYRAMID OF FAITH

I'd like to try and build with you what I call the pyramid of faith. Picture in your mind a pyramid. Pyramids are the most stable of all structures. That is why there are still pyramids standing in Central America, in Egypt, and in other places. They can withstand fairly severe earthquakes. We want our faith and our testimonies to be firm and solid like a pyramid. We want them to be broad-based. When imagining a pyramid with solid foundation stones leading upwards in ever-decreasing layers to a point, divide it into three horizontal sections. The upper section, the highest point, we'll label *testimony* or, if you prefer, *faith*. This is the part of our personal pyramid where we say, "I know." It consists of a number of different stones:

"I know that Joseph Smith is a prophet."

"I know that God lives."

"I know that Jesus is the Christ."

"I know that we are led by living prophets today."

The uppermost layers are the "I know" part of our pyramid of faith.

What does this upper tier of faith rest on? The second underlying section of the pyramid, which supports the upper layer, is described admirably by the Apostle Paul. Paul offers us, I believe, the finest definition of faith in scripture. This is what he said: "Faith is the substance of things hoped for . . ." That is a great word, *substance*. The Joseph Smith Translation renders it *assurance*. The Greek validates that change and also adds the words "basis, foundation" (see Hebrews 11:1*b*). Faith is built on substance, on assurance, on a foundation which is the basis for its support. Continuing on with Paul, we see another wonderful word. "Faith is . . . the evidence of things not seen" (Hebrews 11:1). *Evidence* is perhaps an even greater word than *substance*. In the second layer of our pyramid of faith we can place the words *substance, assurance,* and *evidence.* In my years of teaching I have found that many Latter-day Saints believe that faith is built on a foundation of emotion and feelings, and that can certainly be part of it. But I really love the words *substance, assurance,* and *evidence.* There is a concreteness about them that faith-shaking experiences or people can't remove.

What is evidence built on? Let us now form the bottom and broadest section of the pyramid. This third or lowest layer, the most expansive of the three sections, must be able to bear the weight of evidence. Evidence rests on three things. In the bedrock portion of the pyramid we place the words *reason, experience,* and *authority.* As we examine what we believe in we might say: "My reason tells me this is true," or "My experience tells me this is true," or, "I haven't had the experience, but I trust the authority or the experience or the reason of someone else." Naturally, the combination of all three is desirable. That combination provides us with a very solid kind of faith, one that can withstand some fairly severe spiritual earthquakes.

I KNOW, AND I KNOW WHY I KNOW!

With this background in mind let us see how Alma the Younger handles Korihor, one of the most famous faith-shakers in the Book of Mormon. Alma is, in a manner of speaking, the faith-shaker expert in the Book of Mormon. He faces Nehor, Korihor, and the Zoramites. I suppose there is some appropriateness in this, as he was once a faith-shaker himself. Jacob handles the first one, Sherem, but Alma deals with the above triple threat to spiritual conviction. Alma uses the power of his faith when talking to Korihor. He bears his testimony. What kind of pyramid does he present? "And then Alma said unto him: Believest thou that there is a God? And he answered, Nay. Now Alma said unto him: Will ye deny again that there is a God, and also deny the Christ? For behold, I say unto you, I know there is a God, and also that Christ shall come" (Alma 30:37–39).

That is what we call a testimony, is it not? In testimony meeting we often hear members say, "I know that God lives. I know that Jesus is the Christ. I know we're led by a living prophet." Alma has just offered Korihor that type of intense conviction. Notice the familiar word he next uses. "And now what *evidence* have ye that there is no God, or that Christ cometh not? I say unto you that ye have none, save it be your word only" (Alma 30:40; emphasis added).

If I were Korihor, after having heard Alma's last statement, I would say: "Alma, you stole my line. That's my line. That's what I say to you. That's not what you say to me. You have to provide the evidence." Sometimes we let faith-shakers back us into a corner and say, "Prove your faith! Prove your convictions! Show us your evidence! You have nothing to go on except your own word. Anyone can say, 'I know.'" When this happens, occasionally, the very best strategy is to go on the offensive, as does Alma, and turn it around. This we do politely, tactfully, but firmly. It is calming to realize that there is no evidence that there is no God. There is no evidence that Jesus was not his divine Son who brought the Resurrection. There is no evidence that Joseph Smith did not receive the visit of the Father and the Son in the grove that spring morning.

I have a daughter who was having her faith challenged in a university class by a professor who took great delight, in the name of academic thought and broadmindedness, in trying to destroy faith, especially Latter-day Saint faith. Every week she'd call me on the telephone and say, "Dad, he said this, he said this. And it sounds so good. I don't believe it, but it sounds good. I can't find the way to refute it."

I would talk her through it. After several weeks of this I said to her, "If you're willing to risk a little lower grade, challenge him. Don't let him get away with always putting you and the class on the defensive. You can do this with almost every philosophical question debated in class. Do what Alma the Younger did!" We then talked about his strategy with Korihor. The next week she called me up, and she was just thrilled. I asked her what happened.

She said, "Well, the question of the day was, 'Do we know that there are moral absolutes?' He said: 'We don't know that there are moral absolutes. There is no proof that there are moral, ethical absolutes. Society makes the rules and they can change what is right and what is wrong.'"

"What did you do?" I asked her.

"I raised my hand and I quoted Alma's sentence, applying it to our discussion topic. I said, 'What evidence do you have that there are no moral absolutes? You don't have any evidence. It's just your word.'"

I was so proud of her courage. "What happened then?"

She said, "It was wonderful. The kids all got into it and they kept saying, 'Yeah, what evidence do you have?' And finally he had to admit there was no evidence for his point either."

I repeat: It is calming to know there is no evidence that there is no God. There is no evidence Jesus was not his Divine Son. There is no evidence Joseph Smith did not see the Father and the Son in the grove. There is no evidence the Book of Mormon is not a true account of ancient inhabitants. No evidence!

After having turned the tables on Korihor, Alma effectively said, "I will now give you my evidence, my substance, and my assurance for my belief in God. And my evidence is founded upon experience, reason, and authority." Alma is going to show us the lower portion of his pyramid. He will say: "I know, and what is more, I know why I know." It is a very good exercise to sit down sometimes and say, "These are the things I know, I affirm, I assert, and these are the reasons why I know them." We must learn to put the substance, the evidence, that which is based on reason, authority, and experience under our affirmation of belief.

ALMA'S EVIDENCES FOR GOD'S EXISTENCE

Alma produces four evidences for the existence of God. He gives us one of the finest arguments in behalf of God's reality of which I know. Let us look at them one by one. "Thou hast had signs enough," Alma declared. "Will ye tempt your God? Will ye say, Show unto me a sign, when ye have the testimony of all these thy brethren?" (Alma 30:44). There is evidence number one. What Alma's calling upon here is something we could demonstrate in any assembly of Latter-day Saints. I could say to an audience, "I'm going to give you five or ten minutes to think, and then I'm going to call on some of you. I want you to come up and share an experience in your life that told you there was a God and that he was aware of you." I believe that anyone in that audience could come up with a simple, sweet little experience from his or her life that confirmed that.

I will give you an example from the life of one of my children. When my daughter was twelve years old, we moved to Utah and she entered junior high school. It is my opinion, based on experience, that junior high school is just a horrible time to be alive. I personally suspect that junior high school was invented by Lucifer in hell. At least that is what my experience attests. It's a difficult time, and my daughter was very unhappy during those first months. She didn't feel like she had any friends. She was singled out and picked on—the word *persecuted* may be a little strong, but what she endured was just shy of it. She was a very unhappy little girl. It didn't matter that Mom and Dad loved her because, in her mind, we had to.

She was preparing to receive her patriarchal blessing. In our family, we had our children receive their patriarchal blessing at age thirteen in order to give them a significant source of inspiration and help through their difficult teenage years. My daughter began to pray independently about something she hoped would happen when she received her blessing. She didn't tell anybody else, but she wanted very much for her Father in Heaven to tell her that he loved her in her patriarchal blessing. If he would do that, she thought she could survive the trauma she was facing at school. If she had told us, my faith is such that I probably would have tried to prime the revelatory pump a little. I might have called the patriarch and said, "This is the voice of inspiration! You will tell Kirsten Wilcox that her Father in Heaven loves her."

But we didn't know the contents of her yearning prayers. This was a private matter between her and her Heavenly Father. In time she received her blessing. We could tell that it was a moving experience for her. On the way home, her mother and I asked her about it. How did she feel? She told us about the focus of her prayers and her desire for confirmation from her Father in Heaven. The very first sentence of my daughter's patriarchal blessing, after the formal introduction, says: "Heavenly Father is pleased that you have the desire to know of His feeling and His love for you." What did that say to a thirteen-year-old girl? "I'm aware of you. I know you. You are important and I love you." That story is one of profound simplicity. Some may say it is all a coincidence. But there are millions of such simple things in and out of the Church. These are the tiny miracles, most of which we will never hear about. They represent Alma's first evidence for God. He is basing his evidence, his assurance, on the experience of thousands.

For evidence number two, Alma appeals to the vision of the prophets: "And also [the testimony of] all the holy prophets" (Alma 30:44). This part of Alma's pyramid is based on authority. Most of us have testimonies that are strongly founded in our confidence in the knowledge of others. This is true in every aspect of life. I have never seen God, but I believe in those who have. That belief is strengthened by the realization that there is a marvelous consistency in all of their testimonies and in all they teach. Alma's second evidence, therefore, is the authority of the prophets.

A third evidence Alma relies on is that of the order found in the creation. "All things denote there is a God; yea, even the earth, and all things that are upon the face of it, yea, and its motion, yea, and also all the planets which move in their regular form do witness that there is a Supreme Creator" (Alma 30:44). My reason, Alma says, tells me you can't have all that order and beauty and variety without having something behind it all. My favorite statement from Galileo—the man who first closely looked at all that order—says, "If the sun with all those planets moving around it can ripen the smallest bunch of grapes as if it has nothing else to do, why then should I doubt His power?"[4] The earth is set at the exact distance from the sun so that the tilting of its axis creates the seasons. Move it just a little farther out, and all life dies—too cold. Move it just a little closer, and all life dies—too warm. This type of order does not come by chance. Can you see that Alma is relying on the three foundations of *experience, authority,* and *reason?*

Alma supplies his last proof, which encompasses all three genres of evidence. "The scriptures are laid before thee" (Alma 30:44). The very existence of the scriptures confirms God's reality. The scriptures are filled with authoritative accounts. They also are a catalyst for validating and creating experiences. Let me elaborate on that. Remember Jacob's testimony—he said, referring to Sherem,

"He had hope to shake me from the faith, notwithstanding the many revelations and the many things which I had seen concerning these things; for I truly had seen angels, and they had ministered unto me. And also, I had heard the voice of the Lord speaking unto me in very word, from time to time; wherefore, I could not be shaken" (Jacob 7:5).

Jacob is telling us that revelation is a key in the formation of unshakable faith. We may ask, "Is there someplace else in Jacob where we could find out what created his revelatory encounters? What induced them?" In Jacob 4 we discover the answer. "We search the prophets, and we have many revelations" (Jacob 4:6). Notice that the catalyst for the revelations was the searching of the prophets. The Nephites were searching the scriptures! "We search the prophets, and we have many revelations and the spirit of prophecy; and having all these witnesses we obtain a hope, and our faith becometh unshaken" (Jacob 4:6). Searching the prophets leads to revelatory experiences, which leads to the creation of unshakable faith. I think it is interesting that after Sherem was silenced by Jacob, the people who had once been fooled by him begin to do something they might not have been doing before, at least not to a sufficient degree. "And it came to pass that peace and the love of God was restored again among the people; *and they searched the scriptures,* and hearkened no more to the words of this wicked man" (Jacob 7:23; emphasis added). The scriptures are full of authority. The scriptures create experience, and the scriptures appeal to our reason. They work! The principles and the promises in them are efficacious when we truly live them. The reasonable man will find deep wisdom contained therein.

My own reason tells me that someone like Joseph Smith, with his learning and background, could not have produced what he did. If one does not want to credit him as a prophet receiving revelation, then he is a genius on a level few men in history have ever achieved. Whenever a student comes into the office having had a faith-shaking experience, a little trouble regarding Joseph Smith and the Restoration, I often will sit the student down and say: "I want you to listen for a few moments. I'm going to read some things to you." I choose different passages to share, depending on the circumstances and challenges he or she is facing, but I read to him or her the words of Joseph Smith from the scriptures. Here are some I select from: 1 Nephi 8; 2 Nephi 2; 3 Nephi 17; D&C 88; D&C 93; Moses 1; and Moses 7. Some of these contain very beautiful words, some of them very deep words, some of them very powerful words. They are spiritually and behaviorally motivating. I watch my guest and I can feel the calm settling in. Then it is often simply a matter of just saying, "Could a man who was a fraud, a deceiver, a pretender, write such powerful words?"

In the footnote at the end of Joseph Smith–History, contained in the Pearl of Great Price, Oliver Cowdery described the visit of John the Baptist and his brief words now recorded in Doctrine and Covenants 13. It is a one-verse section, yet if what Oliver Cowdery says is true about a one-verse section, what does that suggest about Section 88, or Moses 7, or 1 Nephi 8, or Section 93? Notice what Oliver says about it:

"No; nor has this earth power to give the joy, to bestow the peace, or comprehend the wisdom which was contained in each sentence as they were delivered by the power of the Holy Spirit! [Notice the three things the Spirit gives—joy, peace, and wisdom.] Man may deceive his fellow-men, deception may follow deception, and the children of the wicked one may have power to seduce the foolish and untaught, till naught but fiction feeds the many, and the fruit of falsehood carries in its current the giddy to the grave; but one touch with the finger of his love, yes, one ray of glory from the upper world, or one word from the mouth of the Savior, from the bosom of eternity, strikes it all into insignificance, and blots it forever from the mind" (Joseph Smith–History 1:71, footnote).

When the faith-shaking contests come, we need to read the words, feel the peace, receive the joy, comprehend the wisdom, and hold firm. I hate to see people give up faith by default when there is so much that could calm their doubts.

The scriptures, then, are Alma's fourth evidence. Can you see in that little exchange with Korihor how he's built his foundation? He knows! More important, he knows why he knows! The why-he-knows is based on reason, experience, and authority. These are all open to us. Our challenge in life is to search for the evidence, the substance to put underneath the "I know" of our faith. Alma will tell us exactly how to do that in one of those powerful chapters that I read to my students, or my children—or myself—when they are having trouble with their faith: Alma 32.

"An Experiment upon My Words"

Alma 32 is one of those wonderful places in the contributions of the Prophet Joseph Smith where I think, "Well, if Joseph made that up, we'd better give him credit for being a genius because there is so much power, dignity, and insight in it." It seems as if Alma saw into our future world and responded with: "I know that your world is going to be a post-scientific revolution world. I am aware that it will be a world of empirical knowledge, of proof, so I'm going to tell you how to create, or search for, or find evidence, on your terms, with a thesis that fits perfectly into your environment."

We can approach Alma 32 in a number of ways. We can view it through an agricultural lens—the planting of the seed and the subsequent growth of the tree. This is the main metaphor employed by Alma because he's talking to an agricultural society. However, let us draw our application from one of the other words Alma uses. That word is "experiment." Alma invites us to try "an experiment upon my words" (Alma 32:27). Let us review briefly the scientific method of discovery, because I'm going to apply that method of discovery in creating evidence and support for our testimonies.

We can simplify the scientific method by dividing it into three stages. We start with a hypothesis. The hypothesis is usually—indeed almost always—stated in positive terms. In other words, we're not trying to disprove something; we're doing just the opposite. The hypothesis of Alma 32 is, briefly stated, "Jesus is the Christ." That's the issue at hand. It doesn't matter what we use as our hypothesis. We could explore "Joseph Smith was a prophet," "Thomas S. Monson is a living prophet today," "tithing is a true principle that creates financial security," "there is a living God," or "the Book of Mormon is a true account of ancient people." In Alma's case, it is "Jesus is the Christ."

The second element in empirical inquiry is running the experiment. There are different words we can use to describe this step. We gather data. We make observations. We test. We prove. In Alma's case, we experiment. That is his invitation, and we're going to examine what he promises we will observe if we try his experiment.

The third component is our conclusion. We need to check our data and come to a conclusion regarding our original hypothesis. We take our conclusion back to the hypothesis and say, "We will have to change it or adapt it." Or, we might look at it and say, "Based on what I've seen and observed, it looks like my hypothesis is holding true. I have not proved it a law yet, but all the indicators are pointing in that direction."

That is the basic scientific method. Most hypotheses rest on what are called "givens." Before we try Alma's experiment on any aspect of truth we wish to know, let us state his four givens.

Given #1

Alma is addressing a crowd on the top of a hill. It is an aristocratic group. A poorer faction timidly approaches with a question. Alma turns around, faces the poorer group, and sees immediately that they are more prepared to listen to him. It is to this less aristocratic assembly that he preaches what is contained in Alma 32. We read in the scriptures, "He beheld that their afflictions had truly humbled them, and that they were in a preparation to hear the word" (Alma 32:6). Our first given, therefore, is that of humility. If we want to find religious truth, if we want to do the experiment, we begin from a position of humility.

According to Alma, it doesn't matter whether we're compelled to be humble or are humble on our own. Our state of mind is the critical factor, regardless of how it was attained. C. S. Lewis once wrote: "In God you come up against something which is in every respect immeasurably superior to yourself. Unless you know God as that—and, therefore, know yourself as nothing in comparison—you do not know God at all. As long as you are proud you cannot know God. A proud man is always looking down on things and people: and, of course, as long as you are looking down, you cannot see something that is above you."[5] I repeat: our first given, if you're going to try the experiment to find religious truth, to discover evidence, is that you must begin in a state of humility.

Given #2

Alma taught: "Remember, that God is merciful unto all who believe on his name; therefore he desireth, in the first place, that ye should believe, yea, even on his word" (Alma 32:22). Given number two is: God wants us to believe. He wants us to find spiritual truth. What if somebody counters, "What if my hypothesis is: 'Is there a God?'" If that is your hypothesis, then assume that if there is a God, he wants you to know, and it will still work.

Given #3

"And now, he imparteth his word by angels unto men, yea, not only men but women also. Now this is not all; little children do have words given unto them many times, which confound the wise and the learned" (Alma 32:23). Given number three is, not only does God desire that we know truth, he will reveal it to us and it doesn't matter whether one is a man, woman, or child. I can't say, "Well, God reveals to men, but he won't reveal to me—I'm a woman."

He responds, "I'll reveal to women."

"I'm just a child. He'll only reveal truth to adults."

"No—men, women, children. All are accepted and can search for truth with full confidence." So we now have three givens. We say, "I'm humble. I remember God wants me to know truth, and I realize he will teach me truth."

Given #4

Given number four may be the most important of all. Alma told the poor Zoramites, "Now, as I said concerning faith—that it was not a perfect knowledge—even so it is with my words." There is such a comfort in these next few words for many members of the Church: "Ye cannot know of their surety at first, unto perfection, any more than faith is a perfect knowledge" (Alma 32:26).

"*Ye cannot know of their surety at first, unto perfection.*" Almost every one of my children, sometime in his or her life, has come to me and said, "Dad, I'm not sure I know the Church is true." I try not to panic, as a parent might at such a moment. We sit down and we talk. It doesn't take very long before they realize they have a perfectly sound testimony. They just didn't think they had one. I remember a conversation I had with my daughter one evening. She came and sat on the bed and said, in tears, "Dad, I don't have a testimony. I don't know if the Church is true." She was fourteen. I tried not to panic. We talked and I said, "How do you feel about Joseph Smith and about Jesus?" She answered and it was obvious that she had a wonderful testimony. She simply thought she had to have it "unto perfection" at age fourteen.

I have discovered—and this is true of many, not just my children or my students at the university—that we have this idea that you either know or you don't know, that it is all black or white. People stand up in testimony meeting and say, "I know beyond a shadow of a doubt . . ." There are a few phrases I would eliminate from the Latter-day Saint vocabulary if I could, and that is one of them. It tends to create guilt or uncertainty in some of those who hear it. I'm not sure how big a shadow of a doubt is. I'm not sure I would recognize a shadow of a doubt. But I am sure that I've had shadows of doubt cross my mind and my heart. Yet we get this idea that it's all or nothing—I either know or I don't know. I pray, and God tells me, and then I have a perfect knowledge. Alma says that I can't reach that point without traveling a substantial distance. Using scientific language, we can't go from hypothesis faith to full-law faith overnight, can we? I think Joseph Smith did in the Sacred Grove, but that was a singular experience in world history. In Alma's analogy, I can't go from a seed to harvesting fruit in a day. That doesn't mean I'm not going to know some things, that I'm not going to see some evidence from the seed turning slowly into a tree, but it releases me from the all-or-nothing, I-know-it-or-I-don't quandary.

When I served as a bishop, many times young men would be nervous about going into the mission field and testifying. They would say to me, "I'm not sure I can say to people, 'I know.'" In conversations with them it was soon discovered that they did know things, or at least they felt deeply about certain truths of the gospel. They were going to be fine missionaries. Well, that's the fourth given. We can't know for surety at first "unto perfection."

"A Good Seed"

If I accept those four givens, I'm ready to test my hypothesis. Alma said, "If ye will awake and arouse your faculties, even to an experiment upon my words, and exercise a particle of faith, yea, even if ye can no more than desire to believe, let this desire work in you" (Alma 32:27). Notice that Alma insists that we test our hypothesis beginning from a positive position. Remember the hypothesis is stated as a positive. We are not trying to disprove something. No one is absolutely, totally, and completely objective about anything. We carry too much bias with us. I know people will say "I'm objective," but I'm always suspicious. In addition, there seems to be an idea floating around in critical circles that the negative is the objective side. So people might say, "You can't really judge whether Mormonism is true because you are a Mormon, and therefore, you can't look at your religion objectively."

And I will say, "Why does not being a Mormon make you more objective than being one? Why is an opposing bias more trustworthy than an affirmative one?"

Because we can't be absolutely totally objective about anything, our civilization has come to the conclusion that it is better, if we're going to err on either the positive or the negative side, to err on the positive. Alma understands this and says, "desire to believe" (Alma 32:27). In a court of law in most of the civilized world, you are innocent until proven guilty. If I can't get total objectivity, I'm going to err on the positive. If I do otherwise, according to Alma, I might "resist the Spirit of the Lord" (Alma 32:28). This will be my fault because I was trying to disprove something. The key in religious matters must always be: "*Desire to believe.*"

Alma continues: "Let this desire work in you, even until ye believe in a manner that ye can give place for a portion of my words. Now, we will compare the word unto a seed. Now, if ye give place, that a seed may be planted in your heart, behold, if it be a true seed, or a good seed . . ." (Alma 32:27–28). Let's pause a moment and reflect on Alma's use of words.

I think it is interesting that from this time on, Alma drops the word *true* and uses only the word *good.* He uses it twelve more times from this point. It was usually easier for my children, my students, and departing missionaries to say, "I know there is goodness in this Church, in the Book of Mormon, in this belief, in this man, in Joseph Smith. I don't have a perfect knowledge of truth, but I know there is goodness. I feel it. I see it." If you look closely in the verses of chapter 32, you'll see that Alma uses the word *good* every time from this point on. We're not saying that we don't know things and can't know they're true. We're emphasizing another word that can be used, that often removes some pressure from people. Is there really a significant difference between saying, "I know this is true" and "I know this is good"? In Western civilization, truth, beauty, and goodness were essentially interchangable.

If it is a good seed, Alma promises, it will do four things for us. These will comprise the bulk of our observations. Each of them has the word *begin* in front of it because, remember, it's not a perfect knowledge at first. *Begin* is also a critical word to watch for in Alma 32. In the Church, we tend to emphasize the first of the four things. There are three other things spoken of, and sometimes, based on what your personality is like, you might respond to the third more than the first, or the second more than the fourth. We want all of them, because together they make the foundation of our pyramid stronger, but let us not forget that there are four things. Let's see what they are.

Swell—Enlarge—Enlighten—Delicious

Alma first tells us that the truth, or idea, or hypothesis that is good, "will begin to swell within your breasts" (Alma 32:28). That is the validation that we generally emphasize. We will know the truth by this feeling in the bosom. We will have a spiritual—physical even—response to truth. I don't much like the word *emotional*. Emotions can be unstable. I'd rather say we will have a spiritual and physical response. We will feel things in our hearts. Alma uses a motion metaphor—swelling—to describe the effect of the Holy Spirit. If that phrase doesn't work for you, then you may pick another that better describes your experience. Taking our cue from another metaphor that describes the same sensation, we might speak of a burning in the bosom (see D&C 9:8). This is a metaphor that draws on the sensation of warmth or heat rather than that of motion. Alma consistently prefers the sensation of motion.

"I don't know if I've ever experienced a swelling," someone might say.

"How about a burning in the bosom?" we ask.

"No, don't know if I've ever had that."

"How about a quaking in the bones?" we try next. That was Joseph Smith's description in Doctrine and Covenants 85:6. I don't know if my bones have ever quaked. If metaphorical language does not work there are other more straight-forward descriptions that might strike home. Have you ever felt joy? Peace? Enlightenment? Love? Goodness? These are perfectly acceptable and used in multiple scriptures. We'll have a physical, spiritual response to truth. That's the first observation.

Alma continues and gives us our second observation, "When you feel these swelling motions, ye will begin to say within yourselves—It must needs be that this is a good seed, or that the word is good, for it beginneth to enlarge my soul" (Alma 32:28). That's our second observation. The truth will enlarge the soul. I take that to mean we will have a behavioral response to truth. If it is good, if it is true, we ought to be better people because of it. If The Church of Jesus Christ of

Latter-day Saints is good, is filled with truth, its members should be some of the best people in the world—which is exactly what you find.

I will give you an example of the enlarging of the soul. When I was on my mission to France we baptized a young couple. The wife was a petite French woman—just tiny. She was married to an almost stereotypical macho husband who was a bit of a bully. They had two little boys, who were afraid of their father. You could see it. When we would enter that house we could feel the tension, the fear of the wife and the children. They did not want to say or do anything that would upset their father. This man, however, took to the gospel like a duck to water. Two weeks after we knocked on their door, they wanted to be baptized.

On the day of their baptism, the wife came to me and said, "Elder Wilcox, I thought you should know I'm filing for divorce from my husband. My children and I are afraid of him. I don't want my children to live that way always. But I won't tell him because if I tell him, it will be very bad." Then she said, "But I have never seen him take to anything like he has to your church. So I'm going to give the church one year to change my husband. If it's right, if it's true, it will change him." That's quite a challenge. Was she being fair? Was her assumption true? I think so! If it's a good seed, it ought to enlarge the soul. That does not mean it will make perfect people overnight. Remember, the key word is "begin." But there should be some changes.

I was transferred a few months later. I came back after more than a year had passed. They were still married. I thought that was a good sign. I went to see the family. They were still active. She was pregnant. I thought that was a good sign. I asked her what happened:

"How are things?"

She said, "Oh, you'll have to see it. My husband will be home in a half hour." A half hour later he came in. The little boys were playing in the corner. As he came in, they jumped up and ran to him. The tension was gone from the house. He still had rough spots, and had a long way to go, but the gospel was enlarging his soul.

Some people feel the Church is true and good because they've had that burning-in-the-bosom answer to prayer, and some people believe it's true because it makes them good people. They look around and they see other good people. They are reassured. The enlarging of the soul is taking place. Would we dare to judge one conclusion as better than the other?

The third observation has to do with the mind. "Yea, it beginneth to enlighten my understanding" (Alma 32:28). That indicates an intellectual response to goodness and truth. Later on, Alma states this same point in the following manner, "Your understanding doth begin to be enlightened, and your mind doth begin to expand" (Alma 32:34). We *should* have a mental response to truth. Answers *should* come to questions. Things should make sense. Wisdom should begin to penetrate. Ideas should begin to flow through the searching mind. Remember, one of the blocks of our foundation is the block of reason. We can anticipate experiencing a mental stimulation of our thoughts.

I remember a sister once coming up to me after a class and saying, "I'm very worried about my husband. I don't think he has a testimony of the gospel." The man was faithful and active, so we talked a little bit about it.

I said, "Is he a temple recommend holder?"

"Yes."

"Does he go to church?"

"Yes."

"Does he teach your family?"

"He's great with the kids."

"Does he pray and read the scriptures?"

"Of course!"

"What's the problem?" I asked.

"He's never felt the burning in the bosom." I happened to know this individual. He was a thinker, and the focus and foundation of his testimony was in his mind. I understand the type because much of my own faith rests here. Is the heart a greater gauge for truth and goodness than the mind? We want both, right? But this particular individual responded to the truth in a more enlightening-of-the-understanding way than a swelling-in-the-breast way. It would be a sad thing if the "mind members" judged the "heart members" who judged the "soul members." We may have different cores within our individual testimonies. The other factors will come if and when they are necessary as our growth continues.

Alma draws his fourth observation from the sense of taste. "Yea, it beginneth to be delicious to me" (Alma 32:28). When something is delicious, you don't have to choke it down. It tastes good. Later on, Alma says, "After ye have tasted this light . . ." (Alma 32:35). That is a great phrase—to taste light. Normally we see light, but in this case you taste light. It's delicious. You want more. The gospel should create a hunger to want to hear and learn more.

What would your response be if you were an investigator learning about the Church and were newly married, or if you had been married all your life and were devoted to your spouse, and your spouse to you, and the missionary said: "Do you know that a revelation was given to Joseph Smith that taught that the love between a husband and a wife is a holy, sanctified thing and will continue beyond the grave? There will be husbands and wives—families—forever!"?

When that profoundly beautiful truth is taught, the response ought not to be, "Oh no! That's a horrible thought." The response should be, "That tastes good. That thought is delicious to us. Tell us more." Do you understand Alma's meaning of truth being delicious?

Actually, if we put the first letter of the four observations together—swell, enlarge, enlighten, delicious—what have we spelled? Seed! That should be enough to make me a believer in the Book of Mormon for the rest of my life! (Of course, it doesn't work in any other language, so I suppose the Book of Mormon is more true in English.) At any rate, it is a handy thing to help us remember the four things that goodness and truth will do for someone running the experiment.

Growing the Tree

If the word is good, the word you used for your hypothesis, you should begin to observe these four things. This is the data you will gather. It's swelling, enlarging, enlightening, and delicious. Now we come to our conclusions, the last step of the scientific method of inquiry. Here are Alma's conclusions: "Would not this increase your faith? I say unto you, Yea; nevertheless it hath not grown up to a perfect knowledge. [Your testimony is not a law yet.] But behold, as the seed swelleth, and sprouteth, and beginneth to grow, then you must needs say that the seed is good; for behold it swelleth, and sprouteth, and beginneth to grow. And now, behold, will not this strengthen your faith? Yea, it will strengthen your faith: for ye will say I know that this is a good seed" (Alma 32:29–30). Those are the words of testimony. You can say "I know."

We can say, "I know there is goodness in the Book of Mormon, in Joseph Smith, in the living prophets, in the Church, in the belief in Christ." We can say this about anything of which we are trying to ascertain the truth: I know this is a good seed. "Are ye sure that this a good seed?" Alma asks. "I say unto you, Yea; for every seed bringeth forth unto its own likeness. Therefore, if a seed groweth it is good, but if it groweth not, behold it is not good, therefore it is cast away" (Alma 32:31–32). "And now, behold, is your knowledge perfect? Yea, your knowledge is perfect in that thing" (Alma 32:34). We have perfect knowledge, but only in the first round of experimenting.

What would we think of a scientist who conducted one set of experiments and immediately, without reaffirming the results at least a few more times, published his findings as though he had discovered some great eternal truth? We would be skeptical of his premature assumptions. What must we therefore do? We must return to our testing, our observations and data-gathering. We do it again and again and again. We keep gathering data, and making observations, and experimenting. That is what Alma tells us to do. He says, "After ye have tasted this light is your knowledge perfect? Behold I say unto you, Nay; neither must ye lay aside your faith, for ye have only exercised your faith to plant the seed that ye might try the experiment to know if the seed was good" (Alma 32:35–36).

At this point, perhaps all I know is that there is goodness in this belief, teaching, religion, or book of scripture. "And behold, as the tree beginneth to grow, ye will say: Let us nourish it with great care, that it may get root, that it may grow up, and bring forth fruit unto us. And now behold, if ye nourish it with much care it will get root, and grow up, and bring forth fruit. But if ye neglect the tree, and take no thought for its nourishment, behold it will not get any root; and when the heat of the sun cometh and scorcheth it [when the faith-shakers come], because it hath no root it withers away [because it had no foundation based on evidence]" (Alma 32:37–38).

Alma has told us how to create founding, solid, assuring evidence. But we've got to do it again and again. The broader the base of our pyramid, the more shaking it can withstand and the higher we can build it. We now take our conclusions back to our original hypothesis and say, "I haven't seen anything yet that makes me believe that what I thought was true isn't true. I'll continue to observe and gather data, and live by what I am learning."

There is a beautiful poem that Robert Frost wrote that I often think about when I visualize my own pyramid and my need to make it strong enough to face the faith-shakers. It is titled "Into My Own." Frost uses the imagery of a journey through a dark forest to stand for the deep things in his mind and heart, things that he knows he will travel through. He hopes others whom he loves and associates with will follow him, and overtake him to see what he's learned. We can see it also as the kind of journey we're discussing here, a journey that may also include dark stretches along faith-shaking paths. Frost ends with these encouraging lines:

They would not find me changed from him they knew—
Only more sure of all I thought was true.[6]

That expresses perfectly how I feel about the gospel we've been given. I've had faith-shaking experiences just as you have. But I've never found anything or experienced anything that made me feel nervous about diving deeper into the gospel, or that the things my mother taught me as a child were not true. Every new round of experimentation solidifies my faith and broadens my base foundation of evidence.

Henry David Thoreau said: "I know that I am. I know that another is who knows more than I, who takes interest in me, whose creature, and yet whose kindred, in one sense, am I. I know that the enterprise is worthy. I know that things work well. I have heard no bad news."[7] *I*, too, have heard no bad news. The more I learn, the more I study—the more the reason, the more the authority, the more the experiences continue to create the evidence.

"Glorious Discoveries and Eternal Certainty"

I began by expressing a prayer that I've prayed every day since my children were born. I continue to offer it. It is that when the faith-shaking experiences come in their lives, they will have a firm and solid foundation, that nothing will be able to shake their faith. A few stones may roll off here and there—we all will be constantly repairing our pyramids as life continues. In truth, some of the stones may need rolling off because they never should have been there in the first place. The important thing is that the building will stand. What can we do, as parents and as grandparents, to help those we love lay the critical foundation layers? Certainly for children and grandchildren we can hope to contribute in establishing some stones of authority. Almost all of our testimonies begin with authority. The trust in the faith of a parent, the trust in a grandparent's testimony. There is something else we can do too.

In *Lectures on Faith,* Joseph Smith describes the passing of faith in God from Adam down to Abraham through the long line of patriarchs. In the second Lecture on Faith there is a beautiful thought. The very last verse of that lecture tells us what we as parents need to do to help our children create their own pyramid. We can be instrumental in guiding them as they lay those first foundation stones. This is what Joseph said:

"We have now clearly set forth how it is, and how it was, that God became an object of faith for rational beings; and also, upon what foundation the testimony was based which excited the inquiry and diligent search of the ancient saints to seek after and obtain a knowledge of the glory of God; And we have seen that it was human testimony, and human testimony only, that excited this inquiry, in the first instance, in their minds. It was the credence they gave to the testimony of their fathers, this testimony having aroused their minds to inquire after the knowledge of God; the inquiry frequently terminated, indeed always terminated when rightly pursued, in the most glorious discoveries and eternal certainty."[8]

That is what I want for my children, for my students, for my grandchildren. That is what you want for those you love. You want them to have glorious discoveries and eternal certainty. Joseph is saying that the spark that begins the questioning, the experimenting, the observing, the gathering of data, is the testimony of the parents, of the fathers in the first instance.

In that same lecture, Joseph used the expression, "what it was that stirred up the faith of multitudes to feel after God." I just love that phrase. As a father, that is what I need to do for my children. I need to stir up their faith to feel after God. And what is the greatest thing, the finest catalyst, for stirring up faith? It is testimony! Next to life itself, which a mother gives a child, the greatest gift you can give a child is the gift of your testimony. So I continue to try and broaden my pyramid, not only for my own sake, but with the understanding that my children's pyramids, in some measure, will begin from that.

May we have the ability to resist all faith-shakers. Wherever they may come, in whatever form, may we not see "cloudy days tomorrow" because we made foolish decisions today in throwing something away which was of great value. May we hold tightly to those most precious truths that dignify us today and will glorify us tomorrow. In his play *Pericles,* Shakespeare wrote these beautiful words with which I will conclude: "For truth can never be confirmed enough, though doubts did ever sleep."[9] May all your doubts be put to rest. May all your truths be confirmed. May you be able to say, "I know," and more importantly, "I know why I know." May that knowledge be ever based on evidence that is based on reason, experience, and authority.

CHAPTER NINE

TAKING THE
TEMPLE WITH YOU

A temple is an outward symbol that testifies of the Lord's desire to dwell with his people, for he has built a house in their midst. It is also our indication to the Lord that we desire him to dwell with us, for we have built a house for him. He is gracious and hospitable. He is always home. This is suggested in the scriptures by the pillar of fire by night and the cloud of smoke by day over the ancient Hebrew tabernacle, just as we would assume a person was home if we saw smoke rising from the chimney in the daytime and a light shining in the window at night. As one who dwells in our midst, the Lord desires our visits and extends to us an open invitation to commune with him in his house.

Early in the Restoration, the Lord commanded Joseph Smith to build a temple, "that your incomings may be in the name of the Lord; that your outgoings may be in the name of the Lord" (D&C 88:120). We enter the temple as invited guests; we leave it as representatives of the Savior.

Over thirty years ago, as a newly called missionary, I experienced my first incoming and outgoing from the temple. I went in somewhat unprepared and my outgoing contained a degree of bewilderment and unease. Now, after more than thirty years of attending the temple, I join my voice with that of David, who wrote, "One thing have I desired of the Lord, that will I seek after; that I may dwell in the house of the Lord all the days of my life, to behold the beauty of the Lord, and to enquire in his temple" (Psalm 27:4).

What has made the difference between my first incoming and outgoing and those at present? A number of factors have contributed to the change. During the intervening years I have learned how to feel and sense the love of our Father in Heaven and our Savior as that love is enshrined in the holy ordinances of his house. To discover that love required some of my deepest ponderings and sensitive reflection. A friend of mine was leaving for the temple recently and was stopped by his five-year-old son who said, "Where are you going?"

"We're going to the temple, son," was the answer.

"Well, when you get there you tell my good friend Jesus, 'Hi,'" the little boy said.

"His mother replied, "I don't think we'll see him there, son."

And he answered with that profound, sweet wisdom of a child, "Oh, I think you will find him if you look very hard for him."

Doing the work for my own ancestors has been vastly significant and has perhaps been the most critical factor in discovering the love of our Father in Heaven and his Son. An ordinance worker once told our family as we prepared to be baptized for names we had researched ourselves, "Many of those for whom you will be baptized today lived hard and bitter lives. Many of them died wondering if God had forgotten them. Today you will show them that he has not forgotten them; he does not forget a single child. For the first time in many, many years their names will be spoken lovingly in his house and they will know of their Father's love for them."

My focus here is on our outgoings from the temple, but in order for us to bring the love and the peace with us as we leave temple doors, our incomings must be done properly. When Jacob returned from the land of Canaan with his family, he was commanded to take them to a mountain called Bethel. *Bethel* in Hebrew means "house of God" (Genesis 28:19a). Twenty years earlier, Jacob had received a dream here of a ladder or a stairway that ascended to heaven. Upon the rungs or steps, angels ascended and descended (see Genesis 28:12). What a wonderful description that is of a temple.

Jacob asked his family to do three things before they went up to Bethel: "Put away the strange gods that are among you, and be clean, and change your garments: and let us arise, and go up to Beth-el" (Genesis 35:2–3). Rachel and Leah were among those who went up to Bethel. What a wonderful example our ancient mothers teach us about incomings and outgoings from the temple. "And they gave unto Jacob all the strange gods which were in their hand, and all their earrings which were in their ears; and Jacob hid them under the oak which was by Shechem" (Genesis 35:4). I do not know what kind of strange gods or earrings this family gave up before ascending the mountain of God's house, but they considered them inappropriate. They considered them things of the world and felt the opportunity to be at God's house worth their abandonment.

Before we go to the house of the Lord to make covenants and receive eternal blessings we must first put away the strange gods, the things of the world. This they did before they ascended, but notice the great lesson inherent in the words, "and Jacob hid them under the oak which was by Shechem" (Genesis 35:4). When they left Bethel they did not pick up the strange gods and trappings of the world, thus returning to old ways. They left them buried by the oak at Shechem. To maintain the calm and serenity of the temple our own outgoings must be the same.

One of the saddest things I experience in my present Church assignment is to see good members of the Church, whom we love, give up the strange gods and earrings of the world at their incomings to the temple only to pick them up again at the time of their outgoings. These may consist in renewing old habits, ceasing to pay tithes and offerings, and becoming caught up in material things. They may consist of inappropriate forms of entertainment or environment, grooming, or styles of clothing that compromise the sacredness of the one physical item that we carry with us as we go out of the temple, which is so deeply connected to the symbols therein. All that is associated with the temple is kept sacred, covered, not revealed outside temple walls. Let us respect and honor that precious gift. Let us consider carefully those things that take place in the temple and allow them to be our guide in regards to that sacred article we promise to wear day and night.

We are told in Genesis that God protected Jacob's family as they left Bethel and journeyed in the dangerous world of Canaan. If we follow their example, we are also assured of the Lord's protection. The scriptures teach that the temple is a place of refuge and safety. When my children were approaching their teenage years, I went into the temple one afternoon to seek guidance as a father. I told the Lord I was willing to offer him any sacrifice if he would protect my children from the worldly temptations and bless them with his Spirit. I believe all of you have, at one time or another, offered this prayer in behalf of your children, your grandchildren, your nieces and nephews. The Lord answered my petition and the Spirit whispered, "This is the sacrifice that I ask of you: Be in this house frequently, constantly, consistently, and the promised protection this house can bestow will be extended to those you love."

This is not a unique promise to me, but to all of us. I knew the Lord was not promising that all my children would grow up without problems, but it was the promise of a powerful influence in their lives, a protecting influence. If we are true to our covenants, our outgoings from the temple carry a protective shield to cover, not only us, but our families—all those we love.

This defensive influence was promised by Isaiah many centuries ago as he contemplated our world. The Lord counsels us in the scriptures to "stand in holy places" when we face the destructive influences of the world "and . . . not be moved" (D&C 45:32). "Not be moved" means more than just "stay in one place"; it also means "don't be afraid," or moved emotionally. *Stand* is not a passive word; it is an active one. It means "make a stand," or fight. Make your stand against the influences of the world in holy places and don't be afraid. Isaiah tells us of three holy places where Latter-day Saints will fight the forces of the world and prevail. "And the Lord will create upon every dwelling place of mount Zion, and upon her assemblies, a cloud and smoke by day, and the shining of a flaming fire by night: for upon all the glory [of Zion] shall be a defence" (Isaiah 4:5; compare 2 Nephi 14:5). Just as the pillar of fire was over the tabernacle when the children of Israel wandered in the wilderness, in the latter days the Lord's spirit will be over every home and every assembly of the Saints to defend them. If we are true to our covenants, the pillar of fire sits over each of our homes by day and by night. It is the pillar of the Holy Spirit.

Isaiah then promises and speaks of the protective power of the temple: "And there shall be a tabernacle for a shadow in the daytime from the heat, and for a place of refuge [a fortress], and for a covert from storm and from rain" (Isaiah 4:6). The scriptures teach that the temple is God's hearth, his fireside, his home. When the forces of the world bear down on us like a hot summer day and we feel we cannot bear it any longer, the Lord says, "Come home. Sit in the shade of my house, enjoy the breezes of my Spirit, feel refreshed, drink from the fountain of love and truth, swim in my river of healing. Now your outgoings can be with greater strength and you can face the heat of the day."

As we protect our part of the defensive line in the great battle between good and evil, holding the sword of truth and justice, sometimes it appears as if all the forces of temptation and worldliness are attacking our single position. We feel isolated, and fear we will be swept away. At these times we can hear the Lord call to us, "Come home. Retreat into the safety of my house of refuge. Put your sword down. There are no battles to be fought in my house, no enemy penetrates these walls. Feel peace for a season. See in panoramic vision the battle for the souls of men; receive instruction in how to hold firm even when others give way; understand the adversary's strategy; be comforted in the knowledge that it was foretold in the Garden of Eden that Lucifer would be crushed. Now your out-goings can be with greater courage. Return to the battle front and swing your sword, confident of ultimate victory."

When the forces of life beat upon you like a mighty storm, when the flood waters of trial, or the pelting hail of day-to-day irritations leave you cold and discouraged and looking for shelter, the Lord gently whispers, "Come home. No stinging hail penetrates the shingles of my house; the flood waters cannot sweep away its foundations; no worldly wind will chill your spirit here. Sit by my hearth; listen to my truths; feast at my table; be warmed by a father's love. Now your outgoings into the storms of life can be without hesitation, without fear."

Our loving Father in Heaven and Savior have given us a sacred triangle of home, stake, and temple, within whose boundaries we can make our stand and not fear.

The Lord revealed to Joseph Smith that he would prepare a "feast of fat things, . . . Yea, a supper of the house of the Lord, well prepared, unto which all nations shall be invited" (D&C 58:8–9). The feast of the temple consists of the richest doctrines, the most nourishing truths, the most life-sustaining covenants and ordinances.

During his earthly ministry, Jesus spoke of godly feasts in a parable. "A certain man made a great supper, and bade many: and sent his servant at supper time to say to them that were bidden, Come; for all things are now ready. And they all with one consent began to make excuse. The first said unto him, I have bought a piece of ground, and I must needs go and see it: I pray thee have me excused. And another said, I have bought five yoke of oxen, and I go to prove them: I pray thee have me excused. And another said, I have married a wife, and therefore I cannot come" (Luke 14:16–20). As a result of this unwillingness new invitations were issued. "And the lord said unto the servant, Go out into the highways and hedges, and compel them to come in, that my house may be filled" (Luke 14:23).

Sometimes our lives become so busy that we realize that it has been quite some time since we've been to the temple. We know the feast is waiting and we sense our need for its spiritual nourishment, but there are oxen to be proved and ground to see and we ask to be excused. Yet the parable testifies that the Lord truly desires that his house be filled. If we are not cautious we may often find ourselves making bricks without straw.

When Moses first appeared in Pharaoh's court, he initially asked that the Israelites be allowed three days' journey into the wilderness to offer sacrifice to the Lord. In other words, in the midst of their brickmaking for Pharaoh, they needed time off for worship. "Get you unto your burdens," Pharaoh said (Exodus 5:4). "They be idle; therefore they cry, saying, Let us go and sacrifice to our God. Let there more work be laid upon the men, that they may labour therein; and let them not regard vain words" (Exodus 5:8–9). He then withheld the needed straw.

Does life sometimes treat you like Pharaoh? Does it demand so much of your time and energy that there is nothing left for feasting and sacrificing? Are we hesitant to make the three days' journey into the wilderness for the needed solitude to worship properly? I believe part of the adversary's plan in the latter days is to see that we have no time left for feasting. The daily tale (or quota) of bricks must not be diminished until, eventually, without the essential nourishment of worship, like the overworked children of Israel we hearken not "for anguish of spirit, and for cruel bondage" (Exodus 6:9).

Jesus' parable of the supper was introduced by these words: "And when one of them that sat at meat with him heard these things, he said unto him, Blessed is he that shall eat bread in the kingdom of God" (Luke 14:15). The word *shall* indicates the man was thinking of a more distant meal, something that would take place in the future. I believe we all look forward with anticipation to our celestial feast in the Lord's eternal kingdom. It seems that the Savior's telling of the parable indicates to us that we need not wait until the kingdom of God to enjoy the feast. We can eat bread with the Savior now in his house if we will not make excuses. And the bread of the endowment is unlike any other upon which we can feast. I believe we can comprehend that with the help of one of the Savior's miracles.

The endowment is like the five barley loaves Jesus used to feed the five thousand. At first it did not appear to be sufficient to satisfy the needs of so many, but Jesus blessed it and each person, we are told, could eat as much as he would until he was filled. When they were finished with the feast, they filled twelve baskets with the fragments, "which remained over and above unto them that had eaten" (John 6:13). The symbolic nature of temple ordinances enables us to constantly return to the twelve baskets for nourishment. This occurs as we learn that symbols can mean many different things at ever-deepening levels and thus nourish us during the multitudinous and changing circumstances of our lives.

We live in such a wonderful time. How many temples can you find mentioned in the scriptures? Upon searching you will discover only a handful. There are now well over a hundred temples scattered over the earth. I have often reflected upon what the ancient Saints would have thought if they could have viewed this dispensation. In ancient Israel, only one man, the high priest, a descendant of Aaron, could pass through the veil of the temple into its most holy place and only on one day every year. How many of us have been in the celestial room of a temple? The celestial room is somewhat similar to the Holy of Holies which was, as described in the Bible, located behind the veil of the temple. We can enter the celestial room as often as we desire. Men and women from every tribe of Israel pass through the veil into the celestial room. What wonder would the ancients feel as they saw thousands of men and women daily entering the temples and sitting in its most hallowed places? Understanding this unique and marvelous aspect of the Restoration will enable our outgoings to always be full of gratitude.

The Lord tells us that his house is a house of learning. He desires that our outgoings be filled with knowledge. Because we are taught through symbols in the temple, we may not understand and receive all the truth the Lord desires us to obtain in only a few sessions. We must learn how to learn in his house through the use of symbols. Let me suggest to you a formula for temple worship that may help. Much of our ability to receive the power of the temple depends on what we do when we are outside its walls. We find a wonderful formula in 3 Nephi 17.

Jesus had spent the day teaching the Nephites and the Lamanites. It had been a full day. At its conclusion, he said, "I perceive that ye are weak, that ye cannot understand all my words which I am commanded of the Father to speak unto you at this time" (3 Nephi 17:2). Are your outgoings from the temple ever accompanied by that feeling? You simply don't understand all you've experienced and been taught. The Savior understands our weakness and teaches us what to do. We are not to be discouraged, doubtful, or apathetic. We are to do five things: "Therefore, [1] go ye unto your homes, and [2] ponder upon the things which I have said, and [3] ask of the Father, in my name, that ye may understand, and [4] prepare your minds for the morrow, and [5] I come unto you again" (3 Nephi 17:3).

Often we only do the first of those five things. We just go home. However, if we desire that our next incoming to the temple be more powerful, we must ponder, which means to deeply reflect upon our temple experience. We must show the Lord our desire to receive the full benefits of his teaching by sincerely asking him specifically to help us understand the symbols and covenants of his house.

There are many ways to prepare the mind to receive the Lord's teaching, but I think the best of all is to go to the temple hungering after insight and knowledge. As a teacher, I know how wonderful it is to teach a class of students who hunger for truth. You desire to give them all you can. The temple is the Lord's house of learning. At the commencement of the endowment we hear what I call "teacher words." Reflecting on those words can help us prepare our minds to learn. We must be *alert* (that's a teacher word) and *attentive* (that's a teacher word) and *reverent* (that's also a teacher word). If these words reflect our attitude, we are prepared to receive. We are hungry for truth and knowledge. Last of all, we must return as frequently as our circumstances allow.

There is a beautiful prophecy in Ezekiel which tells us what accompanies our outgoings from the Lord's house. Ezekiel is shown a future temple in Jerusalem. From its eastern doors, which face the barren, bleak, and dry landscape of the Judean wilderness and the Dead Sea, a river begins to flow. The river brings vibrant life to the desert. Ezekiel sees "very many trees" on both sides of the river (Ezekiel 47:7). He is promised "that every thing that liveth, which moveth, whithersoever the rivers shall come, shall live" (Ezekiel 47:9). The pure waters of the temple flow into the Dead Sea and heal it. Ezekiel sees many species of fish inhabiting its waters. He is shown fishermen spreading their nets all along its shores. He is invited to walk down the length of the river and measure its depth. Each time Ezekiel wades into the river he finds it deeper until finally it becomes, "a river that I could not pass over: for the waters were risen, waters to swim in, a river that could not be passed over" (Ezekiel 47:5).

Whenever I read that marvelous prophecy the Spirit seems to whisper, "What is true of this prophetic temple is true of all my temples." From the doors of every temple a pure river flows. We cannot see these rivers with our natural eyes, but they are there just the same. They are rivers of truth and light. But Nephi also instructs us that the fountain of living waters is a representation of God's love (see 1 Nephi 11:25). These are rivers of love, and they flow from every temple. We can be assured they will give life to and heal "every thing that liveth" (Ezekiel 47:9) They will give life to marriages, to parent and child relationships. They can heal our families and give life to our branches, wards, and stakes. They can heal a parched life rendered dry by the dust storms of trial and heartbreak. One day the combined flow of all the temples will bathe the world in love and light. And finally we will know peace, both individually and as a world.

I believe that these are also rivers of wonderful Latter-day Saint men and women who flow out from the temple with love and inner peace, secure in their covenants, enlightened by revelation and eternal perspective, trusting in promised protection, confident in the nature of never-ending families, and assured of a Father and Savior's great plan for man's happiness. May your outgoings from the temple help to heal and give life to the spiritual deserts and Dead Seas of the world in which you live until one day you will meet your Father in Heaven at the doorway of his eternal, celestial kingdom, there at the top of the stairway, where he will take you by the hand and lead you into your eternal home. Then, as the scriptures promise, there will be no more outgoings forever.

NOTES

〜

CHAPTER 1: WALKING ON WATER:
When the Lord Asks the Impossible

1. Lewis, *The Problem of Pain,* 126.
2. Lewis, *The Silver Chair,* 21.

CHAPTER 2: THE JESUS WE NEED TO KNOW

1. Lewis, *Prince Caspian,* 151–52.
2. Lewis, *The Weight of Glory,* 145.
3. *Journal of Discourses,* 10:174.
4. Angelou, *Wouldn't Take Nothing for My Journey Now,* 73–76.
5. See "More Holiness Give Me," *Hymns,* no. 131.

CHAPTER 3: OF LIONS, DRAGONS, AND TURKISH DELIGHT:
C. S. Lewis for Latter-day Saints

1. Lewis, *Surprised by Joy,* 115.
2. Ibid., 233.
3. Ibid., 7.
4. Ibid., 17.
5. Carroll, *Alice's Adventures in Wonderland* and *Through the Looking-Glass,* 56.
6. Lewis, *The Last Battle,* 227.
7. Ibid., 227–28.
8. Lewis, *God in the Dock,* 112–13.
9. Lewis, *Mere Christianity,* 216.
10. Ibid., 205–6.
11. Lewis, *The Screwtape Letters,* 193.
12. Lewis, *The Great Divorce,* 141.
13. Lewis, *Letters of C. S. Lewis,* 456.
14. Lewis, *Perelandra,* 176.

15. *Mere Christianity,* 199.

16. Smith, *History of the Church,* 3:295.

17. Lewis, *The Screwtape Letters,* 38–39.

18. *Mere Christianity,* 75.

19. Lewis, "Christianity and Literature," in Hooper, ed., *Christian Reflections,* 10.

20. Lewis, *The Weight of Glory,* 172–73.

21. Ibid., 45–46.

22. *Mere Christianity,* 119–20.

23. Lewis, *The Horse and His Boy,* 227.

24. Eliot, "The Waste Land," in *The Waste Land and Other Poems,* 45.

25. Lewis, *The Silver Chair,* 21.

26. Ibid.

27. Lewis, *Miracles,* 221.

28. Grahame, *The Wind in the Willows,* 123.

29. Lewis, "Rabbit or Man," in *God in the Dock,* 112.

30. See *The Great Divorce,* 106–15.

31. Lewis, *The Voyage of the Dawn Treader,* 91.

32. Ibid., 108–9.

33. *Mere Christianity,* 195–96.

34. Lewis, *The Pilgrim's Regress,* 15.

35. *Mere Christianity,* 196.

36. Ibid., 196–97.

37. Ibid., 198–99.

38. Ibid., 202.

39. Ibid., 203.

40. Ibid.

41. Ibid., 205.

42. Ibid., 176.

43. Lewis, *The Problem of Pain,* 46.

44. Ibid., 156.

45. Lewis, *The Magician's Nephew,* 161.

46. *The Last Battle,* 211.

47. *The Weight of Glory,* 29–30, 42.

48. *The Pilgrim's Regress,* 202.

49. *The Problem of Pain,* 150.

50. *The Pilgrim's Regress,* 204–5.

51. *Mere Christianity,* 135.

52. *The Problem of Pain,* 149–151.

53. *The Magician's Nephew,* 210.

54. Wordsworth, "Ode: Intimations of Immortality," in *Intimations of Immortality,* 91.

55. Lewis, "Vowels and Sirens," in *Poems,* 76.

56. *The Screwtape Letters,* 174.

57. Lewis, "The Adam Unparadised," in *Poems*, 44.

58. Lewis, *Out of the Silent Planet*, 130.

59. *Perelandra*, 88.

60. *The Magician's Nephew*, 160.

61. Lewis, *Prince Caspian*, 151–52.

62. *The Voyage of the Dawn Treader*, 156–57.

63. Lewis, *The Lion, the Witch and the Wardrobe*, 68–69.

64. See *Surprised by Joy*, 24.

65. *The Horse and His Boy*, 183.

66. *Surprised by Joy*, 228–29.

67. *The Voyage of the Dawn Treader*, 247.

68. Lewis, *Letters to Malcolm*, 93.

69. *God in the Dock*, 112.

70. *Letters to Malcolm*, 93.

71. *Mere Christianity*, 206.

72. *The Weight of Glory*, 173.

73. *God in the Dock*, 112.

74. *The Problem of Pain*, 156.

75. *The Voyage of the Dawn Treader*, 247.

76. *The Problem of Pain*, 126.

77. *The Great Divorce*, 75.

78. Smith, *The Teachings of the Prophet Joseph Smith*, 255.

79. Lewis, *The Lion, the Witch, and the Wardrobe*, 90.

80. *The Magician's Nephew*, 201.

81. *The Screwtape Letters*, 119–20.

82. Lewis, "Deception," in *Poems*, 90.

83. *The Pilgrim's Regress*, 186.

84. *The Weight of Glory*, 159–60.

85. *The Screwtape Letters*, 16.

86. Ibid., 22.

87. Ibid., 32.

88. Ibid., 155.

89. Lewis, "The World's Last Night," in *The World's Last Night and Other Essays*, 80–81.

90. *The Problem of Pain*, 94.

91. *God in the Dock*, 51–52.

92. *Mere Christianity*, 213–14.

93. Ibid., 121.

94. Ibid., 122.

95. See Benson, "Beware of Pride," 4–7.

96. Lewis, *Mere Christianity*, 122.

97. *The Screwtape Letters*, 69–70.

98. *Mere Christianity*, 124.

99. Green and Hooper, *C. S. Lewis*, 110.

100. *Mere Christianity*, 127–28.

101. *The Screwtape Letters*, 191.

102. Ibid., 193–94.

103. Ibid., 200.

104. Ibid., 65–66

105. Ibid., 60.

106. Ibid., 137–39.

107. *God in the Dock*, 265.

108. Lewis, *The Four Loves*, 137.

109. *God in the Dock*, 92.

110. *The Weight of Glory*, 58–59.

111. *The Screwtape Letters*, 151.

112. Lewis, *The Horse and His Boy*, 186.

113. *The Screwtape Letters*, 6, 8.

114. Andrus and Andrus, *They Knew the Prophet*, 144.

115. *Mere Christianity*, 216–17.

116. *The Screwtape Letters*, 209.

117. Lewis, *Surprised by Joy*, 235.

118. *Mere Christianity*, xv, xvi.

119. Ibid., xvi.

120. Lewis, *The Silver Chair*, 196.

121. *The Problem of Pain*, 106–7.

122. *The Four Loves*, 121.

123. Lewis, *A Grief Observed*, 27–28.

124. Ibid., 17–18.

125. Ibid., 45–46.

126. Ibid., 55–56, 58.

127. Ibid., 58–59.

128. Ibid., 65, 81.

129. Ibid., 82.

130. Ibid., 84–85.

131. *The Voyage of the Dawn Treader*, 213.

132. *A Grief Observed*, 88.

133. *The Weight of Glory*, 140.

CHAPTER 4: THE FOURTH WATCH:
When Your Prayers Seem Unanswered

1. Shakespeare, *The Tragedy of King Richard the Third*, 4.4.22–24.

2. Shakespeare, *The Tragedy of Macbeth*, 4.3.225–26.

3. Lewis, *The Great Divorce*, 69.

CHAPTER 6: SEEING AS GOD SEES:
Discovering the Wonder of Ourselves and Others

1. "The Golden Plates," *Children's Songbook*, 86.
2. Proctor and Proctor, *The Revised and Enhanced "History of Joseph Smith by His Mother,"* 199.
3. Ibid., 201.
4. *Mencius*, 63.

CHAPTER 7: WHEN ALL ETERNITY SHOOK:
Finding Hope and Healing in the Savior's Sacrifice

1. See Wendy Perrin, "Stop Press: Calculating the Odds."
2. Buonarroti, *Selected Poems from Michelangelo Buonarroti*, 129.
3. MacDonald, *Unspoken Sermons*, 93–94.
4. Farrar, *The Life of Christ*, 576–77.
5. Lerner and Loewe, *Camelot*, 69.
6. "God Loved Us, So He Sent His Son," *Hymns,* no. 187.
7. "I Stand All Amazed," *Hymns,* no. 193.
8. "How Great Thou Art!" *Hymns,* no. 86.

CHAPTER 8: YOUR FAITH BECOMETH UNSHAKEN:
Building Your Testimony Pyramid

1. "Cloudy Days in Tomorrowland," *Newsweek,* 27 January 1997, 86.
2. Lewis, *A Grief Observed*, 17–19.
3. Ibid., 20.
4. Galileo Galilei, quoted in http://www.why-the-bible.com/evolution.htm; accessed 6 January 2011.
5. Lewis, *Mere Christianity*, 124.
6. Frost, "Into My Own," in *The Poetry of Robert Frost*, 5.
7. Thoreau, "Letter to Harrison Blake, March 27th, 1848," in *The Writings of Henry David Thoreau: Familiar Letters*, 163.
8. Smith, *Lectures on Faith*, Lecture Two, v. 56.
9. Shakespeare, *Pericles*, 5.1.203–4.

Sources

Andrus, Hyrum L., and Helen Mae Andrus. *They Knew the Prophet.* Salt Lake City: Bookcraft, 1974.

Angelou, Maya. *Wouldn't Take Nothing for My Journey Now.* New York: Random House, 1993.

Benson, Ezra Taft. "Beware of Pride." *Ensign,* May 1989, 4–7.

Buonarroti, Michelangelo. *Selected Poems from Michelangelo Buonarroti.* Ednah D. Cheney, editor. Boston: Lee and Shepard, 1885.

Carroll, Lewis. *Alice's Adventures in Wonderland* and *Through the Looking-Glass.* New York: Penguin, 1998.

Children's Songbook. Salt Lake City: The Church of Jesus Christ of Latter-day Saints, 1989.

Christian Reflections. Walter Hooper, editor. Grand Rapids, Mich.: Eerdmans, 1994.

"Cloudy Days in Tomorrowland," *Newsweek,* 27 January 1997, 86.

Eliot, T. S., *The Waste Land and Other Poems.* New York: Harcourt, Brace and Company, 1955.

Farrar, Frederick. *The Life of Christ.* Portland, Ore.: Fountain Publications, 1964.

Frost, Robert. *The Poetry of Robert Frost.* New York: Holt, Rinehart and Winston, 1969.

Grahame, Kenneth. *The Wind in the Willows.* Bath, England, UK: Palazzo Editions, 2008.

Green, Roger Lancelyn, and Walter Hooper. *C. S. Lewis: A Biography.* New York: Harcourt Brace Jovanovich, 1974.

Hymns of The Church of Jesus Christ of Latter-day Saints. Salt Lake City: The Church of Jesus Christ of Latter-day Saints, 1985.

Journal of Discourses. 26 vols. London: Latter-day Saints' Book Depot, 1854–86.

Lerner, Alan Jay, and Frederick Loewe. *Camelot.* New York: Random House, 1961.

Lewis, C. S. *The Four Loves.* New York: Harcourt Brace and Company, 1960.

———. *God in the Dock.* Grand Rapids, Mich.: Eerdmans, 1999.

———. *The Great Divorce.* New York: HarperCollins, 2001

———. *A Grief Observed.* New York: HarperCollins, 2001.

———. *The Horse and His Boy.* New York: HarperCollins, 1982.

———. *The Last Battle.* New York: HarperCollins, 1984.

———. *Letters of C. S. Lewis, Revised and Enlarged Edition.* New York: Harcourt, 1993.

———. *Letters to Malcolm: Chiefly on Prayer.* New York: Harcourt, 1991.

———. *The Lion, the Witch, and the Wardrobe.* New York: HarperCollins, 1978.

———. *The Magician's Nephew.* New York: HarperCollins, 1983.

———. *Mere Christianity.* New York: HarperCollins, 2001.

———. *Miracles.* New York: HarperCollins, 2001.

———. *Out of the Silent Planet.* New York: Scribner, 2003.

———. *Perelandra.* New York: Scribner, 1996.

———. *The Pilgrim's Regress.* Grand Rapids, Mich.: Eerdmans, 1992.

———. *Poems.* New York: Harcourt Brace Jovanovich, 1964.

———. *Prince Caspian.* New York: HarperCollins, 1979.

———. *The Problem of Pain.* New York: HarperCollins, 2001.

———. *The Screwtape Letters.* New York: HarperCollins, 2001.

———. *The Silver Chair.* New York: HarperCollins, 1981.

———. *Surprised by Joy: The Shape of My Early Life.* New York: Harcourt Brace and Company, 1955.

———. *The Voyage of the Dawn Treader.* New York: HarperCollins, 1980.

———. *The Weight of Glory.* New York: HarperCollins, 2001.

———. *The World's Last Night and Other Essays.* New York: Harcourt, 1987.

MacDonald, George. *Unspoken Sermons.* Charleston, S. Car.: Bibliobazaar, 2006.

Mencius, Revised Edition. D.C. Lau, translator. Hong Kong: Chinese University Press, 2003.

Perrin, Wendy. "Stop Press: Calculating the Odds." *Condé Nast Traveler,* February 2003;

available at http://www.concierge.com/cntraveler/traveltips/5466?pageNumber=1; accessed 30 December 2010.

Proctor, Scott Facer, and Maurine Jensen Proctor. *The Revised and Enhanced "History of Joseph Smith by His Mother."* Salt Lake City: Bookcraft, 1996.

Shakespeare, William. *Pericles.* In *The Oxford Shakespeare: The Complete Works, Second Edition.* Stanley Wells and Gary Taylor, general editors. Oxford: Clarendon Press, 2005, 1059–86.

———. *The Tragedy of King Richard the Third.* In *The Oxford Shakespeare: The Complete Works, Second Edition.* Stanley Wells and Gary Taylor, general editors. Oxford: Clarendon Press, 2005, 183–222.

———. *The Tragedy of Macbeth.* In *The Oxford Shakespeare: The Complete Works, Second Edition.* Stanley Wells and Gary Taylor, general editors. Oxford: Clarendon Press, 2005, 969–93.

Smith, Joseph. *History of the Church.* 6 vols. Salt Lake City: Deseret Book, 1974.

———. *Lectures on Faith.* Salt Lake City: Deseret Book, 1985.

———. *The Teachings of the Prophet Joseph Smith.* Selected by Joseph Fielding Smith. Salt Lake City: Deseret Book, 1976.

Thoreau, Henry David. *The Writings of Henry David Thoreau: Familiar Letters.* F. B. Sanborn, editor. Boston: Houghton Mifflin and Company, 1906.

Why-the-Bible.com.

Wordsworth, William. *Intimations of Immortality.* New York: Houghton, Mifflin and Company, 1895.

INDEX

C

D

M

N

O

Oedipus Rex (Sophocles), 124
Offense, avoiding, 40
Oil, widow and, 15, 35
Olive tree, allegory of, 117–19
Olsen, Kenneth, 194
Overcoat, as source of pride, 87–88

P

Pain, 96–100
Patience: with children, 6; in progression, 163–65
Patriarchal blessing, 203–4
Paul, 11, 17–18, 38–39, 116–17, 151
Peer pressure, 90–91
Perelandra (Lewis), 56
Perfection: commandment on, 4, 69–70; judgment and, 48–49; of Church leaders, 198–99; of testimony, 208–9
Persecution, 37–39
Perspective: of God, 17–18, 145–47, 150–58; surface beauty and, 146–47; individual worth and, 147–48; women and, 148–50; divine potential and, 150–51
Peter: walks on Sea of Galilee, 2–3, 5, 12–13; lets down net, 15–16; as fisher of men, 17; heals lame man, 21–22; love of, 22–24; as chosen vessel, 151–52; desire of, 161–62
Pharaoh, 222
Ph.D. dissertation, 171
Philippi, 11
The Pilgrim's Regress (Lewis), 67–68
Political correctness, 91–92, 199
Pondering, 185
Pool at Bethesda, 42–43
Potential, 17–18, 150–58

Prayer(s): scriptures and, 101–2; unanswered, 102–3, 117–19; fourth watch and, 103–5; Jaredites and, 105–7; forgiveness and, 108–11; delayed answers to, 111–13; unexpected answers to, 113–16; for direction, 116–17; at stake conference, 157–58; from Gethsemane, 172–74; to know of God's love, 203–4
Premortal existence, 72–73
Pride, 85–89, 208
Prince Caspian (Lewis), 27–28, 73–74
The Problem of Pain (Lewis), 85, 96
Prodigal Son, 108–9, 183–84
Progression, 47–49, 150–58, 163–65
Prophets, 125, 204–5
Protection, of temple, 220–21
Pyramid of faith, 200–201

Q

Queen, in chess, 149

R

"Rabbit or Man" (Lewis), 63
Rackham, Horace, 194
Radio, 81, 82
Reassurance, 7–12
Red Sea, 146–47
Repentance, 78–79, 108–11, 134, 137–44, 188
Report cards, 152–53
Resurrection, 31–33
Revelation, 204–5, 208
Revelators, 125
Rock bands, 134
Roller coasters, 166–67

S

T